DONE

DONE

HOW TO WORK
WHEN NO ONE
IS WATCHING

ELLEN GOODWIN

ATTENTION SCHOOLS, BUSINESSES AND ORGANIZATIONS:
This book is available at special bulk pricing. Please send an email to info@ellengoodwin.com for more information.

Any internet addresses, phone numbers, or company or product information printed in this book are offered as a resource and are not intended in any way to be or to imply an endorsement by the author, nor does the author vouch for the existence, content, or services of these sites, phone numbers, companies, or products beyond the life of this book.

Publishers Note: Some names, characteristics, places, and incidents have been changed to disguise the identities of the individuals involved. Any resemblance to actual people, living or dead, or to businesses, companies, events or institutions is completely coincidental and unintentional.

To Chris,
For your infinite patience

*The mind that opens to a new idea,
never returns to its original size.*
-Albert Einstein

Contents

INTRODUCTION

I am a full-time Action Hero.

My Action Hero skills don't include multiple methods of self-defense, speaking obscure foreign languages, or being a mad genius at knife skills. My main Action Hero skill is that I am productive.

Action Heroes are made, not born. I get things done every day because I learned how.

I developed my Action Hero skills during the years I successfully worked while no one was watching.

After working as an advertising creative, I spent the next 20 years working from home as a freelance graphic designer with a full roster of corporate clients. For most of that time, my only office mate was an aging, deaf, calico cat who was not exactly the accountability partner of my dreams.

While this doesn't sound the riveting opening scene of an Action Hero tale, it actually is.

As a designer, I had plenty of work to do, but with no real set schedule (by choice), it was easy to get distracted. If I got things done at 10 a.m. or 10 p.m., no one was the wiser.

When I didn't have deadlines looming, it was easy to give in to what I now know is Parkinson's Law, which states: "A task expands to fill the time available for it." I was pretty much the poster child for this.

Of course, back then, I didn't know there was a name for it. I just knew that I could stretch a 30-minute project into a 4-hour non-billable slog.

Not really a great business model. Or life model for that matter either.

When business got busier, and efficiency and effectiveness were called for, I could consistently figure out the whole "how to get more done in less time" game. And win at it, no problem.

You're probably guilty of this as well. It's the whole feet-to-the-fire, nose-to-the-grindstone kind of thing. But for me, it was always short-lived.

When things would slow down, I would revert back to my old, distracted, time-wasting ways.

Over and over.

Oddly enough, eventually, I found that this just didn't work. It was exhausting. While I knew there had to be a better way to get things done in a consistent, non-exhausting way, it was only when my lack of focus and my procrastinating ways threatened my business and my bank account, that I finally got busy looking for answers.

Being the resourceful type of person I am, I went out hunting and gathering.

My hunting consisted of tracking down lots of research, putting myself through lots of education and training. Going through lots and lots of trial and error on my part, where I gathered information (data points really) and real-life experiences to back up the processes.

I tested out theories. Read studies. Attended conferences. Tried apps. Formulated systems and put them through the wringer.

Eventually, I found the keys to being productive and in action, which meant things really started to get done.

My business rallied and became more fun and more successful, which meant more money and a happier me.

The non-business part of my life began to thrive, too, all because I understood how to be productive when no one was watching. (Cue the unicorns dancing over the rainbows in the middle of showers of glitter). I could make my productivity system as involved or as simple as I wanted. And I did.

I could change it up as often as I wanted, or not at all. Everything I learned and practiced all came from understanding how to work with my brain, and sometime around my brain, and the understanding of when my brain wasn't playing nice at all.

One crucial thing I learned is that all of our brains are fascinating, complex, and wacky as hell.

They are the root of productivity, all procrastination, distraction, and frustration. Confusing, huh?

But because I know what's going on, I can help you. I know this stuff. I've lived this stuff, and now it's here in this book for you to know as well.

So, where does the Action Hero thing come in?

Action Heroes,* the kind you find in movies, video games, books, and comics all leverage three primary skills: they know how to be in Action, how to work with their Energy, and how to entirely, and intently Focus on their task at hand. Which are precisely the three skills you need to get things done, especially if no one is watching. So if that's what Action Heroes do, then I'm an Action Hero.

Sharing the secrets to leveraging the trifecta of Action, Energy, and Focus is what this book is all about. When you know (and master) these secrets, your life will change. You will get things done more efficiently, be less stressed, and feel more in charge of your life-changing how you think about yourself. You'll be proactive about what you do and how you do it. You'll be more in charge of your time and feel better about what you accomplish. You'll be able to effectively and efficiently work when no one is watching.

Will every idea in this book work for you? Nope. This is why, when possible, I've provided alternative ideas and tools for you to try. Some people love doing one thing, and it works like gangbusters for them. For others, the same solution might feel like being forced to eat bugs. But there's always an answer out there, and my goal is to provide you with the solution. (For almost all of the problems, a little brain trick is the answer you truly need.)

So grab a pen, a highlighter, a notepad or journal, and dig in. It's time for you to get things DONE.

---

* Action Heroes often get confused with Super Heroes, but there is a big difference. Super Heroes wear masks, and tights and have capes. They come from different planets and they use their super hero skills to defeat their foes. Without superpowers, Action Heroes have to rely on their wits, their intelligence, and their cunning ways. They can usually think and act quickly, to size up a situation and figure out the solution on the fly, saving the day. It's not always about being the strongest person in the room or having the most firepower.

HOW TO READ THIS BOOK

This book is set up in four sections.

In the first section, you'll learn all about being in Action and overcoming procrastination. In the second section, you'll learn how to leverage your personal Energy and how to conserve it, either by building, or eliminating, habits. The third section takes you on a deep dive into Focus—how to get more of it and how to use it to battle multitasking. Finally, the fourth section brings Action, Energy, and Focus together and boosts your ability to achieve Goals.

Many of the tools and strategies discussed in this book can be used in more than one type of situation. When they are mentioned or show up in more than one chapter, just know I'm not being repetitious. I'm just pointing out the different ways they can be used.

This book is full of actionable exercises, moments to pause and write out ideas, as well as activities to try. Blank copies of all the forms used in the book can be downloaded at EllenGoodwin.com/forms.

Each chapter ends with a review section recapping each of the terms, strategies, and tools that were discussed, as well as Action Items you can complete. Some of the Action Items will apply to your current situation, others may be done as a way to prepare for future scenarios.

At the end of the book, there is a full Action Toolbox Recap, listing not only all the strategies and tools from each chapter but also a Quick Response Section with specific productivity questions. For each question, you'll find a synopsis of what actions you can take, as well as a list of the different tools which will help with each situation (and their page numbers), so you can quickly solve any problem you encounter either now or in the future.

Everything in this book is designed to give you the strategies and tools you need to work more efficiently and more effectively, whether anyone is watching or not. It's all about you, getting things DONE.

ACTION

In this first section, you are going to learn the secrets to being in Action. You'll learn what Action really is, how to be in it, and the one tool you can use to make your Action more effective. You'll also learn about the enemy of Action and how you can consistently triumph over it. Taking Action is how lives get changed, goals are achieved, and things get DONE.

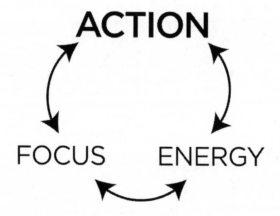

CHAPTER ONE

Action Basics

Action is the foundational key to all success
- Pablo Picasso, *painter, sculptor, poet*

When I was in grade school, my sisters and I shared ownership of a golden hamster named Rosie. Rosie was a typical hamster who had mastered the four hamster life skills of sleeping, seeing how many sunflower seeds she could stuff in her pouches, rattling her cage door (on the chance we had forgotten to lock it), and running steadily on the wheel in her cage.

Each of the first three skills had an end goal. Sleeping? Self-explanatory. Sunflower seeds? Besides entertaining us (which I'm sure wasn't her goal), the more seeds she stuffed in her cheeks, the more food she had for later. Rosie was no fool. Rattling the cage door? Possible escape into the unknown wilds of our toy-filled room. But the running on the wheel didn't really have an end goal.

I mean, it's not like Rosie had a step goal to meet. She could have easily just laid around and eaten sunflower seeds all day. No personal trainer was showing up to check in on her. But still, she got on her wheel and ran and ran (usually at night when the squeaks of the wheel were most likely to keep us awake).

All that running never got her anywhere. The scenery never changed. She never got to the end of a good run in the wheel and found herself miles away from her cage. She ran, and while it probably felt like she was getting somewhere, she wasn't.

She was in motion.

The important difference between action and motion

Being in Action and being in motion feels a lot alike. So much so your brain can't tell the difference, it sees you in motion and classifies it the same as you being in action, when in fact, the two are entirely different.

Action is different than motion.

Action is a little like the game of American football. In football, most of the time the ball is moved, step-by-step, play-by-play towards the goal line.* Each of those plays, no matter how small, is important. The players are in action as they move toward their goal line. It's no different for you. Action moves you closer to whatever your own private goal line is through a series of achievements, either large or small.

Outcomes are achieved through Action, not through motion.

Being able to stop and identify when you're in motion, and then quickly move into action, is a vital skill you need to get things done.

If your goal of running on a treadmill is to get cardio time or log some miles, then your treadmill running is Action. But if your goal is to run to the next town, all your running on the treadmill won't get you one step closer. You're in motion, not Action.

Planning = Motion

A lot of motion is just planning. It might look like Action, but nothing is really getting accomplished. Take, for example, writing out a to-do list. I'm a big fan of having a to-do list of some sort.† Unfortunately, as far as your brain is concerned, the very act of putting a to-do list together is a perfect chance for motion to masquerade as Action, making it an excellent way to procrastinate on actually being in action.

Your brain sees putting your to-do list together as an actual accomplishment, when in fact, you haven't actually moved anything forward at all. Sure, you've thought things through and made some plans, but that's it. You haven't really done anything to move one step closer to accomplishing anything. You have a list, but it is worthless unless you act on it.

---

* It's rare when a play results in the ball being run all 100 yards from one end of the field to the other. But it happens.
† See Chapter Five for a full description of different types of to-do lists.

It's the same with any other kind of planning, whether it's a list of future goals, your plan for the weekend, or a month-by-month plan to get in shape. Your brain thinks you've been in Action the whole time when you really haven't. You've been in the motion of planning.

Motion can feel good, but Action is what produces results. Both Action and motion are necessary when it comes to getting things done, but too many people get caught up in the motion portion of the program and never get into the essential Action part.

How this affects you

How can the difference between Action and motion affect you? Let's say you've decided your office needs to be cleaned up, reorganized, and made a little more efficient for daily use. You know the two options you have here: motion or Action. Planning a new filing system, going online or to the office supply store and finding new file folders, new storage containers, and while you're at it, a new lamp to go on your desk, are all helpful and possibly necessary.* But these are all examples of being in motion, not in Action.

After doing all of this planning and purchasing, is your office any cleaner or more efficient? No. While it's true you have more file folders and storage containers, you haven't used them. You have been in motion.

Action begins when you pick up the first piece of paper and either file it or throw it away. It's when you clear off your desk and get rid of the things you don't need or use any more. It's when you actually start taking the steps that move you towards achieving your goal of having a reorganized and efficient office.

Motion is still important

Don't get me wrong here. I'm not saying motion has to be eliminated. You still need motion. You need the planning and the organizing. You wouldn't take a road trip, start a business, design a website, or build a house without first taking time to plan out what happens when, in what order, and with whom. Doing so would be foolish.

Planning is obviously essential, but always remember it is motion. While it feels like you've accomplished something, you really haven't moved towards

---

* Hey, I don't know how messy your office is

your goal line. It is still only an idea, a vision. Visions are great, but for them to come to fruition, you need Action. All the planning based motion in the world means nothing without putting action behind it.

You probably know people who have "planned" to write a book, open a business, become the next singing sensation, get in shape, travel across the country, or get out of debt. They may have gone so far as to create a schedule, to plot out what has to happen and when, and how they are going to do it. But until they put those plans into Action, they haven't done anything to make their plan a reality. They have been in motion.

To get things done, you need to be able to identify when you are in motion and consciously move from motion into Action, which honestly, isn't as tricky as it sounds.

There are two different methods I like to use. One requires a little preplanning, while the other is a bit like jumping off a cliff. Both work really well and are significant first steps towards getting things done.

Draw your Line-In-The-Sand

When planning (motion) is left unchecked, it can stop all forward progress. A Line-In-The-Sand deadline tells you "enough with the planning and procrastination, it's time to get going!"

Let's say you have a project to complete, either for work or home, and you have a deadline for its completion. It's up to you to decide what happens when, and how much time you spend on each portion of the project. You're very well acquainted with this kind of deadline. It might look a little bit like this:

NORMAL PROJECT

START · · · · · · DEADLINE

MOTION PLANNING · ACTION · MOTION PLANNING · ACTION · MOTION PLANNING · ACTION

The Line-In-The-Sand is a second, much earlier deadline designed to be the stopping point for motion and the beginning point for Action.

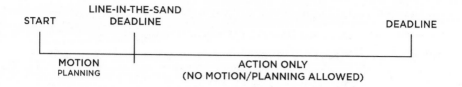

The goal of the Line-In-The-Sand is to make sure you don't spend all your time in motion. You want to be able to give yourself enough time in Action to actually complete your project successfully. When motion isn't stopped, one of two results can occur: there will either be a mad dash to the finish (so your best effort isn't put into the project), or you'll miss your deadline completely (which isn't a great thing either).

Am I catastrophizing? Yes, a little bit. But I'm sure you can think of instances where the motion part of a project or goal completely took over, and Action only showed up in a rush at the end. You probably weren't pleased with the final outcome of your efforts (or lack of efforts).

Putting the Line-In-The-Sand to work

Let's say you have an upcoming project you have four weeks to complete. You choose to make the end of your first week your Line-In-The Sand deadline. The first week you'll be in motion, then you will stop, and the next three weeks will all be Action-based.

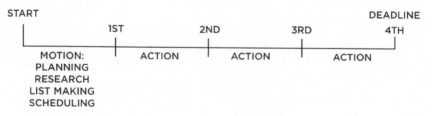

During the first week, you do all your planning, research, and thinking about what could go wrong, and how you can prevent it or solve it if it does happen. This is when lists are made, schedules are outlined, and details are nailed down, all so you can be in Action during the next three weeks. You've given yourself a deadline to stop running on the hamster wheel and move into Action.

Obviously, the Line-In-The-Sand doesn't just work with projects which are a month long. Any project, or any goal you are working on, can benefit from having a Line-In-The-Sand deadline. You just adjust your time accordingly.

Line-In-The-Sand examples

If you have a blog post which needs to be written and posted, then you might give yourself 30 minutes to research, outline, and rough out the post before you get down to writing it out. If you have a proposal which needs to be submitted, you might give yourself a morning to research and gather all the information, then spend the afternoon putting the proposal together.

There is no magic ratio to follow, just use common sense (and a little trial and error doesn't hurt either).

For example, when I know on Monday I have a project due on Friday afternoon, I'll give myself all of Monday morning to prep, research, and plan. My Line-In-The-Sand is when the clock strikes noon. Which is when all motion stops, and I have to move into Action. Unless something happens that requires me to do additional research (potentially opening me up to going down a research rabbit hole), there is no more motion, only dedicated Action to hit my deadline of Friday.

Deciding when your Line-In-The-Sand deadline is and sticking to it is an easy way to ensure when motion stops and Action begins on any project you're working on. This works best when you have the luxury of time, which isn't always the case.

In movies, the hero is always jumping into Action when they didn't think they were ready. Usually, it's because there is no other choice. Jumping In is your second option when it comes to moving from motion into Action.

Jump In when you aren't ready

As a kid, I grew up spending summers with my three sisters on our farm in central Minnesota. Every day around 2 p.m., my mom would pack us in the car and drive over to a nearby lake for a couple of hours of swimming.

One of our favorite ways to get into the lake was to run down and launch ourselves off the dock into the refreshingly cold water. One moment we were dry as we hurtled through the air, the next we were shrieking at the shock of the cold water. Jumping off the dock eliminated any chance of us changing our minds about getting wet. We were committed.

Jumping was the easiest way to get in the water. Walking slowly into the lake was nearly impossible when the water was cold. Even on a hot day, as soon as the water hit our stomachs, we would chicken out and run back to the shore. Then we'd have to decide if we really wanted to get in. Jumping in eliminated any chance for our brains to talk us out of getting in the water.

With the initial cold shock over, it was easy to enjoy whatever came next. Little did I know that those summer afternoons at the lake were training me in one of the tried and true ways to get into Action.

Physics always wins

When jumping off the dock, there was always a moment of inevitability—a moment when there was no turning back. Once we were airborne, even if we changed our minds, there was no way for us to change the laws of physics. No matter how our brains protested that they weren't ready for what came next (freezing cold water), there was no way to go back. There was no way to hesitate, procrastinate, or ruminate. Getting soaking wet was the only option.

It's the same way with jumping into any sort of Action when you aren't ready. While it's not a leap off the dock, it's a leap out of your comfort zone into Action.

Why is this leap necessary? Let's face it, left to our devices, it's easier to NOT be in Action. It's easier to procrastinate, to put things off, to wait until everything is absolutely perfect before moving into Action. Every one of those things keeps you firmly in motion—you're thinking of doing something, but you're not really doing it.

Jumping In when you aren't ready is you giving your status quo (and comfort zone) the middle finger.

What it looks like

Jumping In means you pick *A* place to start, whether it's the perfect place or not. It's *A* place. Not necessarily *THE* place. It's a start. It means you are in Action and actually doing something which is going to move you towards your goal.

It's writing the first paragraph of your book when you aren't even sure how to write a book. It's buying the domain name when you aren't really sure what your website is going to look like. It's booking the one-way ticket to your dream destination without knowing how you'll pay for it. It's taking the first step without knowing what the second step is. It's eliminating the motion and moving into Action. And while it might scare you more than just drawing a Line-In-The-Sand, it certainly gets the job done.

Just like everyone else in the world, I encounter things where I don't entirely know what I'm doing.* But I wouldn't get much accomplished if I sat around and waited until I knew everything before I started. Waiting is the antithesis of Action in every sense of the word.

So I'm much better off just Jumping In, knowing I can learn as I go along or someone can fill me in along the way.

Jumping In is a vital Action tool because you're not waiting for permission from anyone to start, nor are you waiting for things to be perfect. You just start doing. As long as you know what it is you want to accomplish, nothing can really stop you. Once you're in Action, it's easy to keep going. Your brain helps you with this.

Moving from motion into Action isn't an exact science, so sometimes Jumping In is really the only way to get started.

Going Backwards

Now that you know a couple of ways to move out of motion and into Action, I'm going to ask you to go back into motion for a moment because, surprisingly, one of the key Action tools is actually something that puts you firmly in motion. But now you know that just staying in motion is never an option to getting things done, I know you can handle it.

The #1 Action tool

This tool is one that I'm going to reference again and again in this book, not because I like being repetitive, but because this tool works so well when it comes to being stronger than the enemies of productivity. This tool involves planning as a way to help you be prepared for all possibilities, so you save both time and energy. This tool is called an Action Plan, and you'll be using it a lot, both while reading this book, and hopefully afterwards as well.

---

* Shocking, I know.

At its most basic, an Action Plan is a road map to get you from where you are to where you want to be. An Action Plan comes from thinking, "I am here, but this is where I want to be. Ideally, this is the series of small steps I will use. But I know conditions may not (ok, probably won't be) ideal. And situations may arise which could disrupt my path, so here is a plan for what I can do if or when I run into any problems."

Action Plans in your past

When you were a child, your parents and teachers wanted you to become a helpful, kind person. Obviously, that's a long-term goal (and easier to do with some kids than others), so gold stars were employed. Made your bed? Gold star. Did your schoolwork? Gold star. Shared with others? Gold star. Each of those behaviors was part of a system that eventually shaped you into being the helpful, kind person that I'd like to believe you became.

These were small actions that led to a significant outcome. Following an Action Plan filled with small actions is the same thing. Rather than looking to finish a large project, hit a big goal, or trying to achieve something you've never done all in one big leap, work in a series of small steps. When you think about it, every day as you work towards your goal, whatever it is, is another day when you are not actually achieving it. True, you are one step closer, but you technically haven't achieved your goal. You have not yet succeeded.

Soul crushing, isn't it?

But what if you've been looking at it all wrong? Instead of working toward one ecstatic day when the scale hits a certain number, when you cross the finish line, or when your new business launches, what if you concentrate on the success of each of the small actions? Regular success on small goals will eventually lead to success on achieving your big goal.

So, rather than focusing on the success of 20 pounds coming off, you look at the Action Plan success of having a salad every day or watching your portions at every meal. Instead of looking at each workout as something you have to do toward final marathon success, you view it as the Action Plan success of gradually increasing your endurance to the point where you are fully equipped to run 26.2 miles. You are succeeding at the process of achieving your goal.

Start filling out your Action Plan* by listing the small steps that will get you to your goal. For some things, this will be repeating small steps, like celebrating every salad you eat or every time you work out. For others, it will be more of an A to B to C type of thing, like the steps to completing a project where you have to research, write, edit, then present. Which is the reason why there are different forms of Action Plans, as you'll soon see. These small steps are the first part of an Action Plan. The second part is planning for things to get in your way.

Plan for the obstacles

Planning ahead for what could go wrong might feel a little like you are planning for failure, but it's entirely the opposite. Planning ahead for obstacles allows you to be prepared, so the unexpected doesn't stop you in your tracks. If you know that "X" might happen then you can make sure you have the solution to "X" at hand. So as you put together your Action Plans, the second thing you have to do is look ahead to what obstacles might show up and slow you down, or prevent you from achieving your goal. You then decide what strategies or tools you might need to call on, and then build your plan of attack.

You probably already do this, but not in a formalized Action Plan way. For example, if you're going out for the day, you make sure that your phone is charged, and if you're going to be gone a long time, you probably make sure you have a charger available in case you need it.†

Action Plans are that simple. When you plan ahead, you have the luxury of thoughtfully thinking through your responses to unexpected situations. These responses will most likely be better than if you had to come up with an answer on the fly, or if you were under pressure.‡ This is exactly why Action Plans always have If/Then Plans built into them.

If/Then Plans

If I were to ask you to write a research paper on the life cycle of an amoeba, and hand it in to me by next Thursday, besides being a very odd request, you

---

* See plan example on page 16.
† Definitely a first-world problem.
‡ Wouldn't you be more relaxed knowing you had a charger available when your phone hit seven percent battery, rather than figuring out where it could be charged and how long it would take you to get there? Again, first-world issue.

would be much more likely to get the paper to me by Thursday if you did one very specific thing: decide on the time and place when you would sit down and write the paper. For example, you could choose "Sunday afternoon at 2 p.m. while the kids are out playing." This was the discovery of Peter Gollwitzer and Veronika Branstaater[1] in a 1997 study.*

Professor Gollwitzer took a group of students and divided them into two groups. One group was told to write a paper over Christmas vacation describing what they did with their time and how it impacted them. Before leaving the lab they had to write down when and where they would write the paper. The second group was given the same writing assignment but did not have to decide when and where they would actually do the paper.

After Christmas vacation, 67% of the students who had determined ahead of time when and where they would do the paper, actually had the paper completed and ready to turn in. Only 20% of the second group of students had done so.

This study (and many after it) showed that when you decide ahead of time when, where, and how something is going to be done, you are much more likely to make it happen. Because you've identified when it's going to happen, you've also probably identified any obstacles which might show up and what you're going to do to get past them. This is the basis of If/Then Plans.

With an If/Then Plan, you look at what obstacles could show up, and plan how you'll respond with a plan in place. Should the obstacle show up, you're prepared and you don't have to make (usually bad, time-wasting) decisions on the fly. You don't have to stop and think about what you're going to do. You already know. Done correctly, the obstacles actually become triggers for alternate behaviors. You know what you need to do, so you can just get started. Most importantly, If/Then plans keep your Action Plan on track.

What If/Then Plans look like

If/Then plans can be applied to all aspects of your life and used in all kinds of Action Plans.

Let's say your Action Plan is to increase your client base at work. When you set up your Action Plan, you suspected one of obstacles you would encounter

---

* Which had nothing whatsoever to do with amoebas.

would be your frustration with making cold calls and you planned for it. Your If/Then Plan now might be: "If I'm feeling frustrated with cold calling, Then I will take a five-minute walk after the first five calls, and come back and make five more calls." Or it might be: "If I am having trouble with cold calling, Then I will make a game out of it and see how many calls it will take to get to five yeses."

If/Then Plans can apply to anything you're working on. Need to make the most of your downtime? "If I am watching television, Then I get off the couch and exercise during all of the commercial breaks." Very simple. Very specific.

Trying to eat healthy? "If I eat an unexpected treat in the office, Then I will take a 20-minute walk when I get home." Or "If someone brings treats into work, Then I will stay out of the Break Room until they are gone."

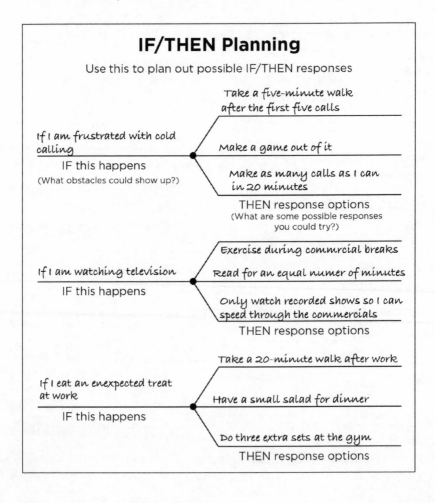

IF/THEN Planning

Use this to plan out possible IF/THEN responses

Take a five-minute walk after the first five calls

If I am frustrated with cold calling

IF this happens
(What obstacles could show up?)

Make a game out of it

Make as many calls as I can in 20 minutes

THEN response options
(What are some possible responses you could try?)

Exercise during commrcial breaks

If I am watching television

IF this happens

Read for an equal numer of minutes

Only watch recorded shows so I can speed through the commercials

THEN response options

Take a 20-minute walk after work

If I eat an enexpected treat at work

IF this happens

Have a small salad for dinner

Do three extra sets at the gym

THEN response options

Setting up If/Then Plans before you need them takes your Action Plans from average to extra strength, so why not try putting a few together now? Think of some obstacles you encounter during the day. Write one or two down, then for each one, come up with three different ways you could positively react or respond and overcome that obstacle. (You'll be doing more If/Then Plans throughout the book, this just gives you some practice in putting them together.)

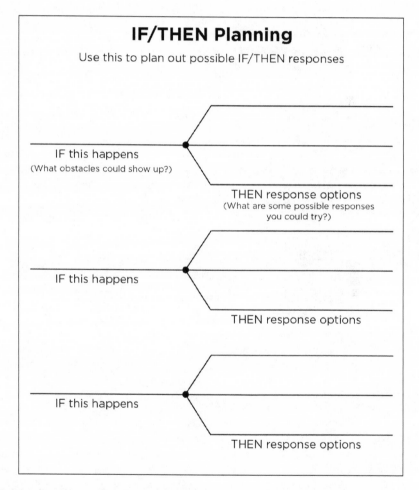

IF/THEN Planning

Use this to plan out possible IF/THEN responses

IF this happens
(What obstacles could show up?)

THEN response options
(What are some possible responses you could try?)

IF this happens

THEN response options

IF this happens

THEN response options

Critical Action Plan information

This brings up another critical Action Plan fact. Action Plans are NOT to-do lists. They are stronger than that. Action Plans are your step-by-step plan to get to where you want to be. Think of a to-do list as a page of directions to build a coffee table from Ikea. You have a picture of how Tab A is supposed to go into Slot B, but there's nothing on the page of directions to help you if Tab A breaks off, or you can't find Slot B, or if one piece arrives broken, or if you're trying to build the entire table with one arm in a cast. The directions assume an optimal situation. Always assume and plan for less than optimal situations, and set up your Action Plan accordingly

Action Plans don't have to be written in stone, nor do they have to perfect. Start with an Action Plan you think is going to work and do it for a while. Then step back and assess if it's working for you. If you feel like you aren't making the progress you'd like, or you're running into problems you didn't think about, take some time and retool your Action Plan as needed. The Action Plan you start with might not be the one you stick with. Action Plans should be living documents that change as needed.

It's always good to have a plan

So, what does an Action Plan actually look like? It can be as simple as a Post-it® Note* which lists what you want to get done, what might be an obstacle and how to deal with it.

GOAL

Spend 45 minutes researching information for my presentation

IF/THEN

If I some of the information I need isn't readily available, THEN I will put it on a list to follow-up on at a future time and keep going.

---

* I will call them Post-it® Notes because that's what everyone knows them by, like Kleenex® and Xerox®, but you can also buy no-name sticky notes. It's up to you. Whether you use the name brand or not doesn't affect anything in this book one bit.

This works great for short-term goals like trying to take care of a one-hour project or maybe a simple one-day project. When you know what might happen and how you'll respond, you are less likely to become distracted or give up.

More involved Action Plans

What about more involved Action Plans? The bigger the project or goal, the better to have an Action Plan in place to prevent procrastination and to guide your actions. But always remember, setting up Action Plans means you are in motion. This is why I think it's always important to have the word START on your plan. Because, while having a plan is great, it's just a piece of paper or a digital file with little black scribbles if you don't move into Action.

On the next few pages are examples of Action Plans. The first is perfect to use for a Multi-Step Project or goal (in this case, going back to school). Because it is big project, it's best to break it down into smaller Action Steps. Every step in this example could be broken down even further if necessary.

Following the Multi-Step Project is an example of an Action Plan for a Repetitive-Step Project, a project that requires consistent repetition of the same task or type of task to achieve your goal (such as running, working out, writing). This type of plan also works well when building habits. Following that is an example of a Small Projects Action Plan. Download blank versions of all of these Action Plans at EllenGoodwin.com/forms.

Different projects and goals call for different types of Action Plans. Figure out which one works for you, then move into Action towards achieving your most important projects or goals.

Filling in Your Multi-Step Action Plan

(NOTE: not all lines have to be filled in.)

This Action Plan works best for projects or goals with sequential steps to accomplish to complete a project or goal.

1. Fill in your project or goal. Be Specific!
2. Write down what success will look like.
3. Note any resources you currently have that you can call on to help you achieve your goal, including individuals, businesses, skills, and tools.
4. Write, in order, each of the steps that will be required to complete the project or goal successfully.
5. Note what the desired outcome for each of the steps is.
6. List any obstacles you might encounter.
7. List possible solutions to your obstacles.
8. Write down your time frames for each step.
9. Why is successful completion of this project or goal is important to you?
10. What is your reward for successful completion?
11. Press Start and move into Action!

ACTION PLAN - MULTI-STEP PROJECT

GOAL: **(1)**
Go back to school and finish degree

RESOURCES: **(3)**
2.5 years completed
Required classes complete
Flexible schedule

WHAT SUCCESS WILL LOOK LIKE: **(2)**
Graduate with a Bachelors in Business

(4) Action Steps	**(5)** Desired Result	**(6)** Possible Obstacles	**(7)** Possible Solutions	**(8)** Timeframe
1. Decide where to apply	Determine where to go	Timing	Clear schedule	2 weeks
2. Apply online for admission	Admission to upcoming semester	May not be admitted	Learn what else I can do	1-2 weeks
3. Sign up for classes	Get the classes I need	Classes may not be available	Look at other available classes	6 days
4. Begin classes	Take classes for my degree	No time to study	Eliminate some after work activities	18 months
5.				
6.				
7.				
8.				
9.				

WHY I WANT TO ACHIEVE: **(9)**
Advance at work
Open up other opportunities
Sense of accomplishment

REWARD: **(10)**
Big Party
Trip to mountains

(11) **START!**

Filling in Your Repetitive Step Action Plan

(NOTE: not all lines have to be filled in.)

This Action Plan works best for projects or goals with repetitive steps you take (daily/weekly) to move you towards your goal. (For example: work out every morning, write every day, go to the gym four days a week.)

1. Fill in your project or goal. Be Specific!
2. Write down what success will look like.
3. Note any resources you currently have that you can call on to help you achieve your goal, including individuals, businesses, skills, and tools.
4. Write out your repetitive task.
5. During the week, cross off each time you successfully perform your task. If you aren't performing the task seven times a week, feel free to cross out the numbers that don't apply to you.
6. List any obstacles you might encounter.
7. List possible solutions to your obstacles.
8. At the end of the week, list your results.
9. Why is successful completion of this project or goal is important to you?
10. What is your reward for successful completion?
11. Press Start and move into Action.

ACTION PLAN - REPETITIVE STEP PROJECT

(1) GOAL:
Run (and finish) the New Year's Day marathon

(2) WHAT SUCCESS WILL LOOK LIKE:
Crossing the finish line - alive!

(3) RESOURCES:
Running club
Running coach
Training books
Running partner

(4) Weekly | Daily Steps To Achieve	(5) Repetitions Performed	(6) Possible Obstacles	(7) Possible Solutions	(8) Result
Follow Race Training Schedule - Week #1	1 2 3 4 5 6 7	Work obligations	Block time in my calendar	5 runs 2 yoga classes
Follow Race Training Schedule - Week #2	1 2 3 4 5 6 7	Out-of-town Conference	Plan running options	
Follow Race Training Schedule - Week #3	1 2 3 4 5 6 7	Work	Run before work	
Follow Race Training Schedule - Week #4	1 2 3 4 5 6 7	Sore/Burnt Out	Light workouts Schedule massage	
Follow Race Training Schedule - Week #5	1 2 3 4 5 6 7	Family in town	Recruit family for runs	
Follow Race Training Schedule - Week #6	1 2 3 4 5 6 7	Vacation	Research and plan routes	
Follow Race Training Schedule - Week #7	1 2 3 4 5 6 7	Tired/Bored	Do new group runs on new routes	
Follow Race Training Schedule - Week #8	1 2 3 4 5 6 7	Work Schedule	Block time in my calendar	
Follow Race Training Schedule - Week #9	1 2 3 4 5 6 7	Conference/ Travel	Research run options	

(9) WHY I WANT TO ACHIEVE:
Sense of Accomplishment
- Run my FIRST
Marathon. What else can I
do?

(10) REWARD:
Weekend at the beach

(11) START!

Filling in Your Small Project Action Plan

(NOTE: not all lines have to be filled in.)

This Action Plan works best for small projects or goals which may or may not be part of a more significant project or goal.

1. Fill in your project. Be Specific!
2. Write down the goal of this project.
3. Why is successful completion of this project or goal is important to you?
4. Write, in order, each of the smalls steps that will be required to complete the project successfully.
5. List any obstacles you might encounter.
6. List possible solutions to your obstacles.
7. List the desired outcome of each step and the deadline for it.
8. Press Start and move into Action!

ACTION PLAN - SMALL PROJECT

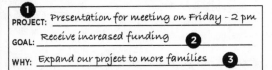

1 PROJECT: Presentation for meeting on Friday - 2 pm

GOAL: Receive increased funding **2**

WHY: Expand our project to more families **3**

8 START!

4 Small Steps Needed	**5** Possible Obstacles	**6** Possible Solutions	Outcome/ Date **7**
1. Gather all needed information	Missing information Missing responses	Alternative research Alternative contacts	All info/ Monday pm
2. Brainstorm outline of presentation	Not everyone can attend meeting	Request additional input via email	Outline complete Tues. am
3. Draft presentation and necessary slides	Time not available	Reschedule 3 committments	Draft complete Wed. 1 pm
4. Review with Division Head	Scheduling conflicts	Review via video call	Full buy-in Thurs am
5. Practice presentation	Unexpected timing conflicts	Practice offsite	Rehearsed Thurs pm
6. Deliver presentation	Unexpected technical issues	Check out conference room 1/2 hour before	Presented and funded

You'll remember I mentioned in the introduction how the brain is the cause of, and answer to, our productivity issues? Using Action Plans plays to one of the secret strengths of your brain, which is how it becomes so powerful.

The Action Plan bonus

Action Plans allow you to employ a secret brain weapon: dopamine. Dopamine is one of the neurotransmitters responsible for the pleasure response when you succeed at a task. And because your brain likes dopamine, it wants to do whatever it can to get more of it. So if your Action Plan is a series of small steps/actions, then each time you succeed at your action, you get a hit of dopamine. With each hit, you feel good, so you want to succeed again, and luckily for you, you have a plan in front of you that tells you what you can do to succeed again in a small way. With enough small successes, you'll get to a big success and a big hit of dopamine. It's an exciting action-reward sequence which powers success.

At this point, you now know your first action skill: identifying motion and moving into Action, and you have your first action tool: the Action Plan. Now it's time to learn about the enemy of your Action.

The Enemy of Action

Being in Action and getting things done is something you aspire to. Unfortunately your Action has an enemy. This enemy's job is to stop you in any way it can. This enemy loves distractions, feeds on novelty, hates leaving its comfort zone, and is responsible for promoting procrastination in all forms.

The enemy? Your limbic system,* located in the region of your brain known as the old brain or the reptilian brain.

This is the part of your brain responsible for your emotions, your memories, and your fight or flight response. This is the part of your brain that wants you to stay in the safety of your comfort zone where everything is safe, secure, and non-challenging. Your limbic system is like a naughty three-year-old, saying "no, no, no" when you need to get things done or you want to try something new.

---

* Or your paleomammalian cortex if you want to get very specific.

Moments of Choice

The power of your three-year-old is most evident during your Moments of Choice, those times during the day where your attention can go in any direction. It's the brief moment where you finish one task and have yet to start another one. Many times, this comes down to a choice between two or more things. Do you click on an email or do you continue to focus on what you were working on? This is the moment where the three-year-old is the most powerful. During your pause, the three-year-old begins suggesting alternative ideas. "Start work on your proposal? Nah! Let's check social media. Now!"

Moments of Choice are a gateway to distraction and procrastination, and they happen so often throughout your day that you don't consciously notice them. This is precisely why time gets wasted, projects don't get started or finished, and procrastination sets in.

The three-year-old is the reason you procrastinate, why distractions are so powerful, and why you think you are a great multitasker. The three-year-old is the primary reason why Action Plans are so important. As roadmaps, they minimize or even eliminate Moments of Choice.

Working with and around your three-year-old is a powerful Action skill you'll be learning more about as we go on.

As we wrap up this chapter, let me first congratulate you! You are now officially on your way to getting things DONE. You've learned the vital difference between motion and Action, and why being in action is so important. You now know how to stop motion by drawing your Line-In-The-Sand, and why Jumping In When You Aren't Ready enables you to overcome the need for everything to be perfect when you start.

Most importantly, you now know the #1 Action Tool: putting Action Plans together so you can overcome obstacles, boost your dopamine, eliminate Moments of Choice, and be stronger and smarter than your limbic system (and the three-year-old that lives in there).

In the next five chapters, we're going to look at another enemy that threaten your productivity on a daily basis and how you can consistently prevail. That enemy is procrastination, and it has the power to stop you dead in your tracks if you let it. Together, we're going to look at the one thing that causes you to procrastinate most of the time, how to deal with distractions, how being organized with your day can change what you get done, and what to do when your goals are too far down the road.

CHAPTER ONE ACTION TOOLBOX: ACTION BASICS

DEFINITIONS IN THIS CHAPTER

Limbic System

The region of your brain responsible for your emotions, your memories, and your fight or flight response. This is the part of your brain that wants you to stay in the safety of your comfort zone, where everything is safe, secure, and non-challenging. Your limbic system is like a naughty three-year-old, saying "no, no, no" when you need to get things done, or you want to try something new.

Dopamine

The neurotransmitter, a chemical released by neurons in your brain, responsible for the pleasure response, acting as a motivational factor in tasks such as when you complete a task.

Moments of Choice

Moments of Choice are a point in time where you have to choose what you are going to do. Many times, this comes down to a choice between two or more things. Do you click on an email, or do you continue to focus on what you were working on? Do you choose to do X, or Y, or possibly even Z? Moments of Choice are a gateway to distraction and procrastination.

TOOLS IN THIS CHAPTER

Draw Your Line-In-the-Sand:

Eliminate procrastination by setting up a deadline where all motion stops and you move into Action on your project or goal.

Jump In When You're Not Ready:

Instead of waiting for everything to be perfect, take a deep breath and jump into Action by starting, knowing that Action is how things get accomplished.

Action Plan:
A series of preplanned, small steps paired with If/Then plans, designed to get you from where you are to where you want to be.

If/Then Plans:
Also known as Implementation Intentions, these precommitments determine what you will do if a triggering event occurs. They can be used to plan ahead for life obstacles or to commit to doing something in the future.

ENEMY OF ACTION:
The three-year-old in your limbic system which loves Distractions and Moments of Choice. The three-year-old wants to keep you safe and in the status quo. All Action Plans and strategies and tools in this book are designed to help you overcome the three-year-old.

ACTION ITEMS
At the end of each chapter are Action Items you can choose to do. Some of the actions may apply to things you are currently working on. Others may be something you will need in the future. Pick and choose what appeals to you knowing, you don't have to do all of the actions immediately.

Identify when Moments of Choice appear
Become aware of and acknowledge Moments of Choice as they show up in your day. Taking the briefest of seconds to identify and tell yourself, "this is a Moment of Choice," will bring you into the present moment where you can consciously make a decision to stay on track.

You can also start to track Moments of Choice and begin to plan for them. Each day, for the next three days, use a blank index card to track when Moments of Choice appear. They may show up after a particular event, such as finishing emails in the morning or returning to your desk after lunch. They may show up randomly, just note when and where they show up.

Example of a Moment of Choice tracking card:

Moments of Choice   Monday
Finishing up morning emails 8:35   At my computer
After morning meeting   10:05   Outside conference room
After half hour of research   11:45   Office/computer
After returning from lunch   1:00   Walking into the building
Mid-afternoon between projects 3:15 Office
End of work   5:25   In my car
Walking in the house   7:10   Front door
After dinner   8:30   Dining room/living room

At the end of three days, go through the three index cards, with your Moments of Choice tracking on them. Note any patterns you see. Circle the three Moments of Choice which most frequently show up. Now, come up with four different ways you can deal with each of these Moments of Choice.

Example: *After finishing emails*

1. *Have a sticky note next to computer with my next 3 tasks written on it.*

2. *Do emails between meetings do I have a hard deadline.*

3. *Establish a ritual for moving to my next task.*

4. *Block distractions before I start emails.*

Frequent Moments of Choice: _____

1. _____

2. _____

3. _____

4. _____

Frequent Moments of Choice: _____

1. _____

2. _____

3. _____

4. _____

Frequent Moments of Choice: _____

1. _____

2. _____

3. _____

4. _____

Build an Action Plan

If you haven't done so already, it's time to build an Action Plan. Download blank Action Plans at EllenGoodwin.com/forms. Pick the one that applies to your project and start filling the Action Plan out as per the instructions on pages 16-20.

When you have completed your plan, press the "Start" in the corner and begin. You've been in successful motion, now is the time to move into productive Action.

Line-In-The-Sand

Set up a simple Line-In-The-Sand deadline for your next project, then hold yourself to the new deadline.

Example:

Project: *Put a presentation together for work*

Deadline: *This Friday (five days from now)*

Line-In-the-Sand Deadline: *End of the Day on Monday: all research, planning, and interviews will be completed.*

Project: _____

Deadline: _____

Line-In-the-Sand Deadline: _____

Project: _____

Deadline: _____

Line-In-the-Sand Deadline: _____

Project: _____

Deadline: _____

Line-In-the-Sand Deadline: _____

Procrastination

Scientists define procrastination as "the intentional delay of an action despite foreseeable negative future consequences." Translated into normal speak this means "not getting things done even if you know it's going to cause problems for you down the road." When you procrastinate, you opt for short-term pleasure at the cost of your long-term goal.

This is not a surprise to anyone.

Nearly everyone procrastinates on something at some time. The key is to be able to identify why you're procrastinating and then use the proper tool (or tools) to overcome it—which is precisely what you'll learn in the next five chapters.

Right now you could easily say "I'll check out those chapters tomorrow" (Ha, ha! A procrastination joke!). But you'll be better off jumping in now and arming yourself with tools and techniques that will enable you to start getting things DONE.

CHAPTER TWO

Procrastination I:
How to get started when starting feels like too much work

Procrastination is the Thief of Time.
- Edward Young, *English poet, philosopher & theologian*

When you break it all down, the basis of procrastination in one way or another is not wanting to leave your comfort zone.

You know what's happening in your comfort zone. There are no surprises to watch out for. Your comfort zone is usually way more, well, comfortable, and fun than what you "should" be doing. So, you stay where you are and don't get started. You're safe.

The main culprit responsible for keeping you in your comfort zone? Your crafty limbic system, of course. Many times when you procrastinate, it is because your limbic system is acting like a naughty three-year-old child and saying "no, no, no" to the things you need to get moving on. (Imagine the crying three-year-old in a grocery cart screaming because he or she can't get their way.) Which, in a nutshell, is your brain on procrastination.

Your limbic system is happy with your status quo, whatever that looks like. You might be lying on the couch, binging on Netflix, doing everything but the thing you're supposed to be doing, and you (and your three-year-old) likes it this way. You like it a lot. So much so that you have no reason or motivation to get started.

Which is not the way things get DONE.

Starting is difficult

The mere idea of getting started could be stopping you. When you look at the project ahead of you, it feels enormous (whether it actually is or not). Maybe you're supposed to be writing a sales report, doing the laundry, putting a presentation together, or something that is actually enormous such as writing a book, losing 20 pounds, going back to school, starting a new business, or any of a million other things.

In situations like this, your limbic system is absolutely no help. Instead of nudging you into action, it's offering up comments like "Oh hell no! That's too much to try to do today. We can't finish that. What's the fun in doing any of that anyway? There's other stuff we can do that's a lot more fun. Let me show you."

Your limbic system can be a bit of a jerk. On the one hand, it wants you to succeed and be rewarded. But it also wants you to hang out where you are, safe and comfortable and not feel challenged.

Since your limbic system is not really helping you prevent procrastination in this scenario, you need to be a little sneaky so you can get started. You're going to need to work with the three-year-old in your brain, and you're going to need to work around it as well. Luckily, there are several things you can try.

One method involves entertaining your three-year-old, while another involves removing one of his or her demands. Another method utilizes the magic of timers, while still another uses a popular competition format. The final two methods have you looking at the importance of where you stop and planning how you'll start. Remember, one size does not fit all, so feel free to experiment and find the tools that work best for you and your three-year-old.

1. How to get started when you don't really feel like it:

Make a Game Out of It

When dealing with a limbic system that is acting like a three-year-old, you often have to treat it like a three-year-old. And what three-year-old doesn't like games?* To overcome procrastination, one of the easiest and by far most amusing things you can do is to make a game out of your project or task. Not

---

* Answer: It's a trick question. All three-year-olds like games.

only will you easily get started, chances are you'll get your task or project done, all while keeping your three-year-old entertained.

Color My World

For years, my neighbor and I have taken hour-long walks in the morning. These walks give us a chance to talk and laugh, and both the time and miles fly right by. But on the odd occasions when she can't join me, all of a sudden my morning walk can become the most tedious thing in the world.

With no conversation and laughter to distract me, the hour drags by. It's just me and my thoughts and the same old scenery. Since my neighbor is not there to hold me accountable, the temptation to cut the walk short frequently pops up—a temptation that is actually my unhappy, inner three-year-old acting up. The three-year-old feels the walk isn't fun, so she doesn't want to do it, which makes it a perfect time to start playing games. My favorite walking game is "Color My World."

It's so simple that, well, a three-year-old could play it.

Before I start my walk, I pick a color* that I'm going to actively look for during the next hour. Not only am I going to look, I'm also going to count how many times I see objects of this chosen color during the walk.

For example, if I pick yellow, I can count fire hydrants and street signs, as well as daisies, cats, kids' toys, traffic lights, rugs, cars, umbrellas, patio seat cushions, and the odd, abandoned baby sock. This silly game makes me more aware of my environment, keeps my brain engaged, challenges me to be more observant, and makes my walk entertaining.

Having a game to play involves my brain-based three-year-old, the very one who would rather stay tucked in bed than walk for an hour the first thing in the morning. The game, as simple as it is, engages the three-year-old long enough for me to get started. It enables me to take something that could be boring and make it mildly entertaining.

---

* You can also pick shapes - squares, triangles, circles, octagons, or for the advanced three-year-olds, tetrahedrons or isosceles triangles.

When you make a game out of your low-priority or possibly dull task, you make getting started much less complicated. This color game doesn't have to just apply to walking in the neighborhood. It can be used in situations where your three-year-old is working very hard to make sure you don't get started. This can range from running errands on a Saturday morning, researching data for a presentation, sitting in a meeting, cleaning out a closet, or doing the laundry.

Picking a color (or a shape) and looking for them can be enough of a game to get you started. And, as you'll soon see, once you've gotten started, chances are you'll keep going. Which is an effective one-two punch when it comes to eliminating procrastination.

Dice, Dice, Baby

When you're overwhelmed with things to do, it's effortless to default to doing absolutely nothing. Moments of Choice represent an almost irresistible opportunity for procrastination to occur. I know I'm not the only one who has responded with a quick click of the television remote, or a jump into the deep end of a good book, or a slide into social media when confronted with a full to-do list. Rather than choose one of the tasks on my list, I choose none of them and go off and do something else. My inner three-year-old doesn't like to make choices, so when given too many, the option is usually clearly in favor of "none of the above." Which always means procrastination wins.

This game makes it easy to get started because you completely remove the default response and your three-year-old from the decision process.

The first step in Dice, Dice, Baby is to give each of the tasks on your to-do list a number, starting with #1 and going up.

There's no set way you have to number your tasks. You can start at the top of your list and start numbering with #1 and go down the list, or start at the bottom and work your way up. You can randomly assign numbers. Whatever works for you.

If you've got 12 tasks or less, raid a board game and get two dice. If you've got more than 12 tasks, grab more dice as needed (or you can be like one of my clients and use a 20-sided Dungeons and Dragons die).

Next, you roll the dice.

Whatever number comes up, you have to do the task with the corresponding number. There are no re-rolls. No over-thinking. You just get started on the task with the corresponding number and do it. Once the task is finished, cross it off the list, then roll the dice again and do the task that corresponds to the number you've rolled. Methodically work your way through your list.

Rolling the dice allows you to randomize your decisions and get started on all sorts of things like your to-dos, your food, your workouts, your clothes, or vacations. It takes the fussy three-year-old out of the equation and eliminates procrastination. It makes getting things done more fun than procrastinating.

BONUS: Roll the dice in other parts of your life

You can use Dice, Dice, Baby for making other choices in your life as well. When you randomize any list in this way, you remove the need to make decisions which conserves brain energy. The fewer decisions you have to make, especially when it comes to small, seemingly inconsequential decisions, the more brain energy you will have available for making more significant decisions in your day.

For example you could roll the dice to help you with:

Exercise. Rather than trying to decide between running, lifting weights, or going to a class, you could number your choices, roll the dice and do whatever number it corresponds to. Same with deciding on individual exercises, or choice of places to run or walk or workout. Write down and number your choices, then roll the dice. Eliminate the decisions and save the energy for your workout.

Clothing. Go through your closet and number every outfit combination you know works, for example, black pants, royal blue shirt, black vintage jacket with black boots could be choice #1, navy-blue A-line skirt, light blue blouse, and navy-blue pumps is choice #2. Roll the dice and wear whatever clothing combination corresponds to the number rolled.

Food. Make a list of your (or your family's) favorite meal choices and number them. Spend a few minutes before your week starts and roll the dice to plan your menu choices for the week. You could also make numbered lists of your favorite restaurants for eating in, taking-out, and delivery. Then when you need to make a decision of where to eat, you just roll the dice.

One of the genius things about numbering restaurant choices is, often times, when it comes time to eat, you already have depleted stores of brain energy and your ability to make decisions is already starting to be affected. Rolling the dice means you have one less decision to make. And, it handily eliminates the age-old conversation of where to eat.

"Where do you want to eat?"

"Anywhere."

"Okay, let's go to the new Thai place."

"Oh no, I don't feel like Thai."

"Then what do you want?"

"Anything."*

Family Activities. Write down options for family activities which you enjoy. Number them, and then before a weekend, a vacation or a holiday, roll the dice to decide what activity to do. This works exceptionally well when there are a lot of people involved. As long as each person has their choice represented, then everyone has an equal chance of getting their choice picked.

Household Chores. List and number household chores. Roll the dice and get started. This is a great way to get everyone involved without anyone feeling like they are being picked on.

Slow day at work list. Everyone occasionally has a quiet day at the office. Whether it's because you're between projects, it's the day before a holiday, or you're just in a low-energy space, there are days when you're not feeling like taking on the world. Before this happens, write down and number a list of tasks you could possibly take care of (especially ones you always seem to put off). It could be as simple as "throw out 20 pieces of paper," "spend 15 minutes throwing out junk emails," "spend 20 minutes writing a list of potential clients to reach out to," or "write ten blog post ideas." When you're feeling restless, unfocused, or unsure what to do next, roll the dice and do your task. You'll eliminate procrastination and you'll salvage the day.

---

* I will neither confirm nor deny this conversation has taken place at my house.

Go Fish

Similar to Dice, Dice, Baby, this game works well when you are faced with several tasks that all have the same level of urgency or priority. In situations like this, it's easy to procrastinate because there is no hierarchy. When you need to get started but you just can't figure out where, it's time to Go Fish.

Cut a piece of paper into 1-in x 3-in slips.* Write down one task on each slip then fold it in half and throw it into a bowl or a hat or a box. If you don't have a container available, then put the folded slips in a pile on your desk or table. Next, close your eyes and pull one slip out of the container or off the table, then get started on the task that is written on the slip of paper.

This is not a game of Catch and Release. You can't throw a slip back once you've pulled it out, hoping you'll pick something better. You have to do the task, and once it's complete, throw the slip of paper away and draw again. Keep pulling out the slips of paper and doing the tasks until you have worked your way through all of them.

Randomizing tasks through the luck of the draw eliminates the overwhelming feeling that comes with having to decide what is most important (especially when everything feels like it is important). Randomizing also works well when you have lots of options to choose from. Rather than spending time weighing the merits of things, just use the luck of the draw.

For example, let's say you're in charge of ordering the catering for an event. Rather than agonize over each of the dinner choices offered, list them all on their own slips of paper and draw out a couple of choices. In this vein, Go Fish works great for making decisions for weddings, new car options, lunch choices, and deciding where your next vacation should be.

Pin the Tail on the To-Do

Like a lot of ideas in this book, this one involves Post-it Notes. You start Pin the Tail on the To-Do by writing each of your to-do tasks on a Post-it Note. One task per note. Depending on how many things you have to get done, you could be writing out a lot of notes or just a few. As long as you have more than two tasks, you can play this game.

---

* There is nothing magic about this size. Make the slips bigger or smaller. I just pick this size as a way to give you an idea of where (no pun intended) to get started.

Next, take the notes and stick them on a vertical surface like a wall, a whiteboard, or a door. You can organize them by putting them in neat rows, or you can just put them up on the surface with no rhyme or reason, or you can group them by type of task. It doesn't matter. You're playing a game here, so you want to make this fun for you, and if neat rows are fun for you, who am I to question it? For the record, I'm not! The more fun you have, the happier your inner three-year-old is going to be, so you'll be able to get started faster and cut procrastination down to nothing.

Cover your eyes with your hand or a blindfold. Whatever you choose, cover your eyes so you can't see anything and point towards your wall, your whiteboard, or your door and touch a Post-it Note and remove it. Uncover your eyes and see what task you picked. It doesn't matter what it is, you have to do it. You don't get to let your three-year-old say, "ahhhh, I don't want to do this now." This is what you are going to do.

Once you've completed the first task, cover your eyes again, and choose another note. Continue until all the Post-it Notes are gone.

Add an additional degree of difficulty

Spinning around before you point to a Post-it Note is entirely up to you. As kids, we always had a "minder" of some sort when we played Pin the Tail on the Donkey so that we put the tail on the wall somewhere in the vicinity of the donkey and not on our little sister. If you decide to spin, it might be a good idea to have someone who will make sure you are pointing towards your notes so you don't end up pointing at a calendar or a photo of your dog, which most likely has nothing to do with your to-dos. You could also fold the notes in half so you can't see the tasks as you place them on the wall, making your selection more random since you don't know which note is where.

Taking time to decide which task has priority over another can be a great way to procrastinate. When you're not sure where you should start, picking nowhere to start feels like the best answer, and your three-year-old self would agree with you. But rather than letting confusion win, establishing some order to the chaos is surprisingly easy and quick thanks to a tool used in competition worldwide.

Bracket your priorities*

Chances are, you're familiar with brackets, especially if you've participated in "March Madness," or your kids have competed in a weekend tournament of some kind. A bracket is a tree diagram that represents a series of games played during a "knockout" tournament.

Basically, a bracket matches and organizes people or teams, two at a time, in a scheduled manner. Whoever wins the game advances to the next round, while the loser is either eliminated or moves over to the losers' bracket. For example, if there are eight teams, after the first round, four teams remain, and after the second, two teams remain and on it goes. Of course, bigger tournaments like March Madness start with a lot more teams.

When you've got a full to-do list with no clearly defined order of task importance, use the bracket structure and start pairing your tasks up and deciding which is the more important of the two.

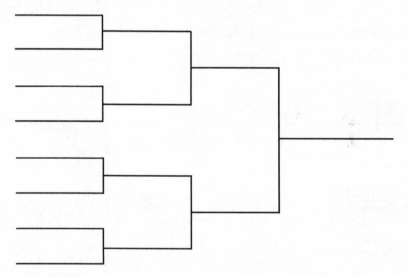

Set up your bracket quickly and randomly, without spending too much time weighing the pairing (remember Moments of Choice represent a chance for procrastination to arise).

---

* **A word of warning:** don't let setting up a bracket take the place of actually doing your work. This is a planning/motion activity that can be interpreted by your brain as you having been in action. Make sure you move into action when your bracket is complete.

Try pairing the first and last tasks on the list. Then pairing the second and the second to the last tasks, then the third and third to the last tasks. You get the idea.

Or you could pick the first two tasks on your list and make them the first pair, the next two tasks are the second pair, and so on. You could randomly select the pairs or even have your kids pair them up. Just pick a method and decide how you're going to pair tasks up without giving it too much thought or too much time.

Once all the tasks are paired up, look at the first pair of tasks, and decide which of the two tasks is more important to do first based on what you want or need to accomplish. Which task has priority over the other? If you feel they are both equal, then look at them based on your schedule and which one needs to be done before the other.

Decide which task wins this bracket, and advance it by putting it on a new winners list. Put the loser on a different list. It now has a lower priority, but the task still exists (you can't get rid of it that easily!).

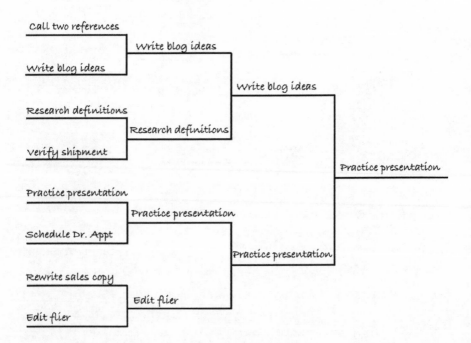

Move on to the next pairing and do the same thing. Make your way through your complete set of pairings. When you're done, you have two new lists: the winners and losers of this round. Pair off the winners and go through the list again and again until you have a clear idea of what task is most important and a hierarchy of the rest of the tasks. Then get started.

The second way you can prevent procrastination by getting started is to get rid of the very false idea that you have to start in the perfect place.

2. Eliminate Perfectionism

I have a friend who spent months putting together a great online program designed to be the cornerstone of her new business. This program could really help a lot of people, and it will, if she ever releases the program out into the wild of the Internet, but so far it isn't looking good. She won't release the program until it is absolutely, completely, no-doubt-about-it, 100% perfect. No glitches, no hiccups, no typos. Nothing can be out of place, and nothing can be incorrect.

In other words, it will never be done, and she will never release it because it will never be perfect. She is effectively using perfectionism to stop herself from starting her new business.

Whether she knows it or not, perfectionism is her chosen way to make sure her business never gets started. Who knows why she is putting off starting her new business. My guess would be fear. Unfortunately, there is no such thing as everything being 100% perfect. Perfectionism is her self-imposed roadblock to getting started.

And she is not alone. Perfectionism affects every one of us at some point because it's a great way to procrastinate. Look at it this way: if you wait for everything to be perfect, you don't actually have to do anything, so you can stay in your easy-to-be-in comfort zone.

"It's not the perfect time to start."

"I want to wait until everything is perfect."

"I can't (insert your choice of action) because it's not the right time."

Your three-year old is the one demanding perfection. It doesn't want you to have to do anything painful, which could get you hurt or make you look bad. If you're the least bit unsure of yourself, your three-year-old is going to use perfectionism as the ultimate tool to stop you from ever putting yourself out there. But here's the thing, for almost everything we do, we can really get by with it being 80% perfect.*

This isn't to say you should be lazy, sloppy, or do things halfway. There is something to be said for making things as good as they can be. But don't use perfectionism as an excuse not to get started. You probably don't need to consult another expert, take another class, or try another rewrite. Honest.

Giving up perfectionism is freeing. It's a great way to make sure you get started. Eighty percent of the time, your 80% is going to be more than enough.

Feeling a little nervous about giving up the perfection excuse? Then here's a shitty technique you can try:

A Shitty First Draft

You know what's easy to procrastinate on? Writing a book. Having to sit down every day and start the process of writing over and over. And then when it's done, everything needs to be in order before going to print. You have to have a layout format that looks good, know that everything is spelled correctly, and have a book cover that makes you stand out from the rest of the books on the shelf. It's enough to paralyze someone. Yet somehow, every year, hundreds of thousands of books get published. So obviously all of these authors are finding a way to move past that paralysis and write despite their desire for perfection

Authors have been dealing with perfectionism issues for centuries, and they have the answer to overcoming perfection-based procrastination, which applies not just to writing, but to just about everything in our world. It's called the Shitty First Draft.† It's the very simple idea that you just write the first draft of whatever you are writing without any judgment. Get the first, imperfect draft done no matter what.

To do a Shitty First Draft, you start writing, knowing your first draft will be terrible, but it will be done. Once you have the first draft written, you go back and edit and rewrite anything and everything and make it better. Draft by draft.[2]

---

* Ok, this probably shouldn't apply to things like flying airplanes, doing brain surgery, or any form of rocket science.
† Kudos to author, Anne Lamott, for giving us this term in her wonderful book, *Bird by Bird*.

It's more important to get the Shitty First Draft done than it is to wait for the perfect time, the perfect ideas, the perfect location, the perfect temperature, the perfect pen, the perfect anything. Start where you are with what you have and get into action.

After the Shitty First Draft is written, authors go back and start to edit, rewrite and reshape their writing, which is when they start working to make their writing good, if not great. But they couldn't start editing if they didn't have the draft in the first place. Their beautiful, highly imperfect, definitely shitty, first draft. And for millions of writers throughout history, the concept of the Shitty First Draft has worked.

So, right about now, you might be thinking, "Well, great, thanks for the interesting idea, but I'm not a writer, so I don't see how this applies to me at all."

Fair enough.

Let's just say writers don't own the exclusive rights to the idea of a Shitty First Draft.

A Shitty First Draft can be the first draft of anything in your world you aren't doing because you aren't perfect at it.

It's true.

Take a moment and think about the Olympics.

Every couple of years, amazing athletes from all over the world descend on a country and compete in sports which you never think about during the years when the Olympics don't occur. Every one of these athletes is impressive in their own right. Their stories are fascinating. Their dedication to their sport is admirable. But what often gets forgotten is every one of those athletes did a Shitty First Draft when they first started their athletic career.

They definitely weren't impressive and perfect the first time they put on skis, hit the ice, did a cartwheel, ran a mile, or did that weird thing with the curling broom. They were awkward and uncertain. They fell and failed, but over time, they figured out what worked and what didn't. They edited their Shitty First Draft over and over. What they didn't do was wait for things to be exactly perfect. They were in Action, learning and relearning, correcting and practicing how to excel in their chosen sport.

You're no different than an Olympic athlete, so quit looking for the perfect time to write your first blog post. Stop believing you have to have all the information before you try sending out your first marketing piece for your new business. Know you don't have to have the perfect exercise routine in place before you start working to get into shape.

Instead, get started and do your own version of the Shitty First Draft. Write the blog post no one reads. Send out the marketing piece no one responds to. Find out you hate all the exercises you thought you would love (then go find some new ones to experiment with).

Congratulations! You have conquered perfectionism and lived to tell the tale.

As you continue to write, market, exercise, or whatever it is you are working on, you will edit and change and grow. You will figure out what works for you and what doesn't. You will get better. You will move forward, without needing everything to be perfect.

My Shitty First Podcast*

When my friend and colleague, Lee Silber,† and I first went into the studio to record the very first three episodes of our podcast, "The Faster, Easier, Better Show," things most definitely did not go as planned.

In our minds, we were going to waltz into the studio and record the most amazing episodes ever. Angels would sing and unicorns would frolic on rainbows in pure, unadulterated excitement.

This, of course, did not happen.

There were issues with the microphones and sound. We stepped on each other's sentences. Our conversation, usually free-flowing and (in our minds at least) hysterically funny, was stilted and hesitant. The voice-over introducing our show sounded slow and draggy, the complete opposite of what the rest of the show was designed to be. Despite what it seems like, this was not a disaster.

---

* This sounds like a terrible toy to give to a child.
† You'll hear more about Lee later in the book.

This was our Shitty First Draft.

Lee is an author and an Efficiency Expert, so both of us know that trying anything new, in any part of our life, will always involve a Shitty First Draft of some sort. And boy did we hit the pinnacle of Shitty that day. But we kept going. We knew we could only get better from where we were, which gave us a goal to strive for. One day, we'll be pros (in our minds at least) and our podcast will be amazing.* We'll do things more quickly and with more confidence. At which point, the unicorns might actually show up. Even if they don't, our Shitty First Draft has served us well. Just like your Shitty First Draft will serve you as well.

There's another way you can overcome perfection-based procrastination. All that's required is for you to adopt a Beginner's Mind: the idea you are a complete beginner who doesn't have to know everything about what you are doing to get started.

Martin Luther King, Jr. said, "Faith is taking the first step even when you don't see the whole staircase."That's a perfect description of the Beginner's Mind.

It's knowing you don't have to know everything to get started.

Beginner's Mind

Last summer, I tried taking a spinning class, something I haven't done in years. My neighbor is a big fan of a local spin gym and goes a couple of times a week. She's always asking if I want to go with her. My answer has always been a resounding, "Why would I?" But then, I adopted a Beginner's Mind and said, "Why not?"

I went into my first class with only two thoughts in my head: first, what was the class going to be like? It's been years since I took anything resembling a spin class. In that time, there have been massive changes. Lights! Music! Stats! Better bikes and fun teachers! Or so I'd heard. But I'd never experienced it, so I was curious to see what everyone was raving about.

Second, I decided it was going to be okay to be the worst person in the class. I had nothing to prove to anyone but myself. As long as I didn't fall off the bike and dangle from my clip-in shoes, I would consider the class a success. In other words, I set the bar for myself incredibly low. So low, I couldn't fail.

---

* Actually, it's pretty good now. Check us out: The Faster, Easier, Better Show Podcast.

Between these two thoughts, I went into the class knowing I was trying something that may or may not work for me, but either way, it didn't matter.*

In the past, I would have let perfection-based procrastination stop me. What if people saw how bad I was? What if I wasn't wearing the right clothes? What if the teacher called me out for not doing things right? What if, what if, what if? The three-year-old in my head could come up with hundreds of scenarios, all designed to stop me from trying something new. But with the Beginner's Mind, my inner three-year-old was silenced, and I went and took the class. And I didn't fail.

I didn't fall off the bike. Thanks to the dim lighting in the studio, as far as anyone could tell, I didn't do anything embarrassing, and I made it through the class. Granted, when the stats came out, I came in dead last compared to everyone else. But, I wasn't comparing myself to anyone else but me. I had a low bar to get myself over, and I did it. I now have my baseline stats, and really, the only way I can go is up from here.

Because of my Beginner's Mind, I did something new and lived to tell the tale. I overcame perfection-based procrastination by being ok with being a Beginner. You can easily do this as well.

Adopting a Beginner's Mind

As adults, we tend to have this foolish idea that we have to be perfect the first time we try something. Not only is this not true, but it's a perfect way to stop ourselves from trying anything new (that we might love) and it's a proven way to procrastinate on just about everything. Adopting a Beginner's Mind means putting aside any fears or questions you have about trying something new. Rather than trying to know as much as possible, or be as prepared as possible, you just have to accept you are an absolute beginner and the only way you can go is up. Teachers, trainers and coaches all exist for a reason: to guide you on your way. So let them do just that. If it helps you, adopt a Beginner's Mind Mantra.

The Beginner's Mind Mantra

The Beginner's Mind Mantra is designed to change how you talk to yourself. Instead of faulting yourself for being a beginner, verbally remind yourself you

---

* I hoped I couldn't fail. I am somewhat clumsy, and the possibility of falling off the bike and dangling was something that could conceivably happen.

will eventually get better. You wouldn't walk into a kitchen and try to make a complicated soufflé right off the bat.* But just because you aren't at your desired finish line (the perfect soufflé) today, doesn't mean you won't be there eventually. This is where the Beginner's Mind Mantra comes in. Okay, it's not so much a mantra as it is a tiny, three-letter magic word that reminds you it's ok to be in the starting phase.

The magic word? Yet.

That's it. Yet. "I can't make a soufflé, yet." "I don't lift heavy weights, yet." "I haven't mastered spin class, yet." When you use "yet" in combination with the Beginner's Mind, there are four additional words that are implied but not spoken. Those words are, "But I will be."

Adding "yet," either out loud, or silently, in your head, reaffirms to yourself you are in the process of getting to where you want to be. While you aren't there at this point, you will be, and more importantly, you haven't given up. One of my favorite phrases to remember is "Never compare your Chapter 1 with someone else's Chapter 17," meaning your journey is different than everyone else's. While they may be ahead of you in skill, they had to get there just like you. They are just further along. Your Chapter 1 will eventually be your Chapter 17 and someone will be looking up to you. You just have to work your way up to it.

Following the Leaders

Actually, it's kind of nice having someone further along in the journey than you are. You now have someone else's trail to follow; you don't have to make things up as you go along. You can see what has worked or hasn't worked, and use it to guide your path, making things much more manageable. As a Beginner, you have nowhere to go but up. You can only get better.

"Yet" is the magic word that makes it ok to be where you are. It eliminates guilt and frustration. You might not be there yet, but with consistent practice and progress, you eventually will be.

Your lack of knowledge or training is just where you are now, you are going to learn what you need to along the way.

---

* Well, you might, and it would most likely be a very messy endeavor, at least it would be in my case.

Using the Beginner's Mind, in whatever form, is very freeing. Your lack of training or education is no longer a reason to procrastinate. You are just starting, and you can only get better from here.

Pick A Place and Start

Having too many choices and not knowing where to start is a perfect scenario for a Moment of Choice and Procrastination. The brain's go-to response when things are overwhelming is to fall back on something comfortable and not challenging. You know, procrastinating. Instead of trying to calm the overwhelm, why not do one simple thing to get started: Pick A Place and Start.

I've definitely been in this situation, and I know this feels wrong, but it's an easy way to eliminate the possibility of procrastination, and why procrastinate when you can be in Action? Action triumphs sitting around looking for the perfect solution every time.

Does the Action have to be perfect? Absolutely not. Perfectionism, as you now know, is seriously overrated. Each year, we host a Christmas party for 60 or so people. While it's a lot of fun, let's just say there is a bit of a mess when it's all over. After the party, there are dozens of used pint glasses, wine glasses, highball glasses, water glasses, and a few shot glasses all gathered on the kitchen counter.* Add in dishes, cutlery, and pans and, well, there's a lot to clean up.

Every year, the morning after the party, I end up standing in the kitchen, having a moment of being overwhelmed when I think it might be easier to sell the house than clean up. After realizing this is not really a feasible option, I think "Where do I start?"† And every year, without fail, I just pick a random spot and start.

---

* If we're lucky. Usually, there are still at least a half dozen or more glasses still scattered on the patio and the porch which need to be tracked down.
† Ok, usually it's more like "Where the hell do I start? And why did everyone stay so late last night? Oh yeah, I told them to."

Less than perfect works just fine

Is it the best spot? Maybe not. But it's a spot. It's my imperfect starting point. Sometimes I start by washing all the serving spoons, then the wine glasses, then the pint glasses and before you know it, everything is cleaned. Other years, I start with the smallest glasses and move up to the largest, then do all the pans. Whichever way I do it, it puts me in Action. Which is exactly what I need to stop being overwhelmed and get started.

This is a no-fail way to overcome procrastination because there is no right or wrong action and no Moment of Choice. As long as I am in Action, I've defeated procrastination. Getting caught up in deciding, "should I start here or there?" is a classic procrastination tactic.

So, seize the bull by the horns, seize the day or the opportunity. Pick your favorite metaphor and pick a place, any place, and jump in. Once you've gotten started, a better path may present itself. If it does, then feel free to follow it. No matter what, you've gotten started, and you've overcome procrastination.

How can you make it even easier to pick a place to start? Make sure any task you start with is very small.

"The secret of getting ahead is getting started.
The secret to getting started is breaking your complex overwhelming tasks
into small manageable tasks, and then starting on the first one."
- Mark Twain (or Samuel Clemons, your pick)

Get small to start

By their very nature, big tasks seem to invite procrastination. They are intimidating to your inner three-year-old. Small tasks make it much easier to be in action. Breaking your big task into a series of small steps makes sure they are easier to get started on and accomplished.

When I get overwhelmed on technology issues,* I procrastinate. Everything I need to do feels big and overwhelming. So I can't even take my own advice and just jump into action. Before I can do anything, I need to make everything very small.

---

* I'm not what you'd call a technological whiz. I'm much too right-brained to feel comfortable with the intricacies of programming, coding, and generally following directions that feel like they were written in a foreign language.

Whenever I encounter a daunting technology issue, I make it a point to break it down into tiny, easy-to-do steps (and I mean tiny, tiny, tiny steps.) Then I figure out where I need help and where I already know what to do.* I block out the necessary time (complete with plenty of breaks to keep my mind fresh) and pick an imperfect place to start.

Of course, once I get going, the technology isn't really so hard.

Do I do each step perfectly? No. But I'm in Action, so I'm not procrastinating. I'm succeeding step-by-step.

My brain isn't getting intimidated by the prospect of trying to accomplish huge things. As a bonus, the small steps mean more rapid rewards in the form of dopamine hits for my brain.

It's easier to envision and get excited about doing 10-20 minutes of a task than it is to think about slogging through two hours of something that might end up being frustrating. Long blocks of unexciting, unfulfilling time make your brain start looking for distractions and ways to procrastinate.

So, be realistic about how big each of your bite-sized pieces of work is going to be. Make each doable but challenging. For example, if you're putting together a work proposal, decide to work on it in a series of manageable 20-minute chunks of time, rather than a straight two-hour session with no breaks. A 20-30 minute time chunk is much more palatable to your brain and is easier to fit into your schedule, so it's more likely you'll actually do it.

No matter the size of the project, you can always break it down into smaller steps. You can figure out the first small step you can take or branch out and figure the next five small steps you can take. Each time you succeed at a small step, your brain will be happy and you'll encourage yourself to keep moving forward. The journey of a thousand miles starts with you knocking one small step out of the park. Succeed, get a dopamine hit, then look to see what you can do next to succeed again.

One Timer to Rule Them All

One of my favorite ways to get started is to give myself a time limit and get moving. So, I am all about the timers. My favorites are old-fashioned kitchen

---

* Most times, this is actually more than I thought I knew.

timers that tick as they count down the seconds.* When I hear the ticking, I know it's time for me to be in action.†

Fortunately, you are surrounded by timers. You've got a timer on your phone, your tablet, your computer, your oven, your microwave, your fitness tracker, even your favorite playlist can serve as a timer if you know exactly how long it is. Timers are available pretty much everywhere you look, and using them is a great way to get started and overcome procrastination.

The most basic procrastination-busting timer technique is just setting the timer for five minutes and getting started on your task or project. Your only job is to work for five minutes, and when those five minutes are up, you are free to move on to something else. Easy, right? The timer tells you it's time to get started, and it tells you whatever you're doing isn't going to be a considerable time commitment.

Five minutes? Piece of cake.

You know who loves this timing plan? The three-year-old in your brain. Five minutes is an easy lift. You're not committing to a full afternoon or a full day. It's just five minutes. 300 seconds. But here's the thing, once you've gotten those five minutes in, chances are you're going to keep going, all because of a sneaky cognitive bias called the Zeigarnik Effect.

Why you hate cliffhangers

The Zeigarnik Effect, which was discovered in 1927 by Russian Psychologist, Bluma Zeigarnik, says we are motivated to complete incomplete tasks rather than having them partially done. The brain doesn't like cliffhangers, it wants closed loops in any sort of story or event, which is why you have such a hard time turning off television shows that leave you hanging from show to show.‡ This means you can easily make the Zeigarnik Effect work for you. If you can work on your task or project for the first five minutes, chances are you'll get your brain engaged in what you are doing. After five minutes, when your timer

---

* I'm using one now as I write this section.

† This is a great solution when I'm by myself and the ticking can't bother anyone. I certainly wouldn't do this in a public place. I don't want to be "that person."

‡ That is why binge watching shows is so satisfying, you can quickly eliminate any cliffhangers as each show automatically cues up. You don't have to wait for the next week for the next show, it's automatically there for you.

goes off, even though you are technically done (even if your task isn't), your brain is going to want you to keep going until you complete the task.

When you time yourself, no matter what timing pattern you use, starting now becomes unemotional. It's just a thing you are doing. Removing the emotion removes the limbic system and your three-year-old. You don't need to be motivated, you don't have to be excited. You are setting a timer and starting.

It doesn't matter what kind of timer you use, just find one that works best for you and use it. Timers work great to help you get started, and as you'll see in other chapters, timers are also a great tool for focus and dealing with distractions.

Another way you can get started more easily is by channeling your inner Sherlock Holmes and leaving yourself some clues so you can easily jump back into your project or task.

3. Take a look at your Hows

A "what" gives you the 30,000-foot view of what you want to accomplish, but the "how" is the boots-on-the-ground, this-is-how-our-shit-gets-done, driver of successful change. You have to know your "how" for the "what" to actually happen.

The "how" is the part that scares people, makes them procrastinate and cling frantically to their comfort zone. Their refrain becomes: "I don't know how to do what I need to do to get where I want to be."

And honestly, that's okay.

As a baby, you didn't know how to walk either, but you learned. You learned through trial and error. You never got to the point where your butt hit the ground and you just gave up. "Nope, I'm good here. No need for me to walk. I'll just sit like this forever. Walking is totally overrated..." You discovered the "how" by finding what worked (or didn't), and it's the same way now that you're a grown-up.

You don't need to know your complete "how" to get started, you only need your first "how." You can discover the rest of your "hows" along the way.

Where then, do you find your "hows"? If you already knew "how" to do something, you probably would already be doing it, right? Not always. Remember, "Beginner's Mind?" Luckily, someone out there in the world has probably already figured out the "hows" of what you want to do, so seek them out.

There are teachers, coaches, and mentors just waiting to share what they know. There are books and classes and groups out there with all the "how" information you need to get started and moving on the right path. Find these people, these classes, these books and learn your first "hows" from them.

When I started putting together my first online course, I didn't have any knowledge of the "how" necessary to put the course together or how to market it or monetize it. So, my first "how" was to talk with some colleagues about what processes they followed with their courses, then armed with that information, I put together my first five "hows" and got started.

Do I need to mention these first five "hows" were really small?

They were so small, they couldn't scare me. They were so small that the idea of not doing them was kind of ridiculous. They were so small, I didn't really feel them gently pushing me out of my comfort zone.

Which is the kind of "hows" you need to get started. Your "what" should be significant and exciting. It should be something that inspires passion in you, so you enjoy every second of moving toward it. But your "hows" should be small, at least in the beginning as you start to find your way. By doing each of those small "hows," the next set of "hows" begin to reveal themselves, and you are on the fast track to achieving your "whats."

4. Leverage the stops to make the starts easier

Working on large projects ensures one thing: you are not going to get everything done in one sitting. You are going to have to stop and start several times.* If you leverage the way you stop, then it will be easier to pick up where you were and get started the next time, you'll eliminate a Moment of Choice, and the option to procrastinate.

Leveraging your stops is another counterintuitive idea. While there are people that find it annoying, there are others that find it to be a fantastic way to save time and eliminate procrastination. Experiment with it to find out which way you feel.

Most people stop on a project somewhere that seems like a normal stopping point, like the end of a chapter or when they run out of an essential supply like paint. They run into a barrier that signals "This is a good place to stop."

---

* Several might be a little optimistic. You are probably going to have to start and stop a lot.

Instead of stopping tasks where it seems most logical, try stopping at a point that makes it easy to pick up where you were and jump right back into the project the next time you start.

Let's say you're writing an outline for a presentation. Instead of finishing a full section, stop in the middle of a bullet point when you stop for the day. When you come back to working on the outline, the mere act of having to finish the bullet point will be enough to pull you into the mindset needed for the outline much more quickly. Ernest Hemingway did this with his writing.

Channel your inner Hemingway

As a prolific writer (despite his best attempts to be otherwise), Hemingway believed in stopping in the middle of a sentence when he was writing well, rather than stopping at the end of a sentence, paragraph, or chapter. This didn't mean he didn't know how to stop. He did. But he felt it would be easier to get started if there were no barriers the next time he got started. He saw the beginning of new sentences, paragraphs, or chapters as barriers since they required him to come up with new thoughts. Completing an idea he had already started made it easier to jump into his writing each day.

Let's say you're doing a physical project, building a shelf, painting a landscape, etc. If you can stop part way through a step, you'll find it easier to get back into the project when you return.* If you are able, stop right in the middle of a step so that when you come back, you have a place to start that doesn't represent a barrier. You'll be able to both leverage the Zeigarnik Effect and bring yourself back into your project much more quickly.

When I sew, I stop my sewing sessions by leaving the fabric on the sewing machine, mid-stitch, when I come back, it's obvious what I need to do next. Without a barrier, I don't need to take the time or energy to figure out where I need to start.

I've essentially left a road map that says "Start here," which saves time and eliminates a Moment of Choice.

Think about how your stops can make your starts easier. It can be as easy as stopping half-way through a step when you're cooking or building something.

---

* Yes, I know this tactic requires you to be able to leave your projects out, which is something not everyone can do.

It can mean leaving a sentence hanging or an illustration halfway done. Anything you can leave as a clue to more easily get started when you come back to your project or task is going to help you overcome procrastination.

Because getting started requires energy, your three-year-old would rather stick with the status quo. Using a Starting Ritual can make a start just a little bit easier for your three-year-old and your productivity. With a ritual, you have a systematized way to get started and get things moving.

5. Build a Starting Ritual

Chances are you have a certain way in which your day rolls once you get up. Mine involves getting out of bed, enjoying a cup of peppermint tea while either reading or writing, then getting ready to work out. But it all starts with the peppermint tea. It's the ritual that lets me know my day has started.

I have other rituals as well. I have a starting ritual for when it's time to write. I move my computer out to where I can see the patio with its flowers, butterflies, and birds. I turn on SelfControl and block the websites that I know distract me, I plug my headphones in, turn on my favorite recording of rainfall,* and I start writing. I begin with a paragraph that starts out with "Good Morning. I'm Ellen Goodwin, and today is a good day, because…"

That is my Starting Ritual. Once I have all those things in place, I know I am in the writing phase of my day and I am entirely focused on that for the next couple of hours. Because I hear "rain" and I am in my writing place, I write. I don't look at anything on my phone. I just write because that's what I do when I have gone through my writing ritual. All of the "writing elements" are in place for me, so I write. When my writing time is done, I remove the "Good Morning" paragraph, and I move on to the next part of my day.

Starting Rituals are everywhere

Having a Starting Ritual (or habit if you like that word better) is a signal to your brain that now is the time to do your specific task. Starting Rituals are

---

* It's monotonous, soothing, and energetic all at once.

everywhere. If you play any kind of sport, getting into your gear is a signal to start. When you put on running shoes and headphones, you know it's time to run. When you pick up your racket and tennis balls, you know it's time to play tennis. If you're a musician, picking up your instrument tells you it's time to practice. If you're a student, opening your books is a signal that it's time to study. Your Starting Ritual should be anything that signals to your brain "Now is the time to start."

When you signal your brain it's time to start, you eliminate a Moment of Choice that could lead to procrastination. Your signal is going to be different for everything you work on. The key is to find the signals that work the best for you.

For me, it's the location and the sound of rain. For you, it could be putting on a piece of jewelry that you only wear when you work on a hobby or are going someplace special to focus. It could be listening to a piece of music or meditating before getting started. I had someone in one of my coaching programs who always put on a particular baseball cap when she sat down to work on the novel she was writing. When the cap was on, there was no email checking or social media posting, it was focused writing time. Filmmaker/writer/provocateur, John Waters, puts on a favorite sweater as he starts his day of writing and uses it to inspire his creativity.[3]

Every Starting Ritual is different. I promise I would never tell you, "The only Starting Ritual that ever works is facing west and bowing four times while wearing a tinfoil hat, then approaching your desk by walking backward." I wouldn't. But you know what? It might be just the kind of ritual you need to get started. I'm not judging.

Experimentation is the answer

A Starting Ritual may take some experimentation to fully develop. For me, it took a while to figure out the environment where it felt best to be for writing. The rainfall background noise showed up as I experimented with different types of white noise, including the sound of a fan whirring, ocean waves lapping, and people enjoying a coffee shop—before that, I just listened to music with no lyrics on Pandora. It worked fine, but it didn't put me into the zone I was looking for. It didn't say to me, "This is your writing time! Get started!" It took a while to figure it out. I experimented until I found what worked. You should too.

Spend some time and discover what feels like a good Starting Ritual for you. Maybe it's listening to a particular song or songs that rev you up and get you excited to start. Perhaps it's the opposite—just sitting quietly and meditating before you start. Maybe it's settling into your favorite chair or window seat and getting comfortable to start on your task. Perhaps it's assembling and organizing all the tools you know you'll need and making sure everything is in place to get started. Search, and I promise you will figure out a Starting Ritual that energizes and excites you and tells that crazy brain of yours now is the time to focus and work on your task.[4]

I shouldn't have to tell you this (sometimes people forget), but your Starting Ritual should be fun for you. It should be enjoyable, it should make you smile with anticipation and be excited about jumping into what you are going to do next. Everything about your ritual should be something that you look forward to. Because, if it is not fun, then you aren't going to enjoy doing it, which, we all know, means you are going to procrastinate by not starting.

In an ideal world, you'd be able to get things done without getting stopped or distracted. Unfortunately, no one gets to live in such a world. When you stop, getting restarted can be as tricky as getting started in the first place. This is why having a Restarting Plan is such a helpful idea.

Restarting Plan

A Restarting Plan doesn't have to be complicated, it just needs to help you do three things:
> **Stop.**
> **Refocus.**
> **Restart.**

Here are five Restarting Actions you can use to get restarted whenever you get off track:

1. Say It - Have a mantra or a phrase you can say to yourself, either silently or out loud, to get restarted. The phrase: "Stop, Refocus, Restart" is concise and straightforward. It helps you acknowledge that you need to stop what you are doing and get back on track.

This one always makes me think of a teacher reminding a student to get back to work. Maybe that's why I find it so useful. In that same teacher-vein, you could ask yourself "What should I be doing now?" or "What is the one small step I could do next?" Both of them can serve as an on-ramp to getting back to work.

2. Feel It - Have a plan of physical action that serves as a way to stop the distractions and help you to refocus and restart. This could be as easy as doing five jumping jacks or two sun salutations to signal the end of being distracted and time to get back on track. You could take a walk around the block or jump up and down three times. The particular action you choose doesn't matter, you just need to signal to yourself that it's time to refocus and restart.

3. Pause It - Stop and give yourself an intentional four-second pause to stop your distraction and refocus on your task. During those four seconds, think about what you should be doing and what you could focus on for the next three to five minutes. Then move into action. Those first three to five minutes of work should be enough to draw you back into the flow of things.

4. Time It - Use a timer to countdown to a restart. Set a countdown timer for one to three minutes. During this time, mentally prepare to restart. At the end of the countdown, set the timer for 5-10 minutes and refocus on your project and restart.

5. Mark It - Mark your stopping point so it's easier to get restarted. Much the same as putting a bookmark in a book, marking where you stop on your project makes it easier to pick up and restart. Marking means you might put a real or virtual Post-it Note on a project at the point you get pulled away or distracted. Or you could take a moment to write a quick note to yourself to indicate what you were doing just before you stopped. It's a little like leaving a trail of breadcrumbs for yourself to follow to get restarted and back on track quickly.

While getting restarted can be difficult, it's not impossible. Especially if you think ahead and have a plan to help you "Stop, Refocus, and Restart."

One of the reasons we procrastinate is because it can seem so damn hard to get started. Moving from motion (or non-motion) into Action can be difficult or uncomfortable, so starting feels good.

The three-year-old in your brain can make or break you, so appease it by making a game out of getting started. Get over the feeling that everything has to be perfect, give into Beginner's Mind, pick a random place to start, and make sure that your starting action is small so your on-ramp to action requires minimal effort. Remember, timers are your friend, and how you stop can affect how you get started again. Sometimes you just have to have a ritual to kick you and your three-year-old in the butt to get started.

Once you know how to get started, you're better prepared to deal with the second major source of procrastination: Distractions.

CHAPTER 2 ACTION TOOLBOX: HOW TO GET STARTED

DEFINITIONS IN THIS CHAPTER

Zeigarnik Effect

A cognitive bias. Humans are motivated to complete tasks rather than having them partially done.

TOOLS IN THIS CHAPTER

Games you can choose from to overcome procrastination by getting started:

Color My World:

Pick a color (or a shape) and count how many times you see it while doing a low-value task such as running errands, attending meetings, doing household chores, or even taking a walk.

Dice, Dice, Baby:

Remove emotions and choices from decision-making. Number your options, roll the dice, then perform the option which corresponds to the dice roll.

Go Fish:

Remove choices from decision-making. Write each of your options on separate slips of paper, put the slips in a bowl or hat, then pull one out. Do whatever is listed on the paper. Then pull out another and repeat. Keep going until all the slips are removed and completed.

Pin-the-Tail on the To-Do:
Write each of your tasks on a separate Post-it Note, put all the notes on a vertical surface, such as a wall, a door or a whiteboard, close or cover your eyes and point. Do the task that is listed on the note you pointed to. Continue until all the notes have been chosen and completed. (Bonus points if you spin around first.)

Bracket Your Options:
Set up a bracket, like ones used in sports tournaments, of your options, then go through to determine the priority of the alternatives. Like March Madness, but not as frantic.

Eliminate Perfectionism by:
Do a Shitty First Draft:
Do the first draft of a project, a new skill, an exercise, knowing that your first efforts will not be perfect, but they will be done, and you can improve on them from where you are.

Adopt a Beginner's Mind:
Accept that you are a beginner when you try new things and know that it is ok not to know everything...yet.

Pick a Place and Start:
Rather than spending time and energy trying to find the perfect place to start, pick A place, not necessarily THE perfect place, and start, confident that it will eventually get you to your desired outcome.

Get Small to Start:
Break your tasks, large or small, into the smallest task possible. Perform the small task, then move on to the next small task, and the next, knowing that the small tasks all contribute to the success of the big task.

One Timer to Rule Them All:
Set a timer for five minutes and start working. Work for just those five minutes, and then you are done. Most of the time, you will keep going because of the Zeigarnik Effect.

Leverage the Stops:
Stop working on your project in the middle of a step, making it easier to jump in and get moving when you return to the project. Again, leverage the Zeigarnik effect and close your loops. (Just think about leaving breadcrumbs for your future self to follow.)

Build a Starting Ritual:

Put together a small ritual that you use to tell yourself it's time to start, whether it's putting on a particular piece of clothing or jewelry, sitting in a certain place, or listening to a specific playlist. Do something that tells you, "Now is the time to start."

Hows:

Not knowing your Hows is no reason to not get started. You didn't know how to walk when you were a baby, but you learned. As an adult, there are teachers, coaches, and trainers who will help you with the Hows. Approach your Hows as small steps to move forward.

Restarting Ritual:

Develop a ritual you can follow when you find yourself off track and need to get restarted. Identify that you are off track, remind yourself of this, then consciously move back onto the track to action.

ACTION ITEMS:
Bracket:

When dealing with options that have the same importance, put them into a bracket to determine their priority. Make a bracket for the "Winner" and the "Losers."

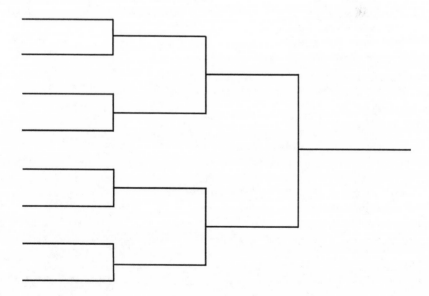

Hows:

When working on a project or goals which feels too big, break it down into small steps. Think of a current project or goal and break it down into 5 smaller steps here:

Project: _____

Small Step 1 _____

Small Step 2 _____

Small Step 3 _____

Small Step 4 _____

Small Step 5 _____

If these steps still feel too big, break each step down further. Once everything is broken down, move into action. Feel free to break a step down even further any time you find yourself procrastinating on it.

Leverage your stops to get started:

Think of your stops as "If/Then" plans designed to leave bread crumbs for you to follow and jump back into your project.

Fill out this form (or write it on a Post-it Note and keep it near any project you are working on.)

For example: *If I am working on an outline, then I can stop in the middle of a bullet point to make it easier to restart.*

If I am _____, then I can stop

_____ to make it easier to restart.

If I am _____, then I can stop

_____ to make it easier to restart.

Put together a Starting Ritual:

Since Starting Rituals evolve by experimenting, list some of the ideas of things you could try for your Starting Ritual. You do not have to come up with something for all of these. Experiment and add or eliminate ideas as needed.

LOCATIONS: _____

(*ex. Library, favorite chair, coffee shop*)

WHEN: _____

(*ex. mornings, after work*)

HOW: _____

(*ex. meditating, chanting, singing*)

WHAT: _____

(*ex. drinking cup of coffee, put on special hat*)

SOUNDS: _____

(*ex. music, white noise, talking*)

SMELL: _____

(*ex. candle, incense, coffee*)

Build a Restarting Plan:

Build a plan to get re-started when you go off track. Make your plan now before you need it.

When I go off track on my project, I will _____ to get restarted:

Say It _____

(choose a restarting phrase)

Feel It _____

(choose a physical action)

Pause It _____

(choose an amount of time)

Time It _____

(choose a timer to use for a countdown)

Mark It _____

(choose a way to mark when you ended, much like a bookmark)

CHAPTER THREE

Procrastination II:
Dealing with Distractions

And every day, the world will drag you by the hand,
yelling, "This is important! And this is important!
And this is important! You need to worry about this!
And this! And this!" And each day, it's up to you to
yank your hand back, put it on your heart and say,
"No. This is what's important."

- Iain Thomas, *author, designer*

Distractions are trouble when it comes to getting things done.

There are two types of distractions that you encounter every day—distractions you can control and distractions you can't control.

Distractions of Choice are the distractions you choose to have in your life, and you could control if you wanted to. These include, but are not limited to, assorted devices such as cellphones, tablets, computers, video games, television, social media of all kinds, as well as anything you do or use that takes away your attention, including books, magazines, or people.

The Unexpected Distractions that you can't control are things such as interruptions by your coworkers or clients or boss that throw off your planned-out schedule; your child getting sick; a repair person taking up your morning as you wait for them to show up in their 9-11 a.m. "window," getting a flat tire, missing the morning train, or fielding calls from random robo callers.

Distractions, whatever their type, are the leading cause of procrastination. They interrupt focus, discourage attention, and frustrate attempts to get things done. Knowing what type of distraction you're dealing with and how to best handle it are skills you'll be happy to understand and use.

So, what distractions are you really dealing with?

Exercise: Track Your Distractions

Once you can identify and classify your distractions, it's much easier to develop a plan to work around them, minimize them, or ignore them. The easiest way to determine your distractions is through the simple act of tracking them.

Just like tracking your food in a food log or tracking your time at work, tracking your distractions helps you to be conscious about the things you unconsciously do every day.

Tracking when, where, and how you get distracted throughout the day is both helpful and eye opening.

The only tools you need for tracking are a piece of paper and a pen. Going analog in this way, instead of using an app or a document on your phone or computer, eliminates a Moment of Choice when you tally a distraction.

For at least three days, write down each time you get distracted. Note where you are, what the distraction is, and what your reaction to it was ("stopped working on my report"). Also note whether it was a Distraction of Choice or an Unexpected Distraction. If you feel so inclined, you can also note how long it took you to bring your attention back to what you had been working on.

That's it. Pay attention to what the distraction was, where you were, and when you got distracted.

TIME	WHERE	WHAT (CHOICE/UNEXPECTED)	RESULT
9:45 a	office	Phone notification Unexpected	Returned call, had to make two more. Lost 1/2 hour
11:15 a	Clients office	Unexpected meeting Unexpected	Rearrange whole afternoon schedule
1:24 p	office	Checked email choice	16 minutes on email
2:12 p	office	Coworker stopped by unexpected	12 minutes
7:40 p	home	Checked social media choice	No time to do research I had planned to do 45 minutes

Why This Helps

Tracking your distractions like this is helpful for two reasons.

First, after completing three days of tracking, you'll have a better understanding of how often you get distracted and by what. This valuable information will help you to be prepared to overcome, ignore, or minimize those distractions in the future.

For example, if you know that you get distracted by notifications on your phone, you can turn all notifications off, or start putting your phone in airplane mode during the time you need to be focused. If you get distracted by favorite websites, you can preemptively block them. If you know a coworker stops by at a particular time every day, you can take steps to make yourself unavailable at this time.

Second, the mere act of tracking when you get distracted will help you to minimize the power of your distractions. Each time you note a distraction, you become more conscious of it. Use this awareness to short circuit the distraction. Let's say you notice that once again a phone notification has captured your attention, you should write it down on your tracking sheet.

Tell yourself, out loud: "That was a distraction, it's over, now back to work."

When you notice and call out a distraction (as weird as it might feel), you are more likely to minimize its ability to take your time and your focus.

After three days, you'll start to see where your mind wanders, and where your automatic response is to give in to distractions. Use this information to make a defensive Action Plan to protect your attention and your focus from distractions of all kinds.

Dealing with the Two Kinds of Distractions

Most Distractions of Choice are best dealt with proactively with actions designed to eliminate or minimize their power. With Unexpected Distractions, your reaction holds the key. Do you let the distraction affect your whole day, or do you respond in a way that keeps you on track? Put another way, do you allow a 10-minute distraction to ruin the next three hours?

This doesn't mean that all Distractions of Choice are always best dealt with proactively. There are times when it's your reactive response, which is important. And by no means is it impossible to deal with Unexpected Distractions proactively. This chapter leans heavily towards ways to take control of your Distractions of Choice, with most of the tools dealing mainly with them. But don't worry, you can quickly adapt the tools to work with Unexpected Distractions as well.

The Basics of Distraction

On average, it takes a person about 23 minutes to refocus after they've gotten distracted.[5] It doesn't matter if they have allowed themselves to become distracted by a Distraction of Choice, or if they have unexpectedly been distracted. If you're getting distracted five times during your work day, this translates into almost two hours per day of your time being affected by distractions (and chances are, you're getting distracted a lot more than just five times each day).

It would be great if you could wear blinders so you couldn't get distracted. And while you might think I'm saying blinders just to be funny, it's actually true, blinders would help because you are biologically predisposed to getting distracted.* You have a tiny, paired structure in the visual field of your brain attached to the optical nerve, called the superior colliculus, which processes and responds to unexpected visual stimuli. The goal of the superior colliculus is to move you toward or away from stimuli, so it either gets engaged or it activates the fight or flight response. Either way, you effectively end up getting distracted.

Distractions of Choice feel good. And you know who loves to feel good? The three-year-old in your brain.

Now, if that three-year-old loves it, how happy is he or she going to be if you take drastic measures to cut out your distractions? Hmmm, I'll take "Not very happy at all," for the win—which leaves you with a couple of options here. You can dig your heels in and work to eliminate all your distractions with a draconian "no distractions at any time" effort. Which sounds great, but you'll be pushing back against your inner three-year-old who will do what he or she can to keep the distractions around.

Or you could choose to set a really low bar for blocking your distractions. This allows you to move into a place where you use small actions to make

---

* If you think you are only getting distracted because you are unfocused, isn't it kind of nice to know there is an actual biological reason for your unfocused state? It's not you, it's your brain!

distractions less powerful in a way that doesn't put your inner three-year-old on the offensive. These small actions are all designed to affect how you interact with your Distractions of Choice.

Minimize Distraction Time

What does the low bar I mentioned actually look like? It looks a lot lower than you probably think. Since you are trying to work around the three-year-old in your brain, you aren't going to try to be 50 percent less distracted, or even 25 percent less distracted. No, small is small. You're just going to try to be 10 percent less distracted.

1. Become 10 percent less distracted

Ten percent doesn't sound like much. Ten percent of an hour is six minutes. Six minutes an hour in a full 16-hour day means a little over an hour-and-a-half of undistracted time, which adds up to 10.5 hours per week. It's not for me to tell you how to use this time, but 10.5 hours per week can be a game-changer. In a month, that's over 40 hours of undistracted time that you can use to do, well, anything. Learn a new language, perfect a skill, go for long runs, read good books, meet new people. All of this by being 10 percent less distracted.*

When you become 10 percent less distracted, you'll start to see immediate results. Really. You'll be procrastinating less so you'll be able to get more done in a shorter amount of time. Once you've gotten 10 percent less distracted, it's easy to start ramping things up to the point where you're 20 percent less distracted. But let's deal with the 10 percent first, and the easiest way to do that is to go for the low-hanging fruit of your digital distractions.

Eliminate Digital Distractions

There are obvious ways to eliminate digital distractions. Unless you've been living under a rock (where I understand the wi-fi is terrible), you already know there are lots of different blockers you can use on your computer to block distracting websites. Apps like Freedom, SelfControl, KeepMeOut and Focus

---

* Is 10 percent too much for you? Then go even smaller. Figure out how to be one percent less distracted. Sometimes I feel like if the whole world was one percent less distracted, we'd be a lot better off. But that's just me. And my soapbox.

all allow you to block sites for amounts of time that you control.* (I've written most of this book with SelfControl keeping me from clicking on to any of my favorite websites when the three-year-old in my brain decides "we" need a break.)

There are apps designed to help you ignore your phone for longer and longer amounts of time, such as Forest and Siempre. Airplane mode is your friend when it comes to blocking and ignoring. And you can easily turn off the audio notification on your email to ensure you don't get distracted each time a new email comes in.

Doing these simple things can easily move you towards being 10 percent less distracted. However, if you want to become 10 percent less distracted without relying on digital help, find ways to make it 20 seconds harder to become distracted by your Distractions of Choice. During those 20 seconds, you interrupt the automatic response to the distraction, making it less likely you'll lose focus and start to procrastinate.

Ways to make it 20 seconds harder to be distracted

Some of these ideas are going to resonate with you and are going to feel like fun. Some are going to make you wrinkle your nose like you did when your mom served her "famous" liver and onions for dinner. Which is okay. Unlike your mom, I'm not offended. Experiment with the options until you find a few that make you stronger than your Distractions of Choice.

Cell Phone

Why should you make it harder to use your cellphone? First, because depending on which study you believe, adults are on their phones, conservatively, between three to five hours a day. Judging by what I see each day, I think the numbers are much higher. Second, because of the addictive behaviors, the safety issues,† and the actual physical strain on your neck. Third, because just having your phone near you lowers your intelligence. The mere presence of a cellphone can change how your brain works.

One study[6] found that college students who took tests while their smart phones were visible on their desks, consistently scored lower than the students

---

* Check Chapter Twelve, the Resources Chapter, for more info on these and other apps.
† Could you please not be looking at your phone while walking in a crosswalk? Thank you.

who took the test with their phones locked in another room. The kicker? It didn't matter if their phones were on or off, they still scored lower. Depending on the study,[7] the scores were sometimes up to a full letter grade lower.

Think about this. It didn't matter if the phones were on or off. The phones just had to be in their line of sight to affect their ability to focus and pay attention.

So, if this is happening in the controlled and seemingly focused environment of academic test-taking, then what is happening to you when you are out in the wilds of your real life and have access to your phone 24/7?

It doesn't take a rocket scientist to know that you get distracted by your phone, so you're procrastinating and not focusing. To overcome this type of distraction, you need to be proactive and smarter than your phone(s), which, fortunately, isn't difficult.

Ideas to make it 20 seconds harder to use your phone:

- Keep your phone in airplane mode during predetermined stretches of time during the day.

- Keep your phone out of sight by putting it in another room or locked in a desk drawer.

- Block distractions on your phone with apps like Zero Willpower, Flipd, and Anti-Social.*

- Buy a minimalist phone. There are several now on the market designed to be nearly distraction-free. Most allow you to phone and text and possibly use GPS. A couple to consider are the LightPhone 2 or the Palm Phone.

- Keep your phone minimally charged so that you can only use it for essential communication.

- Set a passcode on your phone so you have to use the code each time you want to check your phone.

- In social situations, turn your phone off and put it in a zippered pocket or purse.†

---

* Check Chapter Twelve for more information.

† Of course, you could always, I don't know, leave your phone at home? But then how do you call a ride share? Damn, the trials of the 21st century!

- When you drive, keep your phone in the back seat. Of course, if your car syncs up to your phone, this one doesn't apply.

- Engage the "Safe Driver Mode" on your phone so notifications can't come in, and an automatic "I'm driving response" is sent out to whoever is texting you.

- Go black and white. One of the reasons your phone is distracting is because of the bright colors on the screen. Your inner three-year-old is attracted to bright things. Bright distracting things are even more appealing. So, make your phone less interesting by changing the screen to black and white. On an iPhone, go to Settings > General > Accessibility > Accessibility Shortcut > Color Filters on. Now, when you click the Home Button three times, you have the option to change your color filter from color to Black and White. Click three times again to go back to full color. On Android, go to Settings > Accessibility > Vision > Color Adjustment > Gray Scale. Your phone is now black and white until you change it back. With no color, your phone is less appealing, games are downright boring, and everything seems much less fun.

- Discover how long you can go without picking up the phone. Both the Use Carrot or Forest apps can help you find out (and encourage you to work towards longer and longer time frames where you don't pick up your phone).

- Install Siempre, which changes all your icons to simple, boring, black and white icons.

- On any of your devices, turn off or log out of apps and programs each time you're done with them. This way, you always have to go through the log-in when you want to use them. Make it even harder to log-in by making sure the passwords are long and complicated. Now, when you try to remember it or enter it, it's probably going to take you more than 20 seconds to do. This particular tactic works really well because we all have enough trouble remembering short passwords, so long ones effectively shut down any distraction attempts.

- To make it harder to find apps, put them into folders on your phone. Our phones are an extension of ourselves, and we know exactly where things should be, which makes it easy to go right to an app and get distracted. Making this one little change makes your automatic action at least 20 seconds harder to accomplish.

Ideas to make it 20 seconds harder to get distracted by your computer:

- Make it a personal rule to have only one tab open on your browser at a time.

- Utilize blockers like Freedom.to, SelfControl, or KeepMeOut.

- When possible, work in a physical location with your computer but no other devices available.

- Work on a computer that doesn't have access to wi-fi.

- Work on your laptop with no access to a power source. When the battery dies, you have no way to get power, so every moment counts.*

Ideas to make it 20 seconds harder to watch television/movies/ Netflix/Amazon/YouTube

- Monitor and track how much time you spend watching shows of all kinds on all devices during the week. Try to decrease that number by 20 percent each week.

- Disable auto-play on Netflix, HBO, YouTube, etc.

- Place a book, a crossword puzzle, or notepad on your television-watching chair or sofa. When you want to sit down to watch television, you'll be reminded of the other things you could be doing (and do them because they are right there at your fingertips).

- When you are done watching television each day, put it in the closet (if it's small), or if it's too large to move, cover it up.

- Keep the television unplugged and your devices minimally charged.

---

* This is an excellent way to give yourself a hard deadline to get things done.

- Have someone with more self-control than you be in charge of the remote, so you don't automatically start watching the next show.

- Have someone hide the remote.*

- Cut your cable. Stop paying for cable so you have to be intentional about your watching on other sources.

Of course, these aren't the only ways you can make distractions harder to do. You can also do that by making them awkward to enjoy.

Make it awkward

Typically, when you're enjoying your Distractions of Choice, you are physically and mentally relaxed. Your body is at ease. Your mind isn't thinking about work projects or being efficient. Because you're relaxed, it's easy to remain in your comfortable, distracted state. (If you've got teenagers at home, they are pros at this.) If things were uncomfortable, you wouldn't want to be distracted by them as much. This is the whole idea behind making your distractions awkward.

Making my distraction awkward

During any election season, I become a news junkie and consume more information than I really should. I don't like listening to the news or watching it on TV, I need to read it, either in print or online. If given a chance, I would settle into my comfy chair and start going from article to article, which, given the amount of material out there, could eat up a full day, and I would procrastinate on everything.

I know and own this, so to make sure this doesn't happen, I do everything I can to make my news reading awkward and uncomfortable.

When I'm in focus or writing mode, I work with a 20 minutes on, five minutes off schedule. I use an interval timer to stay on track, so a bell rings

---

* Of course, technically, you can still turn the television on. But changing the channels is no longer that easy.

when the 20-minute session begins, then another rings to mark the beginning of a five-minute break.*

The five-minute break is the only time I allow myself to check out any news. But instead of sitting comfortably at my desk and checking out the latest information on my big computer screen, I force myself to use my phone or tablet to read the news. Then, to make it more uncomfortable, I make myself walk back and forth in my living room. As long as I'm reading, I have to be moving. If I stop moving, I have to stop reading. Those are my rules of awkward engagement.

Because I'm walking while reading, I'm not really going to get comfortable, so five minutes is more than enough time for me to catch up on my favorite distraction, and I don't procrastinate on things I need to be doing.

For me, walking and reading keeps me from getting too relaxed and comfortable, so I stay in my "working" state. Walking isn't the only way to do this, whatever your distraction, there's a way to make it awkward.

Look at your Distraction of Choice and pair it with something that makes it awkward to do.

Some options include:

- Standing or standing on one foot

- Standing in the corner (just like taking a time-out)

- Walking (around the house, around the block)

- Holding your hands above your head

- Doing sit-ups or push-ups or squats or burpees

- Enjoying your distraction only if you are outside

- Enjoying your distraction while someone is watching you

- Wearing something that makes it awkward to function like mittens or ski goggles or a motorcycle helmet

For example, let's say video games are your go-to distraction. You love settling in on the couch and getting caught up on the action on the screen all while procrastinating on things you should be doing. To change this up, and make things awkward, try any of the Awkward Distractions listed above.

---

* More about this type of timing interval can be found on page 210 of the Focus chapter.

When you want to binge watch programs or you want to indulge in social media, make it a rule that you have to stand or walk the whole time or do 10 sit-ups or burpees for every minute you're online.

Whatever form of awkwardness you choose, I can almost guarantee that it is going to make it at least 20 percent harder to really get comfortable and give in to your Distractions of Choice.

At the beginning of this chapter, I mentioned that one of the reasons distractions disrupt workflow is because of their randomness. What if you could reduce the randomness of your distractions? You'd stop the three-year-old in your brain from hijacking your attention. You'd no longer need 23 minutes to get back on track. And you'd probably be able to get more done. This tactic works best for your Distractions of Choice (vs. Unexpected Distractions).

2. Schedule Your Distractions

This is going to sound a little counter-intuitive, so stay with me here. Instead of letting Distractions of Choice hijack your attention throughout the day, schedule them and give them their own small, dedicated time block.

You're going to need your phone to do this because you're going to set a whole bunch of alarms. Probably more alarms than you've ever set, so be prepared! (And don't get distracted while doing this.)

Go on your phone and set alarms for five minutes before the top of every hour, for example, 9:55, 10:55, etc. Then set another alarm for the top of each hour. You decide the number of hours you're going to do this throughout the day. If you choose to do this for a full eight-hour day, you're going to have 16 alarms going off throughout the day, but it's a small price to pay for being the boss of your Distractions of Choice.

Is there anything magical about scheduling your distractions for 55 minutes after the hour? Not at all. You can plan them however you'd like. Just be sure you have a defined start and stop time for your distractions. There's also nothing magical about doing this for eight hours in your day. Sometimes it's more efficient just to do this during the hours when you need a strong focus and a little help ignoring distractions. You decide what is going to work best for you.

After the alarms are set, you go about your work for the first 55 minutes of the hour, focusing on your most important work. At 55 minutes past, when the first alarm sounds, you are free to be distracted for five minutes. When the second alarm goes off at the top of the hour, you stop your distraction and go back to work. Your five minute scheduled distraction is up.

The secret behind scheduling

Since you know that you have a break at the end of the hour, and you'll have both the option and the time to indulge in your Distraction of Choice, you're not looking for ways to distract yourself during the time you should be focusing. Your brain is able to settle down, safe in the knowledge that you WILL have time to look at a favorite website, or play a game, check notifications, or talk with a coworker.

Because you have a set time to start and finish, you have boundaries to follow, and you're more likely to be able to force yourself to get back to work, you don't need to rely on feeling "motivated" to get re-started.

With your distractions scheduled, there is nothing random or unplanned. There are no unexpected Moments of Choice where you can lose both focus, and 23 minutes out of your day. You go into your distraction time knowing it's limited, and there is nothing random to contend with. Scheduling your distraction time is one of those ideas which sounds weird, but is really very effective. Experiment with different timing schedules to see what works best for you. Maybe getting distracted for 10 minutes every 45 minutes is better for your schedule. If so, great. Just make sure you schedule your distraction time and only interact with your Distractions of Choice during this time.

3. Leverage the power of hard deadlines (or build some artificial ones)

Last summer, my husband and I invited friends over to hang out on the deck and BBQ with us. These people had never been to our house before, so, of course, we wanted to make a good impression. Before they arrived, we took care of a whole bunch of low-value chores that we had been putting off: a picture got hung, a shelf got cleaned off, a box got moved to the garage, and the porch got swept.

Was there anything that had stopped us from doing any of these tasks before? No, not at all. We had just become immune to the sight of the picture sitting on the counter and the cluttered shelf. With no hard deadline to push us into action, these things just kept getting put off. The upcoming visit from our friends changed a soft, undefined deadline into a hard and fast one that we had to meet.

The power of a deadline can never be overemphasized.

Having an absolute, must-be-done-by deadline not only compels you to get things done, but it also makes it really easy to ignore distractions. Graduations, weddings, holidays, birthdays, reunions, conferences and meetings all serve as hard deadlines for getting things done. When a task doesn't have an absolute hard and fast deadline, you need to be able to create your own.

In my case, the visit of our friends provided the short-term deadline we needed: we wanted the house to look nice for our guests when they arrived. So, 2 p.m. on the day of their visit became our hard and fast deadline. We knew what needed to be done, and by when, so we couldn't get distracted.

Having guests over is just one situation you can use as a hard deadline. There's plenty more that you can leverage.

- **Upcoming vacations make great deadlines.** Knowing that there is a definite time when you are leaving town makes it easy to accomplish things on the to-do list all while ignoring distractions. Since your time is limited, it's easier to prioritize what has to get done.

- **Shorten your workweek.** If you have control of your work schedule, try shortening your week by a day or occasionally shorten your work day by an hour or two by going into work late or leave early (like you would for a doctor's appointment or your kids' soccer game). Less available time means making smart choices about how you use the time you do have.

  I used to go to 1 p.m. "Businessman's Special" baseball games during the summer, which meant I had to leave work by 11 a.m. on game days. I started work by 6 a.m. so I could get my work done for the day by 11. The compressed day made it easy to ignore any and all distractions while working.

- **Use a reward as a deadline:** Get tasks done in the morning by using something you really enjoy as a reward. For example, no coffee or social media or gossip with coworkers until you have finished a task or achieved a predetermined goal.

- **Co-create deadlines:** Get together with a friend or coworker and declare a hard deadline for a project that currently only has a soft one. Back up your commitment with money or some other penalty for missing the deadline.

- **Action Hours:** Leverage the power of your peers and join with several friends in person or online and commit to an hour where you work individually on tasks of your own choosing. Check in with each other before the hour begins. Discuss what you plan to accomplish during the hour. Do your work for an hour, then check back in with each other when the hour is up. Share what you accomplished, then repeat as needed.

  This can also be done virtually via a video call using Zoom or Join.me.* Everyone joins the call at a preset time. After a quick check-in and discussion of what each person wants to accomplish during the next 30 minutes to an hour, everyone turns off their microphone (but leaves their cameras on) and starts working. Everyone has their video on so you can easily see if someone is not doing what they said they would be working on. At the end of the preset time, everyone checks back in and says how they did.

- **Work in a location with a physically hard deadline.** Go to a coffee shop two hours before it closes and commit to having a rough draft finished before they kick you out. Park in a two-hour parking spot when you go to a co-working space and commit to having the rewrite of your business plan done before you have to move your car. Take your laptop to the library without a charging cable and commit to having a quarterly plan for blog posts in place (and outlined) before the battery dies.

Deadlines are the kryptonite that eliminates any space for distractions to thrive. Of course, eliminating any opportunity for distractions to show up works pretty well too.

---

* For more information on both platforms, please see Chapter Twelve.

4. Work like you're on a plane

Every day from my home in San Diego, I see plane after plane take off from the airport, and unlike most people, I don't think "Ah, wouldn't it be great to be flying somewhere?" No, I look at those planes and think "Those lucky people up there. Think how much work they can get done in the next few hours."

When planned correctly, you can get a lot done when you're on a plane. No one can really interrupt you with a call or text you, or just pop into your office when you're up there. Unless you spring for the wi-fi, you aren't really searching the web. You can just be getting work done in stealth mode: writing, planning, reading, outlining. Overall, you have the potential to be undistracted for a large block of time.*

While it would be awesome to be able to jump on a flight every time you wanted to avoid distractions, it's probably not feasible, so instead, take the best element of air travel—the undistracted time—set a timer and get things done (all without any of the annoying aspects of security checks, crowded planes, and fighting over the armrest).

Step-by-step: how to work like you're on a plane (when you're really not):

1. **Plan your "flight":** Figure out when you want to "take off" and for how long. An hour in the morning? Two hours after lunch? More? Less? Block this time out on your calendar, consider this as important as a doctor's appointment. Take some time to plan what you want to accomplish during this time. Make a detailed list of what you specifically want to accomplish. If you want, you can schedule your actions hour by hour, or half hour by half hour. .

2. **Pack your bags:** Make a list or gather what you're going to need: notebooks, laptop, charger, pens, printouts, books, journals. Pack everything up so you're ready to go.

---

* My friend, Peter Shankman, has been known to book long flights (New York to Hong Kong) so that he can get drafts of his books done. Extreme? A little. But highly effective.

3. **Set an alarm:** Set an alarm on your phone for 15 minutes before your chosen "flight" time. When the alarm goes off, grab your bag with the items from #2 and head out.

4. **Get on the "Plane":** Go to a location where you won't be interrupted. If you're working in an office, this might mean shutting the office to your door with a note on it saying "Do Not Disturb" or commandeering an empty conference room. If you work at home, you could move to a different room in the house, or head to a coffee shop, a library, or a co-working space. You might even try the lobby or poolside at a local hotel or find a park with picnic tables. Really need "undisturbed airplane time?" Consider checking into a hotel.

5. **Get into "airplane mode":** Make this time as functional as you can. Turn your phone off, or at the least (unironically), put it into airplane mode. If you're using a laptop, turn notifications off and turn on an app like SelfControl to block distracting applications, news feeds, and games. If necessary, put in earplugs or put on noise-canceling headphones.

6. **Focus:** For the next hour (or more), focus on working without distractions. Get up every hour or so to get some water and stretch your legs, just like you would on a plane, then get back to work.

7. **Landing:** When you've hit your predetermined time limit, pack up your belongings, turn your phone back on, take the blocks off your browser and return to your regularly scheduled work.

8. **Plan your next "flight":** so you can continue leveraging working without distractions.

Putting yourself and your work into "airplane mode" is a great way to overcome distraction-caused procrastination, without having to buy a ticket, deal with TSA, or overpay for bad airplane snacks.

You now have several ways to be stronger than procrastination causing distractions. You can be 10 percent less distracted by making it 20 percent harder to get distracted, or you can make your Distractions of Choice awkward. You can schedule your distractions, set up hard deadlines or work like you're on a plane. All of these are great plans of Action, but you still might need a solution that's a little extreme.

5. Go to the extreme

I once heard motivational speaker, Jack Canfield, tell a story where he said that 100 percent was easy, but 99 percent was a bitch. It's the idea that we have to go 100 percent in on something (for example, no ice cream) for it to work because 99 percent (ice cream only on the first of the month) opens up too much of a slippery slope. This can apply to distractions as well. For some people, having their Distractions of Choice under control is good enough, but for others, the only way they can be confident about not getting distracted is with 100 percent removal.

Studies have shown that completely avoiding situations where you need to rely on self-control (not eating ice cream on days other than the first of the month, or picking up your phone when you're supposed to be focusing on something else) is more effective than relying on self-control alone.[8] Removing yourself from any chance of temptation is always going to work better than relying on restraint. If you feel like you are helpless in the face of distractions, you can turn to these very extreme measures.

[WARNING: Use with caution! These may cause severe anxiety in some people.]

Give someone else the power

- Have someone you REALLY trust reorganize your phone or desktop, so it's at least 20 seconds harder to find your automatic distractions mindlessly. Have them do it every three weeks, so you don't get too used to things.

- Go the Nuclear Route and make it impossible to be distracted by having someone change the passwords on your go-to distractions. Agree that you will receive the new password when you have achieved a predetermined goal. Author, James Clear, has his assistant change his social media passwords every Monday morning. On Friday afternoon, if he's gotten everything done that he wanted to for the week, she gives him the passwords so he can sign on to social media over the weekend. On Monday, the process starts all over again.[9]

Knowing how to be stronger than your distractions—by making them 10 percent harder to do, scheduling them, employing hard deadlines, acting like you are on a plane, or going to extremes—will always help you to be in Action. But there is one more way that you can be stronger than your distractions and that's through accountability. Accountability is such a strong way to overcome distractions, it gets its own chapter.

CHAPTER THREE ACTION TOOLBOX: DISTRACTIONS

DEFINITIONS IN THIS CHAPTER
Distractions of Choice
The distractions in your life that you choose. Your devices all fall neatly into this category.

Unexpected Distractions
The distractions that show up in your life, such as coworkers popping into your office, phone calls, and unexpected problems that take time to resolve.

Superior Colliculus
A paired structure located on your optical nerve designed for reacting to visual stimuli.

TOOLS IN THIS CHAPTER
Become ten percent less distracted by making it harder to be distracted. Put together ways to make it 20 seconds harder to use your cellphone, computer, television.

Make it Awkward:
Make it awkward to give in to your distractions of choice by only doing them when you ARE not comfortable. Walk around, stand in the corner, wear a motorcycle helmet, wear mittens—do whatever you need to do to make the performance of your distraction less than optimal.

Schedule Your Distractions:
Set a timer for the last five minutes of each hour and only allow yourself to give in to Distractions of Choice during this time.

Leverage Hard Deadlines:
Use the power of hard deadlines to get things done. If you don't have a hard deadline, then set one up. Shorten the time available to get things done.

Work Like You're on an Airplane:
Schedule work time as if you were taking an airplane flight. Plan on being where no one can bother you with an email, or by coming into your office. Settle into deep focus and get things done.

Go to the Extreme:
Give someone the power to be in charge of the things that distract you. Have them hide remotes or anything else that's a distraction, or have them decide log-in passwords, and agree not to give them to you until you've done your work.

ACTION ITEMS

Plan ahead to be less distracted:
Think of ways you can be less distracted by your Distractions of Choice, then begin experimenting with them to control your time better.

Phone

Computer

_____

_____

_____

_____

_____

_____

_____

_____

Other Devices

Other Distractions

_____

_____

_____

_____

_____

_____

Make your Distractions of Choice awkward:

If your Distractions of Choice are awkward to do, you're less likely to do them. Think of three to five ways you can make your favorite distractions awkward. Choose one and try it out for the next two days. Work your way through your list. When you've experimented with all of them, choose your favorite and start using it daily.

1. _____

2. _____

3. _____

4. _____

5. _____

Schedule when you will distracted:

Plan when you will distracted, then set up appropriate alarms to keep you on track.

Some examples:

"I will allow myself to be distracted - at the end of each hour for five minutes."

"I will allow myself to be distracted - from 1:45 pm to 2:00 pm each day."

"I will allow myself to be distracted - after I've done the first five tasks on my to-do list."

"I will allow myself to be distracted _____

_____

"I will allow myself to be distracted _____

_____

"I will allow myself to be distracted _____

_____

Extreme ways to stop distractions:

Think about who you could call on to make it impossible to become distracted. What would they need to do for you?

Who	What
_____	_____
_____	_____
_____	_____
_____	_____
_____	_____

Once you have a complete list, start asking people to help you out.

CHAPTER FOUR

Accountability:
The best way to be stronger than your distractions

Accountability separates the wishers in life from the action-takers that care enough about their future to account for their daily actions.
- John Di Lemme, *business coach*

I haven't always been a fan of accountability. I first learned about the concept of accountability from the book *Think and Grow Rich* by Napoleon Hill. My initial reaction when I read about it was a resounding "Hell no!" Why did I need someone telling me what to do?* I was convinced that I could do anything and everything to run my business, and my life, by myself without someone looking over my shoulder.

And how did that work out for me?

If you remember my story from the introduction, not so well. So, of course, I learned my lesson, right? Wrong. Instead of looking into getting some accountability (via a business coach or a partner), I just kept bumbling along. I watched the same unhelpful patterns of a little success, a lot of stress, and more failure, repeat over and over. I marked the repetitious failures down to "that's how business works" when, in fact, it was "just how Ellen works."

Eventually, I did break down and hire a business coach, well, actually two of them, and, as expected, I disliked them because I saw them as authority

---

* Which shows you just how well I understood what accountability really was at that point.

figures (like my former teachers or cranky bosses) rather than partners on my path to success. I resented seeing my coaches just like I disliked going to oboe lessons with my band director in high school. And why did I hate those lessons? Because I didn't do the work and I knew I would be called out on it.

What I missed

Those lessons were there to hold me accountable for my practice so I could do better, they were there to be helpful, even though I didn't see it that way at the time. I looked at those lessons as punishment, not as a way to make myself better—the same way I started to look at my homework assignments from my coaches.

I was missing a huge point: accountability is most definitely not a punishment. It's guidance when you aren't sure what should come next. It's a touchpoint when you are adrift. It's an anchor to keep you on track. But most of all, it is a fantastic gift that you give yourself to help you get to where you want to be.

I really can't say enough good things about accountability and how it's worked in my life and the lives of others.

If you're like I used to be, please stop now! Don't look at accountability as a bad thing. Look at it as the tool that is going to make you go further faster, help you stop procrastinating, build better habits, focus more...and, well, everything. Accountability is really that potent of a tool.

Think back to when you were in school. Your teachers held you accountable for learning the material, and exams held you accountable for really remember it. Your parents held you accountable for becoming good citizens who weren't jerks in public, who shared with others, and who said please and thank you.

As adults, your family holds you accountable for making money so you have food on the table and a roof over your head. If you have one, your boss keeps you accountable for getting your work done and your friends hold you accountable for getting out and having some fun once in a while. If you run your own business, your clients keep you accountable for honoring contracts (both social and business), getting work done on time, and growing the business.

You are held accountable every day in different ways. But it's time to take it one step further and start leveraging accountability in all areas of your life.

Can you be successful without accountability? Sure. Would it be easier if you did have accountability? Absolutely.

Accountability airlines

If you were getting on an airplane in 48 hours and flying somewhere for a couple of weeks where you needed a passport and an electrical converter, you would have a lot of things to be taking care of right now. You'd be finalizing timing with the house sitter, talking to the dog sitter, finishing all the last-minute things at work, packing suitcases and dealing with all the little last-minute minutia that pop up when you travel.

What you wouldn't have is time for distractions like social media, video games, or emails. There would be no time to leisurely sit with friends over coffee or to binge watch a series on Netflix. You would be focused entirely on the goal of getting on the plane and heading out of town. Your upcoming flight is holding you accountable for your actions right now. Having outside accountability functions much the same as that flight. It enables you to ignore distractions and focus on what you need to be getting done. It's like putting blinders on so you can't be distracted (as we discussed at the beginning of Chapter Three.)

There are many different forms of accountability you can use in many different situations. Sometimes you need immediate accountability, sometimes you need long-term, ongoing accountability. Sometimes you need a group to keep you on track, sometimes a little one-on-one accountability works best. All accountability is a tool, so choose the tool that works best for your situation.

You've Got Accountability Options

Social Accountability, by definition, is very public. And that's where its power lies. You are putting yourself in front of others, which can make you feel vulnerable, but it can also be powerfully motivating.

1. The power of the group

Studies have shown that we act differently and make better choices when we know others are watching.[10] The Observer Effect, or the Hawthorne Effect, as it is formally known, basically states people modify their behavior because they are being observed. When we're being watched, we act as we want others to think we genuinely act.* The Social Accountability of the Group does the same thing.

In its original form, Weight Watchers® was a very much in-person, social accountability system. Once a week, you showed up at a meeting and you weighed in. Right then and there, you would know whether you achieved your weekly goal or not.† Since everyone at the meeting was on the same path of trying to lose weight, everyone shared in each other's triumphs and disappointments.

The set up of the meeting was designed to keep you accountable for the process of losing weight. The weekly weigh-in was intended to keep your goal of losing weight in the forefront of your mind, with the idea of making it easier to say yes to both healthier foods and exercise, and no to the off-limits foods.

While I'm certainly not pitching Weight Watchers, I am all for the type of Social Accountability it epitomizes.

To feel the power of Social Accountability, all you need to do is take a class or join a group.

The class of accountability

Last fall, I started taking an exercise class near my house two times a week. The classes are small (only seven people), last 45 minutes, and are intense, fun, and they are holding me accountable for my fitness goals.

I didn't think of the classes as a type of Accountability Partner, but they definitely are. When I'm tired in the morning, I get up and go because I know that if I'm not there, my absence will be publicly noted, and I'll miss out on the good discussion and laughs the class is known for. Since I've paid in advance, I also don't want to waste my money.

Whether you're joining an exercise program, taking an adult-education class at a college, or sitting through a week-long certification training, you are being held accountable for your goal. By taking the course you're benefiting from the knowledge of the instructor, there's camaraderie with the other students, which makes it a little more fun (and easier) than doing it on all on your own. More importantly, organized classes eliminate any chance which

---

* Think of how much better you drive when there is a policeman behind you.
† To the great relief of everyone, weigh-ins were done privately.

your brain can jump in and distract you from what you are doing with random Moments of Choice. You have a set time to show up and a defined path to follow, all of which work together to keep you accountable.

Join the club

What if you want Social Accountability, but you're not up for structured classes? Then look into joining a group or a club that's centered around an interest you have.

Want to be reading more? Join a book club and read and discuss books with people who are equally passionate. Want to travel more? There's a travel club out there that will hold you accountable for getting off your couch and visiting those exotic locations you've always been talking about. Want to run a marathon or two? Join a running club and participate in bi-weekly group runs. Want to work on your photography? Find a photography club and push your skills. Whatever your interest, there's a club out there for you that will provide you with Social Accountability.

You'll be more committed and inspired by surrounding yourself with people who share your same interests. You'll learn more than you would if you tried to do it on your own. You'll have the support of the Group when you get frustrated and want to give up (or give in to distractions). You'll have a backup system that will keep you on track when you get caught up in the everyday things that can derail your progress.

The meeting of the minds

One of my favorite forms of Social Accountability is a committed Mastermind Group. I first learned about Masterminds in the same place as I learned about accountability, *Think and Grow Rich*. And my initial reaction was pretty much again, "no, thanks." The idea of a Mastermind just didn't do it for me, until I finally got involved in my first Mastermind group. Then my eyes were opened and I was sold on the idea.

There are formalized ways you can do Masterminding, which work well in small groups of four to six people where everyone gets a certain amount of time to share their wins, look to the group for help, and appreciate what they've been doing.

Less structured than a formalized Mastermind is a group within LinkedIn, Facebook, Instagram, Reddit, or any other social media platform. Within these types of groups, it's easy to request someone to hold you accountable. Just post, "Hey, I need to have X done by 3 p.m. Can someone check in on me to see if I got it done?" Or "I need to have X done by 3 p.m., I'll be posting back here when it's done." Pretty simple. But again, it works on the principle that someone knows what you are supposed to be doing and someone (or multiple someones) are watching you and your progress.

Currently, I'm more of a fan of a larger online Mastermind formula, where things aren't so structured. In this type of group, the members function more as a trusted Board of Directors, where you can bounce ideas off of each other, offer each other support, and most importantly, hold each other accountable for accomplishing things.

Do-it-yourself Social Accountability

If you really look, Social Accountability is available all around you. Besides joining classes or clubs, you can go to your coworkers for Social Accountability. Let them know what you are planning to do and have them check in on your progress. For example, at the end of the day, tell them what you want to accomplish that evening and ask them to follow up with you the next day to see how you did. You could do this with a trusted friend or neighbor (and offer to do the same for them).

2. Get an Accountability Partner

The gold star, the shining pinnacle, the ace in the hole of accountability is the dedicated, one-on-one Accountability Partner.

I have one. We've been partners for over eight years. We met online in a coaching group that we were part of, and we've never actually met in person. Which is kind of perfect (as you'll soon see). We talk every business day for about five to ten minutes. We check-in, say what we did or didn't get done the day before, where we're having problems, and what we want to get accomplished during the upcoming day. Then we say goodbye and go about our day. Simple and straightforward.

But here's the thing, it's tough to tell my Accountability Partner that I'm going to do something and then have to tell him the next day I didn't get it done because I chose to play online games for three hours. Knowing I have to tell someone what I did or didn't accomplish keeps me on track. Could I just lie and say I did things when I really didn't? Of course, I could, but I don't. The whole point of an Accountability Partner is to be honest and use the power of accountability to get things done.

Finding your own Accountability Partner

To find an Accountability Partner, you don't have to be part of a coaching group like I was. Instead, look around you. You have friends, coworkers, people in networking groups, neighbors, friends at the gym, fellow parents at your kids' school. Potential Accountability Partners are everywhere. For the record, I am not a big fan of asking a spouse, a significant other or a family member to be your Accountability Partner. With family, there are too few filters and too much emotional baggage involved.

The great things about friends or coworkers is that they do have filters and boundaries, and they usually don't have any agendas, and they genuinely want to help you out. Chances are, they also have something they would like to be working on as well. Having you as their partner helps them just as much as it helps you.*

Since, by definition their job is to hold you accountable, a coach, a trainer, or a teacher can also serve as an Accountability Partner. Unlike a friend or coworker, with a coach (trainer, teacher), you don't have to hold them accountable. It's all about you.

Coaches, trainers, and teachers are available for any category of accountability that you might need. We all know athletic coaches or trainers, but there's a coach, trainer, or teacher for almost anything you might need to hold you accountable for your progress. Need business help? There's coaches,

---

* You can also look for Accountability Partners in social media groups you belong to. (If you don't belong to any, find one that appeals to an interest you have, follow the group for a while to see who might be a good person to reach out to in a very non-stalker kind of way.) You can find Facebook groups to check out by searching for "10 best (name of your social media) groups for ____[insert your interest]" in your favorite search engine.

trainers, and teachers for every issue you might need help with: planning, finances, managing employees, growth, the list goes on and on. Need help with a new skill, hobby, or life goal? Guess what? You don't have to go it alone. There's a coach, trainer, or teacher out there to not only help you but to hold you accountable for your progress, all cleverly disguised as anything but an Accountability Partner.

Most likely, your relationship with a coach, trainer, or teacher will be a paid relationship, which isn't a bad thing at all.

When you pay for the accountability, you're more likely to be invested in and accountable for your progress. With this in mind, let's look at the third (and one of my all-time favorites) way to be accountable.

3. Putting Your Money Where Your Mouth Is

For this accountability process to work, you need a firm deadline, some money, one helpful person, and a group of other people you can't stand.

This process works great on tasks or goals that are large and are going to take a while to achieve. Think writing a book, losing weight, learning a new skill, building an online program, anything that is measurable and is going to take longer than a few days to accomplish.

Basically, "Putting Your Money Where Your Mouth Is" is a variation on the theme of betting against yourself.

For seven years during high school and college, I spent my summers working as a counselor at summer camps. Camps, as you know, come with mess halls that make all sorts of food which is designed for powering young campers through their days of activities, training and general all-out exuberance that comes from being in the great outdoors surrounded by friends without the pesky presence of any parents.

The food was calorie-dense, with tasty favorites like pancakes, sugary cereals, hot dogs, potato salad, pasta, brownies, and bread, lots and lots of bread. This was kid food, and what the kids ate, the counselors ate as well. All of which meant, without fail, at some point during the summer, the camp staff and counselors would all get together and make a weight-loss bet.

Usually, the bet was something like losing 10 percent of your body weight in a specific amount of time.

We would make a chart of everyone's starting weights, put a designated scale in the nurse's office (with masking tape marking the precise spot where the scale had to sit) and collect money. Everyone would put in $20, with a male winner and a female winner splitting the pot. The weight-loss bet was friendly but competitive. We watched what everyone ate, tried to tempt each other to cheat, and exercised as if our lives depended on it. Whoever won the money at the end of the bet was still our friend, and we were all happy. There were no dire consequences, and the worst-case scenario was that you lost 20 bucks (and hopefully, a few pounds). Our money showed our commitment to the project and its process as well as our belief in ourselves.

How it works

"Putting Your Money Where Your Mouth Is" is a little like our summer weight-loss bet, but it has an interesting twist that makes it an even more powerful accountability tool. Instead of betting that you will be victorious against your friends, you are betting that you will be victorious against people you don't like.

To Put Your Money Where Your Mouth Is, you first define the project or goal you need to achieve. What, specifically, (with specific being the keyword) do you want to do or accomplish? This is where the measurability comes into play. You don't want to lose "some" weight, you want to lose "no less than 10 pounds." You don't want to "work on your book," you want to "finish four chapters." You don't want to "start a business plan" for your new business, you want to "complete your business plan." You don't want to "plan a workshop," you want to "outline a precise timeline and full contents of a workshop."

You get the idea. The more specific you can be, the better. After defining your goal, you decide on your deadline. Again, specificity is necessary. Rather than something vague like "a week to 10 days," be specific. "Wednesday, June 21st, at 3 p.m. PST" is more like it.

Choose someone who will serve as a temporary Accountability Partner for this project or goal. A friend, a neighbor, or a coworker are all excellent choices for this role. Let this person know your specific goal and deadline and what sort of proof of accomplishment you will show them. "By Wednesday, June 21st, at 3 p.m. PST, I will have four chapters of my book written, proofed and edited and will show you the complete four chapters in a Word file."

Next, decide how much money you are willing to forfeit if you don't accomplish your goal on time. This needs to be an amount that will really inspire (or terrify) you, so $10 is not going to cut it. Depending on how deep your pockets are, I suggest you start with a minimum of $100 and rapidly go up from there.

The fun part

Now, the fun part. Pick an organization, a charity, a religious group, a candidate, or a political party that you *don't* believe in.

This is going to be some group that, because of their beliefs, you would never in a million years give your hard-earned cash to. This organization, charity, or political party will get your money if you don't succeed at your goal in your specified time frame. Yep, your money will go towards helping the efforts of people or organizations that make you cringe.

Write a check to this organization, charity, or political party in the amount you previously decided and put it in a sealed, addressed and stamped envelope and give this to your temporary Accountability Partner. If you don't accomplish your goal by your deadline, it is now their job to put the envelope in the mail and send your money to the organization, charity, or political party that you despise.

The idea behind this is every time you think about giving in to distractions, encounter enticing Moments of Choice, or put off working on your project, the thought of your money going to "those" people and their efforts will encourage you to focus on the task at hand and do whatever you can to be successful.*

If you finish your project or achieve your goal within your time frame, you go to your temporary Accountability Partner, show them that you've done what you've said you were going to do and they either hand your envelope back to you, or they rip it up for you. Your money stays in your account. You're happy, you've ignored distractions, you've achieved what you wanted to, and you haven't enriched the coffers of anyone who makes your stomach turn.

If you don't finish your project or achieve your goal, the envelope is mailed and your procrastination just cost you real money, and perhaps a little bit of your dignity.

---

* BeeMinder and Stickk are apps that work in much the same way as Putting Your Money Where Your Mouth Is, only you don't get the option of giving your money to a group you don't like. Learn more by checking out the resource section on page 282.

I've used this process many times. My clients use it. People in my Mastermind use it. And it works every time. It's simple, powerful, and way more effective than betting $20 as we did at camp.

Left to our own devices, big projects just sit there, so when you are serious about getting things done, Put Your Money Where Your Mouth Is.

4. Put Some Skin in the Game

Which is more motivating to you: hanging on to what you already have or getting something you currently don't have? If you're like most people, you are more motivated by the idea of hanging on to what you already have. Fear of Loss* has been proven to be a more significant motivator than the potential for reward when it comes to many things.

We are designed to want to keep what we have, which makes Loss Aversion a perfect tool to use for accountability, and is the basis for Putting Some Skin in the Game.

This tool works really well if you're one of those people who respond well to process goals, meaning you like achieving and celebrating mini-goals along the way to the final goal, instead of just waiting to hit that one big goal.

Again, there's money involved. And again, the goal is to keep your money and not give any money to those you don't believe in. But this time, instead of having to achieve one big goal, the money comes into play as you achieve (or don't achieve) predetermined milestones on the way to achieving your goal.

Just like earlier, you make a financial commitment by deciding on an amount of money you are betting that you will get things done. But you're also going to be putting a plan together which consists of the milestones you plan to (or need to) hit on your way to achieving your goal. Each time you hit a milestone, you get some of your money back. Each milestone you miss means some of the money goes to those you don't want to have it.

Deciding on your plans and milestones

Let's say your goal is to put together and publish an ebook on your favorite hobby, "Raising Ladybugs for Fun & Profit." Rather than having your single

---

* Technically, it's called Loss Aversion. A term coined by psychologists, Amos Tversky and Daniel Kahneman, in the early 90s.

goal be the publishing of your book on Amazon, you are going to set up a series of milestones that you have to meet along the way to publication and the deadlines for when you are going to meet them.

For example, you could set one milestone for when you've finished the research for the book, one milestone for when the first draft is done, one for when the second draft is done, one for when the copy is sent to the editor, and one for when everything is uploaded and published. All of these are essential steps in the book-writing process, and all of them can serve as milestones where you keep your money, or you lose it.

Next, you would use these five milestones to determine how much money each milestone is worth. If you're putting $500 up against yourself, then every one of these milestones is worth $100 to you. You will either get $100 back each time you hit a milestone, or forfeit $100 if you miss a milestone. Now, just like "Putting Your Money Where Your Mouth Is," you pick a group, a charity, an organization, a candidate, or a political party that you don't believe in. Miss a milestone, and they get your money.

Next, you choose a no-nonsense temporary Accountability Partner/Holder of the Money, who will be the keeper of the funds. This is the person to whom you will report your accomplishments (or lack thereof) to. Give them your list of dates and milestones and, of course, your money. In this case, because each milestone is worth $100, you give them five addressed, stamped envelopes ready to be sent off to the group that you don't believe in—each with $100 in it.

You and your temporary Accountability Partner must agree on the verification process for hitting each milestone. This will vary from person to person. You can self-report, knowing you need to be honest. You can determine an external verification such as showing your partner your finished drafts or having your Accountability Partner check in on you and your progress regularly. Just define the verification process that works for you and your Accountability Partner.

Then it's time to get started.

How it works

You know your milestone and deadlines, so you start your research and finish one day ahead of schedule (yay you!). You show your partner your research notes and are rewarded with the return of $100 of your money. Next up, you need to finish your first draft, which takes longer than you thought it would and you miss your milestone, so your Accountability Partner mails off $100 as per your agreement. While you're a little disappointed, this motivates you to finish your first draft and work doubly hard on hitting the last three milestones, so your money comes back to you and doesn't end up in the hands of those you don't believe in. Your Fear of Loss fires up the engine behind your success.

This isn't the only way to leverage the Fear of Loss. You can do it in smaller ways as well, through precommitments that make it harder for your future self to sabotage your efforts. You could use a financial precommitment such as prepaying for gym classes, educational training, or theater tickets. Since you've paid the money, you can't get a refund. You can use a precommitment of automatic money transfers to build your retirement fund. A financial precommitment increases the chances that you are going to follow through on what you said you were going to do. If you know that you've already paid for a class at the gym, it's a lot harder to roll over in the morning and pull the covers back up over your head and bail on your class.

Whether you set up a plan of milestones backed by money, or use smaller financial precommitments, having some skin in the game is a great way to leverage your natural aversion to loss and get things done.

Accountability, like many tools in this book, performs lots of roles. More than anything, it's a fantastic way to overcome all types of distractions: the ones that make you procrastinate, the ones that steal your focus; and, the ones that prevent you from achieving your goals.

Accountability exists in lots of different ways, from individual partners to groups, to Social Accountability, to coaches, teachers, and friends. Experiment to find what works best for you. When it's right, you'll know it. You'll start getting things accomplished, you'll be more focused, and you'll feel better knowing that someone is watching. You'll be one step closer to consistently getting things DONE.

CHAPTER FOUR ACTION TOOLBOX:
ACCOUNTABILITY

DEFINITIONS IN THIS CHAPTER
The Observer Effect or Hawthorne Effect:
People modify their behavior when they know they are being observed.

Fear of Loss/Loss Aversion:
Being more motivated to hang on to what you already have, rather than getting something you don't currently have.

Precommitments:
A commitment made in the future that makes it harder for your future self to sabotage your efforts.

TOOLS IN THIS CHAPTER
Power of the Group/Social Accountability:
Leverage groups to become accountable. Tell people what you're going to do, and by when, then follow through and let them know.

Accountability Partner:
Have one-on-one accountability with a person/coach/teacher, which may include daily check-in calls, or weekly get-togethers to stay on track. Tell them what you are going to do, then report back in when you've accomplished it.

Put Your Money Where Your Mouth Is:
With the help of an Accountability Partner, set up a plan where you must pay money to a person, group, charity, or organization that you don't believe in if you don't finish your predetermined task on time.

Put Some Skin In The Game:
Plan out milestones to achieve on your way to your goals and attach an amount of money to each one. For each one you hit, you keep your money. For each one you miss, your money goes to a person, group, charity, or organization that you don't believe in.

ACTION ITEMS

Get Social:

Think of various forms of social accountability you could begin using to accomplish your goals.

Example: *Goal: to read more*

Social Accountability: *join or start a book club*

Next Step(s): *Ask friends, check Meet-Up to see if a group exists, check the library bulletin board, check a book store website.*

Goal: _____

Social Accountability: _____

Next Step(s): _____

Goal: _____

Social Accountability: _____

Next Step(s): _____

Goal: _____

Social Accountability: _____

Next Step(s): _____

Goal: _____

Social Accountability: _____

Next Step(s): _____

Become Accountable: Find a Partner

First step: answer some questions:

What do you hope to get from working with this Accountability Partner:

_____

How will you work together: _____

How often will you talk: _____

Now, think who you could ask to be your Accountability partner. (*Remember Significant Others and family are not good choices.*)

Possible Accountability Partners

_____

_____

In the next three days, contact these people and set up a time to meet and discuss the possibility of becoming Accountability Partners.

———————————

Putting Your Money Where Your Mouth Is:

Prepare to Put Your Money Where Your Mouth Is by answering these questions:

My task or project (be very specific): _____

Deadline (be very specific): _____

Proof of completion: _____

Temporary Accountability Partner: _____

Amount of money: _____

Group, Organization, Charity, Political Party you don't believe in:

_____

Their mailing address: _____

Putting Some Skin in the Game:

Prepare to Put Some Skin in the Game by answering these questions.

My task or project (be very specific): _____

_____

Milestones:*

1. _____

Date_____

2. _____

Date_____

3. _____

Date_____

4. _____

Date_____

5. _____

Date_____

Amount of money each milestone is worth: _____

Temporary Accountability Partner: _____

Group, Organization, Charity, Political Party you don't believe in

_____

Their mailing address: _____

* Add more milestones as needed.

CHAPTER FIVE

Procrastination III:
Being Organized

Organizing is what you do before you do something,
so that when you do it, it is not all mixed up.
- A.A. Milne, *Author*

Back in my designer days, my darkest, most non-productive times were when I didn't have a lot of jobs to work on. Rather than get my small amounts of work done and then move on to something else, I would procrastinate on everything. I could sit in motion all day long, trying to make decisions. "I need to find photos, but I'll do that this afternoon." "I should get the proofs to the client, but it's okay if I wait another day." "I could reach out to potential clients, but not today." My day, by choice, had no structure, and without structure, nothing got done.

On the other hand, when I was slammed with work, I got everything done every day. Yes, I had more work to do, but I got it done, even though I struggled when I didn't have much to do at all.

The reason? When I was busy, I organized my days. I made sure I had time scheduled and blocked out for everything. I left nothing to chance. I was in action because of organization. I was in my best work mode.*

In this chapter, we're going to look at overcoming procrastination by being organized, but don't panic! When I say organized, I'm talking about organizing your days, not organizing your desk, office, or living room.

---

* Eventually, I learned to apply all of my organizing and structuring to every day—whether I had a lot of work to do or not. And it made everything much better.

If you don't love the term "organized," you're not alone.* "Organized" has bad connotations for me, so I rarely use it. Instead, I prefer to say that I "become deliberate" about my time. Through deliberate planning, I know what I want to accomplish, and I have a path to do just that. So, if it feels better to say "deliberate" or use words like "intentional" or "boundaries" or even "proactive," please, please, please, go with it. When it comes to organizing your day (week, month, year), it all means the same.

Organizing Can Be Dangerous

In and of itself, the idea of organization can be enough to cause procrastination. When you organize or plan, you are in motion. Which, as you know, is a dangerous place to be. Therefore, it's vital the organization tools you use are easy to work with and minimize Moments of Choice, so you can effortlessly move from motion into Action.

What do I mean by being organized to beat procrastination? I mean having some boundaries to your day to ensure you accomplish what you want, whether that's doing amazing things at work, having a great time with your family, or laying in a hammock reading a book. I also mean knowing what needs to be done, and when, so you can easily minimize or eliminate any distractions that can pop up during the day and lead you down the path of procrastination.

Each of the tools I am going to discuss in the following pages enables you to become intentional about how you are going to spend your time. But, before we go further, there is a cognitive bias we need to address, since it can impact the intentional design for your time.

Don't Trust Your Brain: The Planning Fallacy

While doing some research for an upcoming project, I had an appointment to meet with a woman who runs a networking group for entrepreneurs. We were going to discuss information that would answer questions I had about group dynamics.

---

* I know the word organization can strike fear into the hearts of people. The whole idea of "In-box zero" makes me cringe with the same ferocity as when someone says, "there is some math involved."

On the day of our meeting, I got to the specified coffee shop 10 minutes early, grabbed my coffee, and waited for her.

And waited.

And waited.

She showed up 15 minutes late. Not because she forgot our meeting time, but rather because she fell victim to a problem that all of us as humans are subject to, called The Planning Fallacy.

The Planning Fallacy is a cognitive bias first proposed by psychologists, Daniel Kahneman and Amos Tuersley, in 1979. This phenomenon makes us consistently underestimate the amount of time necessary to complete tasks. Mainly, this is because we tend to look at tasks as one thing (going to the store, writing a term paper, getting ready for work, driving to the coffee shop) when, in fact, everything we do is made up of many separate parts.

Each of the parts has the potential to take longer than we first imagine. Put them all together and, suddenly, what you thought would take 10 minutes ("I'm running to the store for milk") ends up easily taking 20 or 30.

The trip to go get milk can involve you going out to the car, getting in the car, driving to the store, getting out of the car, walking into the store, walking to where your item is (or where it should be), walking to the check-out, waiting in the check-out line, waiting, waiting, finally checking out, walking out to the car, getting in the car, driving the car home, getting out of the car, and finally, walking back into the house. In an ideal world, this might just take 10 minutes, but the chances are pretty good that any one of those actions is going to take more time than you think, throwing your time estimate right out of the window.

In this woman's mind, she was just driving to the coffee shop. How long could that possibly take? (Answer: a lot longer than she thought.)

If we're born with this cognitive bias, how are we supposed to overcome it?

Look at your tasks differently

Rather than looking at your task as one complete event (going to get milk), look at it as the accumulation of many small events, each of which not only takes time to accomplish but could also have unforeseen, time-consuming obstacles added to it. Estimate your time based on each of the small events, not as one singular event.

Make a quick estimate of how long you think something is going to take. Then double it. You'll be surprised how close you are to the time it actually takes.

Or, you could just time yourself

Use the stopwatch on your phone and time your task from beginning to end. Once you know how much time a task or event actually takes, you'll be much more likely to overcome the Planning Fallacy next time and get things done on time.

I finally broke down and did this. For way too long, I underestimated how long it took me to leave my office for meetings. I thought I could easily be out of my desk chair and behind the wheel of my car in a total of five minutes. I was horribly wrong on my estimate.

When I timed all the necessary things I had to do to get out of the office, I realized that I needed to start getting ready to leave a full 14 minutes before I need to be behind the wheel of the car. Now that I know, not only am I now consistently ahead of schedule, I'm also less stressed and more courteous on the road.*

Since you now know that the Planning Fallacy can trip you up, you'll be better prepared to plan your time accordingly. In the upcoming pages, I'm going to suggest options to help you start organizing your days. Remember, organizing usually involves motion, so it's important to make sure you move into Action when you're done.

You don't have to use all these options. As a matter of fact, DON'T use all of these options. There are too many, and your chances of being stuck in motion will exponentially increase. Instead, read through them, pick one or two that appeal to you and try them out.

1. Plan your day the night before

This is just as simple as it sounds. Make your plan for the day, before you need it. With your day planned out the night before, you can hit the floor running first thing in the morning. You're protected from distractions that can quickly derail your day, and you can become unstoppable for the first couple of hours (if not all of them) in your day.

---

* As a bonus, my husband is happier since I use my newfound timing knowledge to get me out of the house on time when I go places with him.

Making this morning magic couldn't be easier.

At the end of your work day, or before you go to bed, take five to ten minutes and write up your list of what you need to accomplish the next day.

How you organize your list is up to you. Feel free to make your standard to-do list (whatever that looks like) or write out your list with concrete time blocks for everything so you have a strict schedule.

You can make a list of the five most important things you have to accomplish. You could set up "Must do" and "Nice to do" lists.

You know what works best for you when it comes to planning your day. How your list looks is up to you.

Just write it out, so it's complete and available when you start your day. (As always, you can go analog and do this on a piece of paper, put it in an app, or on a list on your computer. Whatever feels best for you, just do it.)

Planning like this works on a lot of levels

1. At the end of the day, your ideas are fresh in your mind, so it's easy to list what needs to be done the next day.

2. Your ideas and plans for the next day are out of your head, so they aren't circling around using up mental energy and attention. Your brain is for thinking, not storage.

3. You overcome the potential for distractions and procrastination first thing in the morning. Because the list is done, there are no decisions to be made. There are no Moments of Choice. You have an objective list already completed and ready to follow. You don't need to rely on emotions and motivation to get going. You just start.

I make my list right before I go to bed so I get all the ideas and thoughts out of my head. I'm not thinking about them while trying to sleep, and when I wake up, the list is right there telling me what my day is going to look like.

Another way you can plan your time is by Thinking about Friday on Monday.

2. Think about Friday on Monday

On Sunday night or Monday morning, I make it a point to take some time and think about the upcoming Friday afternoon.

I'm not wishing the week was over and the weekend was already here. I love what I do too much to wish the week away. What I'm thinking about is what I want to have accomplished by quitting time on Friday. I am backtiming my week.

When you backtime, you decide what you want to have accomplished at a certain time in the future, then you work backwards, step-by-step, from the finished task to where you are now. It's similar to the thinking you would use when planning a big event or a vacation. You know what the outcome is, so you work backward to make sure everything gets taken care of.

For example, let's say you wanted to have everything for an upcoming presentation completed and ready to go by 5 p.m. Friday.

Backtiming tells you that by Thursday, you need to be formatting the presentation, so on Wednesday, you need to design the layout. You could only create the layout if the content were written, so that is what has to happen on Tuesday, and the content could only be written if you had done the research, and that is what has to happen on Monday. Obviously, this is a simplified schedule, but it illustrates how taking backward steps can help you build a schedule ensuring everything gets done in order and on schedule.

By planning in advance, you overcome the Planning Fallacy and make sure you give yourself enough time for each step.

Your Friday goals don't have to be something you have to work on every day during the week. They just have to be something that, at the end of your Friday, you'll be happy you've completed them.

If planning for an outcome for the week feels like a little too much, why not just plan your outcomes for the day?

3. Plan for your outcomes

For some people, a standard to-do list is very much a hard "No, I'm not going to do it." For whatever (valid) reason, to-do lists don't appeal or work for them. This is where I instead recommend going small and putting together an Outcome List.

An Outcome List is a list of three to five outcomes you want to achieve during the day. It's a scaffolding you use to structure the actions of the day in such a way that you accomplish the outcomes without needing a step-by-step list or guide to follow. You know the outcomes you want and work accordingly to achieve them.

Ideally, your Outcome List should be so short that it can fit on a standard-sized 3-in x 3-in Post-it Note. You know what your end goals for the day are and you work toward them in whatever way necessary to ensure they get accomplished.

These aren't "Have my whole book written," nearly impossible types of Outcomes. They are smaller and more achievable Outcomes such as "Have Chapter Six outlined," or "Walk 10,000 steps," or "Practice my presentation two times." These Outcomes don't spell out the details of what has to be done to achieve them. You determine and plan for this as you go through the day.

> ### OUTCOMES
>
> **1.** Have Chapter 6 outlined
>
> **2.** Walk 10,000 steps
>
> **3.** Practice my presentation 2 times
>
> **4.** Schedule 3 client calls
>
> **5.** Plan schedule for Friday

If this were my list and my Outcome was to hit 10,000 steps, I'd have to think about where and when I could get steps in. I might decide to take a walk at lunch, take the stairs whenever I could or walk instead of drive to the grocery store. I wouldn't list these actions on my Outcome List. I would just figure out which ones would help me to ultimately hit my target outcome of 10,000 (or more) steps.

Shooting for Outcomes enables you to operate in a proactive mode. Actions have a consistent record of becoming Outcomes. Take, for example, the Outcome of writing this book. Only through the act of consistently sitting down to write every day did the outcome of adding page after page to my draft occur. That draft eventually became this book.

Author, Stephen King (who, trust me, I am in no way comparing myself to), has an Outcome Goal of writing 10 pages a day, seven days a week. So, 70 pages a week is his Outcome Goal. When he consistently hits this goal (and he does), he produces books. He is in Action. His Outcome List says "Write 10 pages today," and he finds a way to do it.

Variation on a Theme

Sometimes even a three to five item Outcome List can be a little too distracting. If that's ever the case, try writing down each of your desired outcomes on separate Post-it Note (or you can use index cards). When you are finished, you should have three to five Post-It Notes each displaying one Outcome.

Next, review the outcomes then stack them in the order you want to accomplish them. Once stacked, you can only see the one task that's written on the top sheet.

This is now your non-distracting Outcome List for the day.

Your job is to focus on the one outcome printed on the top note and work on it until it is finished. Once completed, you pull off the top sheet on the stack, crumple it up and throw it away. Your next outcome is now revealed and you can begin working on it.

Working this way allows you to focus on only one thing at a time. You aren't looking at your to-do list and thinking about how you can get this or that thing done. You have complete focus, so you get more done, more quickly.

While I love Outcome Lists and swear by them, there are also two other lists I use to beat procrastination and be more intentional about my time. They are the Back Burner List and the To-Don't List.

4. The Back Burner List

What happens to you when, in the middle of focusing on one thing, you suddenly think of something else that needs to be done? In theory, this shouldn't be a problem. You should be able to continue doing your first task despite this new thought that has crept into your brain. In reality, thanks to your limbic system, this new thought can quickly become an enormous procrastination problem.

As you now know, the three-year-old in your limbic system craves new and exciting things, so while you're furiously working away on one project and a thought pops up for something new that needs to be done, your limbic system wants to do it RIGHT NOW.

According to your limbic system, you "need" to drop what you are doing and give all your attention to this new thought immediately. On the one hand, unless something is on fire, or someone nearby needs immediate medical attention, you really don't have to do anything. On the other hand, you now find yourself distracted because you are thinking about the new thought that popped up. So, instead of focusing on your task, you find yourself thinking "Oh yeah, I have to call the dentist (or doctor, or florist, or mom) today."

On a conscious level, you know you don't have to make the call at this very moment. Your prefrontal cortex, which exercises control over your conscious actions, is hard at work trying to keep you on your current track and ignore this Moment of Choice. Your limbic system, which exercises no sort of impulse control whatsoever, wants you to not only think you have to act now, but it wants you to actually go and immediately make the call. It wants you to believe that it is absolutely the most important thing you can do with your time.

Without a plan to combat the limbic system, you are going to go off on a time-sucking tangent where you hunt down the needed phone number and make the phone call only to end up waiting on hold or leaving a voice mail. After which, you are back trying to remember where you were before you got distracted. (Which, as you know, can take up to 23 minutes to happen.)

Corralling Your Three-Year-Old's Thoughts

A Back Burner List is just what you need to combat your impulsive limbic system.

A Back Burner List starts each day as an empty document or piece of paper that moves through the day with you. When new, uninvited thoughts pop up about tasks to take care of or ideas you want to act on, you merely pause and add them to the Back Burner List and return to what you were doing. The whole process should only take a few seconds of your time.

By writing those intruding thoughts down, you've gotten them out of your head, freeing up valuable brain space you would otherwise be using trying to remember them. You've also acted on the thoughts even if only to note it on your list. The mere act of recording the thought satisfies the limbic system because you have done something. The intruding thought has been noted and captured, and you can now deal with it in a way that fits into your schedule without derailing what you are currently working on.

It's easier to be organized if you don't have as much to organize in the first place. So, start saying No more often.

5. The To-Don't List

A To-Don't List is one that evolves over time (vs. writing it up daily, like a to-do list). Because it's essential to identify tasks and eliminate or delegate tasks that are not worth your time or in your best interest, keeping a To-Don't List is a great way to be in charge of your time. The To-Don't List becomes a brain filter that instantly identifies undesirable tasks when they show up and enables you to pass on them without any guilt quickly.

A To-Don't List is based on you deciding to say No to things in your life that don't serve you. You've probably heard that saying No to one thing means you are saying Yes to something else. When it comes to getting things done, this is absolutely true.

One of my favorite ways that anyone ever has said No is the way author, E. B. White did. White was a prolific writer for the *New Yorker* and wrote the children's classics *Charlotte's Web* and *Stuart Little*. He also suffered from high levels of anxiety.

In September of 1956, he received an unexpected letter requesting that he join The Committee of the Arts & Scientists for Eisenhower. This was something that wasn't in White's plans. He wanted to be out of the public eye and working on his writing. So, he said, No. But on his terms.

In response to the formal request, White replied: "I must decline, for secret reasons."

Secret reasons. How awesome is that?

He didn't elaborate on what they were (how secret would they be if he shared them?). Just that they were secret, and because of them, he was saying No. He did this, so he could say Yes to the important thing in his life, writing.

Building your To-Don't List

This is what you are going to do as well: you are going to keep a list of all the things that aren't effective or productive in your life that you have said No to.*

Since To-Don't Lists become a manifesto to live by, build them for different parts of your life. You can build a To-Don't List for only work or business. It can be as abstract as "I don't get caught up in emotional madness in the office," or "I don't participate in office gossip," or as specific as "I don't schedule meetings between 1 p.m. and 3 p.m.," or "I don't check e-mail until after 10 a.m."

You can build a list for your personal life with things on it such as "I don't buy clothes that require dry cleaning" or "I don't make plans to go out on Tuesday evenings."

You can build a list dedicated to health with items like "I don't eat anything after 7 p.m." or "I don't hit the snooze alarm," or "I don't miss a day exercising."

Everyone's To-Don't List is going to be different. The key is to make sure that your list eliminates things in your life that don't work for you (either physically, mentally, emotionally, or productively). Once you have your list started, it's critical that you hold your commitment to yourself and don't do the things you don't want to do. This list is very much alive and evolves as you figure out things you don't do. Say No either publicly, or for secret reasons. But keep track of what you are saying No to.

Moving past lists, we get to scheduling as a way to overcome the Planning Fallacy and procrastination by being intentional with your time. And it starts with an odd question: How do you schedule your Free Time?

---

* And I don't see any reason why you can't tell people "No, for secret reasons." Let them wonder.

6. Honor your Free Time

Most people are good at scheduling things like appointments, meetings, family outings, and kids' activities. If they are lucky, their unplanned (but always appreciated) Free Time slips in between all of this scheduled time.

Planning Free Time feels weird because most of the time you think of Free Time like "extra money," a unicorn of an idea that doesn't really exist. You think that when/if you have Free Time, you'll do something you never seem to get around to.

Most of the time, that plan (or really, lack of a plan) just doesn't work. That's because our old friend, Parkinson's Law, shows up. Parkinson's Law states that a task expands to fill the time available for it. So, if you've only scheduled time for work tasks, then that is precisely the time that is going to get filled. If you schedule your Free Time as well, you put boundaries in place to protect this Free Time. Your work time now can only expand so much before hitting a predetermined, Free Time boundary.

But what if you changed this and began scheduling your Free Time first and made it just as important as a doctor's appointment? When I bring this up in workshops I teach, people always make this confused face. Their nose wrinkles up, and they look at me like I've possibly lost my mind. (Chances are, you're making this face right now as well.) We're all so used to thinking of Free Time as something that only shows up when we've finished all of our "have tos," that we've never really looked at it as something we can plan for. And just to reassure you, I haven't lost my mind!

When you schedule a doctor's appointment, your kid's soccer game, a job interview, or a weekend at a conference, these appointments become set in stone and all your other tasks have to flow around them. You schedule your time and activities so you can get to your doctor, the interview, the conference, or the game on time without the chance of anything interrupting or intervening. Each of these things are not just appointments, they are also deadlines.

If you schedule your regular appointments and honor them, then why not schedule your Free Time and honor it?

Building your Free Time into your schedule

At the beginning of the month or even at the start of the quarter, look at your calendar and block out when you want to have Free Time. Maybe it's every day after 4 p.m., or for full weekends twice a month, or every other Friday morning, or a three-day weekend every two months. Perhaps it's just an hour every other night when the kids are in bed. You decide what works for you. Block this time out. If you're using a paper calendar, block this out in red pen. If you're using a digital calendar, block it out in some menacing color that tells you that this time can't be touched. Commit to this time, just as you would for a doctor's appointment, your kid's soccer game, or a conference.

Now the important part: decide what you're going to do with this time. Have a rough outline of what you'd like to do with the time. It could be as simple as "reading time with the kids," "explore a museum I haven't been to," "work on my hobbies," or "hang out with my friends." Both of these steps are important for a couple of reasons:

1. These blocks of Free Time aren't just there to give you something to look forward to. Just like your other appointments, your schedule now has to flow around your Free Time as well. More importantly, these blocks now serve as a deadline to get your other things done so you can move into your Free Time without any feelings of guilt. Since it's scheduled, you have to do it.

2. Since it's easy to downplay the importance of scheduled Free Time and let other tasks take over, it's important to have a plan of how you're going to use your time. Without a definite course to follow, your three-year-old brain can jump in and convince you to either ignore your planned Free Time, or to waste it on something that's not really important to you. Without a plan to use your Free Time, you give your brain a Moment of Choice, which is where procrastination and other bad choices can occur.

Bonus: Studies have shown that both knowing when you're going to have Free Time and how you're going to use it can actually make you happier.[11] So there is no reason not to plan for your Free Time. You deserve it.

Planning your Free Time might feel weird at first, but once you start doing it regularly, you'll see how effective it is. You're giving yourself deadlines and planned breaks. Definitely a win-win.

7. Mind the Gap

On the subways in London (or more correctly, the Tube), the melodious, disembodied voice constantly reminds passengers to "Mind the Gap," the space between the platform and the subway car. The gap is the empty space that can trip you up and ruin your day if you aren't paying attention.

Sort of like gaps of time in your day.

Gaps are your transition times. The time between when you've finished one task, and before you start the next. Gaps by definition are Moments of Choice. They lack structure and they force you to make choices about what to do next, which is where you can easily become distracted or procrastinate. As you know, the fewer Moments of Choice you have, the less likely you are to procrastinate.

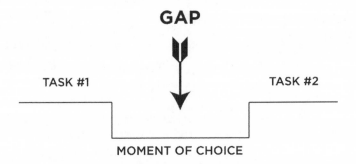

A gap between the end of one meeting and the starting of another one can easily become a moment where you take the opportunity to "jump onto email for just a second" and get lost in an email thread.

You can experience a gap between the time when you drop off the kids at school and now need to shift into work mode, but first, you decide to put a load of laundry in.

My gap used to be the time between returning home from the gym in the morning and getting ready for work. This gap was when I had choices to make about how I was going to use my time. Unfortunately, it was also when my guard was down and I was most easily distracted. Between showering, making and eating breakfast, watching the news, and checking in on my email, I could get lost in my gap for hours.

Once you start looking for gaps in your day, you'll be surprised by how many there are. Try using this four-part plan to navigate them:

- **Have a ritual or a routine** that moves you from your Task A into your Task B with no gap time. To eliminate the gap I had after going to the gym, I put together a solid routine that had me go straight to the shower when I got home. No turning on the television to check the news or stopping by the computer to check emails. Once I was showered and ready for work, I would reward myself with a favorite tea and breakfast as a prelude to jumping into work. This meal represented my transition from the early-morning-me to the working-with-clients-me with no stop included for procrastinating.

- **Build a habit.** Once you've figured out where gaps show up in your day, build a habit that you can follow that allows you to navigate the gap without falling into it. Your habit can be something as easy as setting a five-minute timer when you complete a task. Use the five minutes to physically and mentally transition to your next task. Or you could build a habit of listening to a favorite song when you complete a task. When the song ends, you start working on your next task.

- **Establish personal rules.** It's not the gaps in time that can derail you, it's how you choose to use them. So, make personal rules about what you can and can't do in the gap.

  If "quickly checking emails" always turns into 20 minutes or more online, make a rule not to check emails during transition times. Instead, decide on a set time when you check emails and stick to it. If you know playing a video game in a time gap is going to take you down an entertainment rabbit hole (at least until you run out of lives), make a rule of no games during work time. Or remove the temptation all the way and take the game off any of your devices. If you know that gap time exposes you to too many distracting options, always have a list nearby of what you need to do next.

- **Recite a mantra.** Have a mantra to bridge the gaps in your day. It can be as easy as "Mind the gap" (bonus points if you do it in a British accent) or "Here's a gap." All you need to do is acknowledge the gap so you can react appropriately. When you've consciously labeled the gap, you'll be much more likely to avoid falling mindlessly into it.

You can make your mantra more of a positive affirmation if you like. Try something like "This is a gap, I know what I need to do next, and I'm starting it now." Experiment with a few different mantras to see what works best for you and helps you to successfully mind the gap.

Knowing that the transition between Task A and Task B is full of moments where you have to make choices, having a predetermined structure to deal with the gap is your best possible defense of your time and your forward momentum.

When you're not organized or intentional about your time, it's easy to procrastinate and waste time—definitely not the way to get things done! Luckily, there are lots of ways you can become organized, even if you hate that word. Keep an eye out for the Planning Fallacy so you can stop it from tripping you up.

Take pressure off your brain by planning out your day the night before, think about Friday on Monday, know what you want to accomplish each day, have Back Burner Lists and To-Don't Lists, schedule your free time, and remember to Mind the Gap. Any or all of these, will help you conquer procrastination.

Experiment with one or two ideas at a time and see what works or doesn't work for you. I think you'll find that being organized is a skill that's pretty powerful to have (and not as painful as you might think.)

CHAPTER FIVE ACTION TOOLBOX: ORGANIZATION

DEFINITIONS IN THIS CHAPTER
Planning Fallacy:
A cognitive bias that causes humans to consistently underestimate the amount of time necessary to complete tasks.

Parkinson's Law:
A task expands to fill the time available for it.

TOOLS IN THIS CHAPTER

Plan Your Day the Night Before:

Take time at the end of your workday, or the end of the day, to plan out exactly what needs to happen the next day. Set up whatever plan works for you, then jump into your next day at full tilt, completely eliminating any option of procrastination.

Think about Friday on Monday:

Think about what you need to have done by the end of the week, then back-time your schedule to ensure everything gets done.

Plan for Your Outcomes:

Decide what your desired outcomes for the day are. List them on a Post-it Note, schedule your day in a way that the Outcomes are achieved.

Back Burner List:

A list of ideas and thoughts that pop up during the day that need to be acknowledged and remembered, but that you don't need to drop everything and take care of immediately.

The To-Don't List:

An ongoing list of tasks and obligations that are a hard "No" for you. These tasks and responsibilities are no longer attractive, are time-wasters, or no longer serve your desired goals. When they pop up in your life, refer to your To-Don't list and say No.

Honor Your Free Time:

Plan out your free time, not only when it's going to happen, but also exactly what you are going to do. Then hold to that schedule like it's a doctor's appointment.

Mind the Gap:

Eliminate the gaps in your day that are Moments of Choice, where you can get easily distracted and start procrastinating. Choose from:

Have a Ritual or Routine to Mind the Gap:

Establish a ritual or routine that helps you to identify gaps and then smoothly move past them without getting distracted. Don't leave this up to choice; when you see a gap, call it out so it can't waste your time.

Build a Habit:

Put together a habit that takes you through the gap without getting lost in it.

Establish Personal Rules:

Set up personal rules for how you deal with gaps. Follow them whenever you encounter a gap.

Recite a Mantra:

Have a Mantra or an affirmation that you repeat to yourself to keep from falling into a gap. Something as simple as "This is a gap, and I don't have to fall into it" will work.

ACTION ITEMS
Plan Your Day the Night Before:

Decide when you will plan out your next day.

For example: *I will plan out my day the last five minutes at work. I will plan out a 5-item outcome list and add to my To-Don't list.*

I will plan out my next day at (time) _____

Where I will do the planning: _____

The format I will use for planning: _____

Use this schedule for the next five days, then adjust as necessary.

Plan for Friday on Monday:

Set up a plan to Backtime a project.

For example:

Project: Presentation

Due Date/Deadline: 5 p.m. Friday

Backstep 1: Run through presentation (Friday morning)

Backstep 2: Format presentation (Thursday)

Backstep 3: Design the layout for presentation (Wednesday)

Backstep 4: Write content (Tuesday)

Backstep 5: Do all research (Monday)

Your turn:

Project: _____

Due Date/Deadline: _____

Next to the Last Deadline (Backstep 1):_____

Backstep 2: _____

Backstep 3: _____

Backstep 4: _____

Backstep 5: _____

To meet your deadline, work backward starting first with Backstep 5.

Outcome List:

On a sticky note, write the numbers 1 to 5, then write down the outcomes you would like to have for the day:

OUTCOMES
1.
2.
3.
4.
5.

Follow this list during the day. Do what is necessary to achieve each of the Outcomes (without using a detailed To-do list.) You can also list each outcome on a separate sticky and then stack the outcomes in the order you'd like to achieve them. That way you are only looking at one Outcome at a time.

Start Your To-Don't List:

Write down your first five known To-Don't. When complete, transfer to your notebook or write on a piece of paper and post where you will see it often. Add to the list as you think of more items.

1. _____

2: _____

3: _____

4: _____

5: _____

Plan for your Free Time:

Look at your schedule for the next week or next month, schedule, and securely block out three Free Time sessions. Decide what you'll do during each session, and who, if anyone you'll do it with:

Date and Time: _____

What you will do: _____

Who you will do it with (optional): _____

Date and Time: _____

What you will do: _____

Who you will do it with (optional): _____

Date and Time: _____

What you will do: _____

Who you will do it with (optional): _____

Overcome the Gaps:

Pick one way you will overcome the Gaps in your day and how you will do it. Refer to page 119 for more information.

RITUAL   HABIT   RULES   MANTRA   OTHER

My plan will be: _____

_____

_____

_____

Chapter Six

Procrastination IV:
Putting things off

Amateurs sit and wait for inspiration,
the rest of us just get up and go to work.
- Stephen King, author

The future always seems like a long way off, no matter how old you are. When I was a kid, I remember thinking how far off the year 2000 was and wondering whether we'd have hover cars and live in houses in space like the Jetsons (sadly no to both). The year 2000 showed up and even with all the fanfare, it still felt like the future continued to be unimaginably far away.

That's the problem with the future, we can't really see it, so we procrastinate on doing things that will be beneficial to us in the future.

No matter how I try, the future-me and the present-me are never going to be friends. I'd like to think I do things with the future-me in mind, like go to the gym, eat healthily, and save money for a rainy day, but if I'm honest, I don't do them nearly as much as I should. And you probably don't either.

I don't think of future-me as an older, hopefully wiser version of myself. Future-me is an unknown stranger. I'm not the only person who thinks this way, science[12] has shown everyone thinks of their future self as a stranger as well, which poses a problem.

As humans, we are wired to put our current self before everyone else, especially strangers. We basically treat strangers differently than we treat ourselves and if that stranger is your future self, problems arise. It's easy to put off doing what needs to be done today because the future person who is going to benefit from your efforts is currently a stranger to you.

You're more likely to put things off, like exercising, saving money, going back to school, switching jobs, or working towards future goals, in favor of what benefits you today. While you know you shouldn't put things off today, when the beneficiary of those tasks is going to be a stranger, you're less likely to be excited to do them.

For example, if the future-unknown-me wants to be 10 pounds lighter by the time summer rolls around, and the current-me wants to eat a donut today for breakfast, chances are current-me is going to win. This means nine weeks down the road, future-me will be disappointed and annoyed when my jeans still don't fit. But right now, current-me doesn't care. The immediate payoff for the current action (eating the donut) is greater than the payoff further down the road (future-me easily sliding into a pair of jeans).

Scenarios like this play out all the time, and it's not just with food, and it's not just me. How's your retirement account look? Yep, thought so. It's hard to save for your future-retired-self when that self is a stranger to you. At this point, current-you would rather spend your money enjoying a vacation now instead of socking money away for the stranger 20 years down the road.

Why would you do this?

There's a name for this, and it's not "misguided selfishness," it's Hyperbolic Discounting. The term originally comes from Behavioral Economics and states that we can easily see ourselves today, but not tomorrow or a week or 10 weeks from now. A major part of Hyperbolic Discounting is the "Present Bias" which refers to the "tendency of people to give stronger weight to payoffs that are closer to the present time when considering trade-offs between two future moments."[13]

This is precisely what happens when current-me is chowing down on a chocolate glazed donut, while future-me is throwing her hands up in disgust.

If you want to achieve your long-term goals, the ones that are 10, 21, 30, 90 days, six months or more away, then you have to make friends with your future self to overcome the Present Bias, then make it a point to keep your goals in front of you, and make them concrete.

1. Make friends with your future self

You've probably walked into a meeting, a party, or a classroom and encountered a group of strangers who you know next to nothing about. Then, over the course of time, you learn a few names, shake a few hands, make a few friends. These people are strangers no more. You know their faces, you've learned a few tidbits about them, you feel some sort of commonality with them. While they may never be your best friend, they are no longer strangers to you.

One of the ways to overcome the Present Bias is to meet, face-to-face, the stranger who is your future self. After all, putting a face to a name is one of the first steps in converting a stranger to a friend.

You can imagine what your future self might look like, but you'll probably do it in the most idealized way possible, a story-book version of you in the future with everything beyond perfect. Or you can look at your face 30 years from now through the magic of technology and apps. There are several to choose from, including AgingBooth, Life Advisor: Personal Test, or Oldify. Just search for "Aging Apps."

All of them work pretty much the same way: snap a picture of yourself and the app does an age progression for you. Yeah, kind of scary, but helpful. Looking face-to-face with me 30 years down the road makes me think more carefully about what I'm doing today. Is what I'm doing now going to be helpful to this older version of me? What could I do today (and tomorrow) to change things?

With a glimpse into what my future self might look like, it's easier to make choices that will make my future self happier.

Since this face is now my friend, what are some of the ways I can help my future self? I can remember actions have consequences and while present me really loves hanging out on the couch, future me is going to like that I can move and lift things, so getting to the gym today is a very good idea. Future-me is also going to like having money to buy things, so working with a financial planner and having a solid savings plan is a good thing (even though I want to spend the money now).

But knowing I should do these things and actually doing them are two different things. So, just like sometimes having to be smarter than the three-year-old in our brains, we sometimes have to be smarter than our current-selves in order to make our future-selves happy.

Planning ahead and using precommitments

Planning ahead isn't really anything new. It's something everyone has done before. Only, this time, you're doing it with your future self in mind. Think of it like preparing to go camping or on a trip where there are lots of variables and unknowns to consider and plan for.

You have to think about where you're going, what you're doing, and what you are absolutely going to need (swimsuit) and what you might need (lotion to soothe a sunburn or stop poison ivy from itching). You have to take the time to imagine what your future self is going to want to eat and is going to need to be happy. Then you have to pack accordingly. Now, if you can do this for a short-term event like a camping trip or vacation, then you can do this for events that are further down the road, where your future self is counting on you to have planned ahead and acted accordingly.

You can plan ahead for any scenario and any goal, whether it's something that's going to happen next week or two years from now. Take some time to think about what future-you is going to need and make sure current-you does what's necessary to overcome the Present Bias and be successful.

Many times, you'll find the best tool to help you with planning ahead is using precommitments.

The power of precommitments

Precommitments help you commit, in advance, to doing things that will make it easier to ensure your future self's happiness. Think about it: your future self is going to hope you have prepared for retirement by systematically setting aside money, or you've done what's necessary to lose weight, learn a new skill, or have a job that you love.

Using precommitments will increase the probability of current-you making future-you happy. If precommitments sound familiar, there's a reason: they are a form of If/Then Plans.

By their very nature, precommitments make it harder for current you to give in to the Present Bias since the intentional actions you take now limit (in a good way) your future options. Precommitments can be things like setting up an automatic savings plan so current-you isn't in charge of putting money into your savings or retirement account. You can't spend your future money if you don't see it in the first place.

You can precommit to eating well by having someone shop for you, so no junk food comes into your house, or you could pay to have healthy meals prepared and delivered to you.

You can precommit to working out by paying for personal training, classes or your gym membership in advance.

You can precommit to your health by scheduling future doctor and dentist appointments before you leave a current appointment.

You can precommit to continuing your education by signing up and paying in advance for a course you've been meaning to take.

You can precommit to not smoking by not having cigarettes in your house.

You can precommit to blocks of distraction-free time on your computer or phone by scheduling "block out sessions" ahead of time using apps like SelfControl, Freedom or FlipD. (This also means precommitting to having time to focus.)

Future-you isn't that far in the future

Making your future self happy doesn't have to be complicated, and it doesn't have to be for your future self months or even years in the future.

For example, my favorite way to make my future self happy is to change the sheets on my bed before I leave for a trip. When I return home, I appreciate that I thought ahead to make my future self happy with fresh, clean sheets as a welcome home gift. It's a small thing, but it works.

Making sure your future self isn't a stranger makes it easier to do the things you need to do with long-term outcomes. Anything you can do to overcome the Present Bias, even if it's as simple as looking at your potential future self on your phone, is going to enable you to make your future self much happier and more productive.

You'll be less likely to procrastinate or sabotage your efforts, it will be easier to say no to the donut, no to spending all the money, and no to being lazy on the couch.

2. Keep Things in Front of You

The second way you can prevent procrastination when your goal is too far off is to Keep Things in Front of You. When you've got a goal that is going to take a while to achieve, not only is it difficult to see the finish line because it is far off, but there's usually a lack of urgency to it as well. Six weeks can seem like plenty of time to accomplish a task, especially if you're still only on Week One. When you feel like there's still lots of time to get things done, it's hard to remember that each day counts. But that's exactly what you need to do.

The second way you can overcome the Present Bias is to make sure every day you are aware of your goal and the actions you need to be taking. One of the best ways to do this is to keep yourself aware of your goal and the actions you need to be taking, and then track or measure them.

What gets measured, gets done

Keeping track of your progress is a time-honored method for keeping your goals in front of you every day. You've probably heard the phrase "What gets measured, gets done."* If you can track the actions you're taking towards achieving a goal, then you're much more likely to achieve it.

Trying to lose weight? Record what you eat each day and keep a chart of your weight as it goes down week to week. Want to get in shape? Keep track of when, where and how you exercise each day. Want to increase your knowledge in a new field? Track what you read, watch, and who you listen to. Want to build a new habit? Give your self a gold star for each successful repetition of your new behavior. You get the idea.

When you have a goal that's too far in the future for current-you to imagine accomplishing, measure and track your progress. This allows you to overcome the Present Bias because when you mark things down, either on a chart, a calendar, a spreadsheet, in an app or on a website, you reinforce the idea that what you do each day DOES matter, whether you can tell it or not. Current-you is doing the things that future-you will appreciate. Your tracking method doesn't have to be elaborate, it just has to be consistently done. A simple chart, notations in a notebook or a tracking app on the phone all work great, or you can get more elaborate and use one of the following two methods:

---

* This quote is usually attributed to the late Peter Drucker.

Red dots vs. green dots

One way you can keep track of how you're doing is as easy as red dots and green dots. This idea comes from my friend and podcast co-host, Lee Silber. As I mentioned before, Lee is an Efficiency Expert, so he knows a thing or two about getting things done.

Lee tracks his progress with a system of sticky green dots and red dots. He decides what he wants to be tracking, for example, eating less pizza, working out consistently, drinking less beer, writing more, practicing drums, looking for speaking gigs. He figures out precisely how daily success looks for him in each of those areas (for example: absolutely no pizza, 30 minutes of exercise, one or fewer beers per day, one hour minimum of writing, a half an hour on the drums, one hour reaching out to people who book speaking gigs) and then finds a calendar, and some red and green dot stickers.

At the end of every day, he looks at each of the items he is tracking* and gives himself a dot based on how he did for the day. Green means he succeeded, and red means he didn't. That's it. No journaling, no soul-searching—just a simple green dot or a red dot goes on the calendar.

Tally them up!

At the end of the week, he tallies the number of green dots and red dots for each task. In an ideal world, there would be seven green dots for each of the things he is tracking, but that's not always the case, especially when life gets in the way. Some days, pizza gets eaten, or practice gets skipped, and red dots show up. But all is not lost.

Lee is not looking for the specific number of red and green dots he gets each week, but rather he's looking to see how they are trending. If he's doing things well, then the green dots will show him that. If he's not doing so well, then there are more red dots than green dots showing up. When that's the case, he knows there is work to be done in a particular area.

What's great about this is over a period of a few weeks or months, he can follow his progress (or lack thereof) and course-correct, as the dots can serve

---

* For the record, you don't have to be tracking a lot of things like he is in this example. He's been doing this a while. It's perfectly acceptable to start tracking just one or two things. Make it easy and don't overwhelm yourself.

as an early warning system that shows if he is veering in the wrong direction. Too many red dots over too many weeks tells him he needs to make some changes.

Is there anything magical about red and green dots? Not at all. You could do yellow and purple dots. Or black and white. Whatever colors work for you. Honestly? You don't even need to be using sticky dots. You could use a markers and make circles or squares or triangles on your chart or calendar pages. Colors and shapes aren't really important, the fact you are tracking your progress is. Are you consistently getting more of one color than the other? Are you consistency making forward progress? Or do you need to make some changes and tighten things up a bit?*

The green and red dots are one way to measure your progress, another is just by simply making Xs.

Don't Break The Chain

Another color-related way to track yourself is to use a tracking plan that has been attributed to comedian, Jerry Seinfeld (although he denies he came up with the idea or even uses it). According to the story,[14] Jerry wanted to be consistent in writing jokes every day. He knew if he was consistent in writing, he would be a better comedian. Rather than sitting down and thinking, "I'm going to write jokes for two hours on Monday and two hours on Friday," he wrote jokes every single day. He then (in theory) devised something called "Don't Break The Chain." Each day he was successful in sitting down to write jokes, he put a big red X on a calendar, with the goal of the Xs eventually forming a chain across the weeks and months, signifying his consistent accomplishment.

Even if Seinfeld didn't come up with the idea, somewhere, someone did and it's still a great way to track things.

---

* Yes, there's probably an app you could use as well. Lee is just an analog kind of guy. The system works, so why not try it?

To do your own version of "Don't Break The Chain," you need a calendar and, ideally, a red marker. Decide how you are going to define success.

Making it both very specific and something that will move you towards achieving your goal, not just something that is easy to do. It could be writing a certain number of words, doing a certain number of exercises, limiting your calorie intake to a certain level, or reading a certain number of pages. Each day that you succeed at your task, mark a big red X on the calendar (you can pick any color marker but red works really well). The next day, when you succeed, you mark another X on the calendar. Ideally, you will repeat daily. By the end of the week, if you've been consistent, you'll have a chain of red Xs signifying your own personal streak of accomplishment.

Challenge yourself to see how many days in a row you can succeed. Focus not on the outcome of your actions, but on your consistency, knowing the process is how the outcome is achieved and that each day counts.

Where and how doesn't matter

It actually doesn't matter where you track your progress or how you do it. You can track on a physical calendar with check marks, or on an app with digital high fives. You can track with hash marks on an index card or with detailed notations in a journal. You can do big red Xs on a wall calendar or tiny red Xs in a pocket calendar. You can meticulously log your efforts in a notebook, or jot them on sticky notes. When you consistently track, you'll find it's almost impossible to procrastinate on working towards the things your future self will appreciate.

The third way you can overcome the Present Bias is by making your faraway goals concrete.

At this point your future goal is just an abstract idea somewhere on the horizon. Obviously, you want to get to the place where you've successfully completed your goal, only you don't know what that place or you yourself are going to look like when you actually get there. To combat the abstractness of your goal, you need to find a way to make the goal concrete in your mind so it's easier to remember that every day counts. This will make it harder to procrastinate on the consistent steps needed to achieve the goal. Luckily, making your goals into something concrete isn't as hard as it sounds.

3. Make your goals concrete

My friends, Rob and Trish, had a big, abstract, far away goal: they wanted to pay off their credit card debt. Now, this is a tricky kind of goal, not only does it feel abstract, but paying down your credit card debt is not something you think of every day. Usually, you think of your credit card balance only when it's time to make the payment. It's rarely top of mind every day.

But for Rob and Trish, it really needed to be an every day thought since they were carrying a hefty load of debt. Together, they decided the best way to keep their goal concrete was to literally keep it in front of them every day. Their first step was to get two poster-sized pieces of paper, tape them together, and make a chart.

On one end of the chart, they wrote a very high number: the total amount of money they owed on all their credit cards. Actually writing it out and acknowledging it was a big step. On the other end of the chart was a zero, representing the far-off day when all of their cards were paid in full. They then divided the chart into the number of months they figured it would take to pay the debt down, and how much they would be paying each month to make it a reality. Once this was done, they could now look at the chart at any time and see where they were with their goal and what they needed to do next to stay on track.

So far, pretty straight forward. Right?

Then Rob and Trish took one additional, very critical step: they taped the chart to their living room wall.

Yep, the chart was out there where they had to look at it. Every. Single. Day.* Now, it's not like this chart blended in with their living room decor. It stood out like a beacon, which was the whole idea. Their goal to pay off their debt was no longer abstract, it was concrete, and in their face.

Putting in the work

For the first few months, they were diligent about following their plan and paying the exact, predetermined amount on each of their bills. When they were paid, Rob or Trish dutifully marked their progress on the chart, and together, they watched the numbers slowly, slowly go down.

---

* As a bonus, anyone who stopped by could see how deeply in debt they were. Nothing was hidden anymore.

But then something happened right around the fifth month. Seeing the chart every day forced them to think about their credit card debt even more. They were looking at it every day, how could they not? The main thought they kept coming up with: what could they do to achieve their goal even faster? They put their heads together and revised their plan of attack.

They stopped eating out so often and instead made an effort to cook more at home. They pulled their coffee maker out of the garage, dusted it off and started making their morning coffee at home. They took their lunches to work and started driving less and walking more. They checked books and movies out of the library and stayed at home instead of going out for entertainment. As they saved more, they were able to pay more money each month on each card, so they began to reduce their credit card debt much more quickly.

This simple chart on their wall kept their goal in front of them all the time so it was very concrete in their minds. And it worked better than expected. Thanks to the chart, they paid off all their credit card debt seven months ahead of the date they originally anticipated.

Then, with the success of the first chart in mind, they turned around and made a new chart for a new abstract goal. This one started with zero and went up to a high number as they started saving money for a down payment on the house. They used the same in-your-face-every-day process, and again, it worked perfectly. They now live in their own house, where there's probably a chart on the wall as they move towards some other goal.

Their chart worked for several reasons. It made the abstract become concrete with a precise, consistent action, "this much money gets paid or saved each month." Rob and Trish were able to measure and move themselves because they were able to track their progress each month. They were able to keep everything in the Present Day because they saw the chart every time they walked through the Living Room.

There was no way to ignore it.

A chart, whatever it looks like, and for whatever goal you're trying to achieve, is a great way to make any goal concrete. It shows you where you are, where you want to go, and what you need to get there. As long as you put it somewhere you will see it every day, it becomes the way your current-self works to make your future self happy.

One fitness company has found a way to use this principle in their program. If you purchase the P90X workout system,* somewhere, amongst the DVDs, the tape measure, the recipe and fitness guides you receive, there is a 90-day calendar that tells you exactly what workout you'll be doing each day for the next 90 days. This calendar goes on your wall, and it becomes the place for you to keep track of your workouts and your progress. You can see all 90 days in one glance, which makes the abstract goal of getting in shape in 90 days a concrete concept. And it keeps you more accountable by seeing every day what is expected, and allowing you to plan ahead for future workouts.

Keep things in front of you

While a chart worked great for Rob and Trish, it might not be the tool for what you're working on. Rob and Trish had one thing to focus on, but if they'd had a lot of things to keep in front of themselves, clipboards would have been a better idea for them.

In my office, I have six different clipboards hanging on my walls. Each of these clipboards has a list on it for something I need to pay attention to and keep in front of me.

For example, one list attached to one clipboard is titled "Far Away." On the list is things I need to accomplish, but the deadline for each one of them is six months or more in the future. In the past, I might have made a list like this (motion at its best), then put it in a file on my desk and forgotten about it. Now that it's on my wall, I see it every day. And while I'm really not acting on any of the items yet, they aren't lost in a pile on my desk.

The great thing is, if I think of something or see something that pertains to an item on the Far Away List, I note it on the list so the idea isn't lost. Sometimes

---

* Or really any workout system. And yes, you can still buy most of them as DVDs.

I'll use a Post-it Note to create a more detailed description of the thought or idea then stick it on the clipboard with the Far Away List. When it's time to revisit these faraway ideas, all the information is there, I only have to pull the clipboard down and review my notes. I don't have to start from scratch since it's been in front of me, it hasn't been forgotten, and the ideas have kept coming.

Clipboards to the rescue

Clipboards are also an excellent way to keep long lists of things that need to be done, in front of you. If you've ever hosted a large event, managed a large project like launching a business, or putting on a conference (or a wedding), you probably had a considerable Master List of everything that had to be done. Your brain is not designed for remembering every single detail, so while getting all your thoughts and ideas down on paper is a great way to corral them and make sure nothing gets lost, it's also a great way to become overwhelmed by the sheer number of tasks.

One part of your brain knows that everything on the list doesn't have to be done immediately, while another part (your inner three-year-old) is trying to run in the other direction from sheer panic.

If you pause and look closely, you'll see there is a hierarchy to the list, of what has to happen and when. A must be completed before C can be started, and D can only occur if B has been taken care of. But sorting all of that out can be difficult. You need to cut through all of the chaos of the Master List and establish some order. This is where double clipboards come into play.

Take the Master List and put it on a clipboard, then pick six to eight items of the that need to be taken care of immediately or in the next 24 hours and write them on a blank piece of paper. Now put the clipboard with Master List on it somewhere where you can still see it, but is out of your way. Take this new list, with the six to eight items on it and attach it to a new clipboard. This is the new shortlist that you are going to refer to and focus on. This shortlist of six to eight items is going to feel a whole lot less overwhelming, and more importantly, doable. Your only job now is to focus on taking care of these six to eight tasks. Once they are all complete, go back to the Master List and cross them off, then put together another shortlist with six to eight more items on it and work through them.

Since the Master List is always in sight, it won't get lost in the shuffle of life, but since you are pulling only the immediate tasks from it, the chance of getting overwhelmed by its sheer size (and possibly procrastinating) is significantly reduced.

These are not the only ways you can use clipboards. You can put up multiple clipboards (like me) and dedicate each one to something different: family, hobbies, chores, work. You can use clipboards to track your progress on various goals or as a place to keep random thoughts and ideas that you don't know what you're going to do with yet.

It's very easy to procrastinate on doing the things you need to do when your goal is too far away. Because you deal with the double whammy of Hyperbolic Discounting and the Present Bias, you have to be smarter than your brain. You have to make friends with, and take care of, your future self. You need to keep your goals in front of yourself every day through measuring and tracking, and you need to do what you can to make those far off goals concrete so you can do everything, every day, to ultimately achieve them.

We now move on to the next skill: Energy. Specifically, how to manage it, conserve it, and leverage it to make you efficient and effective so you can get things DONE.

CHAPTER SIX ACTION TOOLBOX: PUTTING THINGS OFF

DEFINITIONS IN THIS CHAPTER
Hyperbolic Discounting
A term from Behavioral Economics that says we can easily see ourselves today, but not in the future.

Present Bias
The tendency of people to give stronger weight to payoffs that are closer to the present time when considering trade-offs between two future moments.

TOOLS IN THIS CHAPTER

Make friends with your future self:

Because your future self is a stranger to you, and as humans, we don't like strangers, use an Aging app to get an idea of what you might look like in the future. When you know what your future self looks like, it's easier to do things that will benefit you in a future time.

Use Precommitments:

Decide ahead of time when you are going to do things that will benefit your future self. Make it even easier by automating activities, which eliminates the need for making choices.

Keep Things in Front of You:

Keep actions and goals in front of you and top of mind, so you are more likely to accomplish them.

What gets measured, gets done:

Track, measure, and follow your daily progress, so you don't forget and go off track. Choose from:

Red dots vs. green dots:

Decide what things you want to change or track in your life. Decide what daily success looks like for each item you follow. At the end of the day, put a green dot on a calendar if you succeeded, and put a red dot if you didn't. At the end of a week, or month, tally the dots to see how you are doing.

Don't Break the Chain:

Each day you succeed at a predetermined task, make a red "X" on a calendar. Try to keep the X's going by continuing to succeed. The goal is an unbroken chain of red Xs.

Make your goals concrete:

Find a way to keep your goal or a representation of it in front of you every day. Use a picture, a saying, or chart, anything to make far off goals a part of your everyday experience.

ACTION ITEMS
Make friends with your future self:

Download an Aging app (check page 283 in the Resources section for a list of apps) snap a picture and look at your older self. Now list five things you would like to start doing today for your future self.

1. _____

2. _____

3. _____

4. _____

5. _____

Red dots vs. green dots:

Find a calendar (or download one at EllenGoodwin.com/forms). Pick two to four things you want to track for three weeks. Decide what daily success looks like for each one.

_____ Success _____

_____ Success _____

_____ Success _____

_____ Success _____

Next, pick two colors, whether it is with sticky dots, or with markers. One color will represent daily success ("good"), the other will indicate you need more work ("bad".) Begin tracking each on the calendar. At the end of each week, tally the number of "good" dots versus the number of "bad" dots. If the "good" dots outnumber the "bad" dots, you're doing a good job. If it's the other way around, determine what you can do to become more successful.

Don't Break the Chain:
Find a calendar (or download one at EllenGoodwin.com/forms), decide on one thing you would like to track, and what daily success looks like when it comes to this task. Get a red marker. Each day you succeed at your task, put a big X on the calendar. When you don't succeed, no X's. Your goal here is to build a streak of red X's across the calendar.

Find additional ways to make your goals concrete:
Get creative to make your far-away goal concrete, so you work towards it every day and overcome the Present Bias:

- Make a chart that shows where you are now and where you want to be eventually. Decide what actions you need to take to move you towards your goal and build them into the chart. Hang the chart somewhere you will see it every day.

- Find a photo of what completion of your long-term goal looks like to you. Use the photo as your home screen on your phone or as your screen saver on your laptop. Print the photo out and put it on your refrigerator, in your car, or on your wall at work. Put it where you will see it every day.

- Write down what it will be like when you achieve your goal. Go all in and write how it will feel, what it will mean, what will be different, why it will matter. This is you defining what your future self will be like. Writing it down will help you to start making friends with your future self, so you're more likely to do the things you need to do each day to make your future self happy, and your goal a reality.

- Record (either just audio or full video) yourself reading the above list. Listen or watch it every day, once or twice. Make the future part of your current day.

ENERGY

As you move into this second section, you'll begin to see how managing your energy is essential to being in Action, and how leveraging your energy is the second important skill to master so you can successfully work when no one is watching.

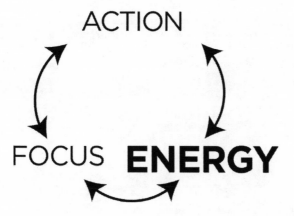

CHAPTER SEVEN

Energy

When you can't change the direction of the wind,
adjust your sails.
- H. Jackson Brown Jr., *author*

Energy can be called a lot of things: motivation, self-control, and willpower. Whatever you call it, it all boils down to utilizing it in a way that is most effective and efficient for you. Which means you're being intentional with how you use the ebbs and flows of energy throughout the day and you aren't using energy up on things that aren't important to your goals and.

What personal energy means

Every day when you wake up, you have a certain amount of energy. It doesn't matter if you are someone who wakes up before the sun is up and starts to take on the day, or if you stay up all night and don't roll out of bed until after high noon.

Not only do you have energy, but you also have a set pattern (more or less) of how your energy will increase or decrease throughout the day. This is your chronotype.* Your energy pattern might be very high in the morning, then diminish after lunch to a point where you don't really want to do anything, only to have it revive as the end of the day approaches. Or you are someone who wakes up with low energy but gets more energetic as the day goes on. Neither one of these energy patterns, or really any other, is inherently better or worse.

---

* By definition: a person's natural inclination with regard to the times of day when they prefer to sleep or when they are most alert or energetic.

In this chapter, we're going to look at energy patterns, why they are important, how you can leverage your energy levels, and how you can be stronger than the energy stealers in your life.

The flawed science of Willpower

You've probably heard the fact that you have a finite amount of willpower (brain energy) at any given time, and when you run out of that energy, you run out of the ability to make decisions and get things done. Unfortunately, at this point, the science is kind of muddled on whether this is true or not.

For years, this fact was taken as gospel. In a 1998 study done by Roy Baumeister of Florida State University, hungry college students* were told they were going to take part in a study about food perception. The students were individually taken to a room where they were presented with foods for the study. In the room was a table with a stack of fresh, hot, chocolate chip cookies, as well as a bowl filled with radishes. They were told these two foods were chosen because they had highly distinctive tastes, which the students would be questioned about the following day.

One-third of the students (Group One) were told to sample two or three cookies, but no radishes. Another third of the students (Group Two) were told to taste two or three radishes but not to touch the cookies.

The final third of the students (Group Three) served as the control group and didn't participate in any of the food tasting.

Following the tasting portion of the study, the students were told that they needed to wait for 15 minutes to for the sensory memory of the food to fade. During that time they were asked to help with another study. This one had to do with determining who had better problem-solving abilities—high school students or college students.

The (college) students (including the students in Group Three) were then given a series of puzzles to solve, which, unbeknownst to them, were unsolvable and actually designed to measure persistence. The researchers were looking at how much time each student would spend trying to figure out the right answers before becoming frustrated with their efforts and giving up.

---

* Students were told to refrain from eating for at least three hours prior to reporting to the lab.

Chocolate changes things

The lucky chocolate chip cookie-eating students from Group One and the students from Group Three, who didn't do the taste study, all worked on the puzzles for an average of 20 minutes before giving up. Remember, both of these groups had not had to exercise any type of willpower or self-control before working on the puzzles.

Not so for the poor students in Group Two, the students who had to exercise their willpower and self-control, ignoring the warm chocolate chip cookies.

It should come as no surprise, that on average, the students in Group Two, on average, gave up on the persistence puzzle a mere eight minutes after starting.

While there is a long scientific explanation as to what this experiment seemingly proved, the short description is this: utilizing willpower and self-control in one area of your life, in this case, not eating cookies, depletes the amount of willpower and self-control you have available for other parts of your life—like solving puzzles that require persistence.

Other studies

Numerous other studies along these lines have been done at universities all over the U.S. and Europe. Not just to torment students, but to confirm the whole willpower and self-control issue. Some studies had students watch emotional movies without changing their facial expressions, then had them squeeze a hand exerciser for as long as they could. Again, the students who exercised willpower and self-control (not changing their facial expressions) were unable to squeeze for as long as those who had been free to express their emotions while watching the movie.[15]

Then there is the "White Bear" challenge.[16] Students in one group were told NOT to think about a white bear, while the students in the control group were told nothing about a bear and were free to think about whatever they wanted to.

When it came time for both sets of students to work on a series of puzzles, the white bear thinkers gave up more quickly than the other students.

Questioning the science

Over the past 21 years, things have changed due to how the studies were conducted,[17] and the belief that we only have a limited amount of willpower has been called into question by the scientific community. Whether it can be scientifically proven or not, you know that throughout the day, you have a certain amount of energy available at any time. And, when you've used up that energy, it's difficult, if not impossible to be civil, to make reasoned choices, or to concentrate.

You don't need to be a member of any sort of test group to remember when something like this has happened to you: you've spent a morning working on a project that required your concentration or you've been in a particularly testy meeting with coworkers where you expended a lot of energy not saying what you really thought. When lunchtime rolled around, your depleted energy levels made saying "hell yes" to a hamburger and french fries so much easier than sticking to the plan you made earlier in the day, when you had lots of energy, of eating a healthy salad followed by a walk.

You are (temporarily) out of energy, which compromises your ability to function. You're tired, annoyed, grumpy, and not motivated. Until you reenergize yourself, or your next wave of energy appears, you're not going to be as effective as you'd like to be. Which is a fact you can prove to yourself any day you want. No cookies, radishes, or white bears necessary.

Luckily, there are ways to work with (and when necessary, around) your energy levels to ensure you are energized when you need to be. If you're going to be leveraging the trifecta of Action, Energy and Focus, it's a really good idea to actually know when you have the most energy, the best ways to use it, and how to avoid losing it.

First, let's talk about your energy levels.

When is your best time?

Think about when you do your best creative thinking.

Are you better at analytical tasks first thing in the morning or later in the afternoon?

When is the best time for you to work with others versus working alone?

When do you feel physically most powerful?

Most importantly, why does any of this matter?

Knowing your chronotype or your energy pattern is essential to being able to get things done. It allows you to be more effective with your time, which will, in turn, impact all areas of your life.

According to author Daniel H. Pink's book *When*, everyone, shares a very consistent pattern of energy throughout the day.[18] For Larks (or Early Birds—people who get up early and go to bed early) and what he calls "Third Birds" (not really Early Birds, not really Night Owls), there's a big surge of energy in the morning followed by an afternoon dip, then a re-emerging of energy in the late afternoon/early evening.

Night Owls, people who get up late and stay up late, follow this pattern as well, only it's reversed: they have a small surge of energy whenever they get up, followed by a dip, then a big wave of energy that goes late into the night. Once you know what pattern you most closely follow, you can start to plan your time in a way that most effectively leverages available energy.

Schedule by levels

Take, for example, working out. If your exercise goal is to lose weight, then, according to Pink, working out first thing in the morning is the best, but if you intend to be more limber and enjoy your work out more, then afternoon/evening workouts are best for you.

If you're an Early Bird and you know you have high energy in the morning, you'll be most efficient if you schedule tasks that require analytical or creative thinking for the morning, rather than trying to work on them in the afternoon when your energy levels dip. If possible, avoid using your peak morning energy on things like answering emails, monotonous meetings, or tedious, mindless tasks. Save the low energy tasks to match your low energy afternoons. (If you're a Night Owl, simply reverse this schedule.)

Since everyone is affected by near-universal energy patterns, it also pays to think of the energy levels of the people you interact with. Schedule your doctor's appointments before noon to ensure alertness and engagement on behalf of the doctor. Schedule tests (of all kinds, medical, education, interviews, etc.) for the morning as well. Both you and the test administrator/interviewer will likely have more energy and self-control.

Scheduling by energy level can make a huge difference. I've had clients who have endlessly agonized over the "how" and the "what" of their days, only to be pleasantly surprised to find scheduling by their "when" changes how much they accomplish each day. Pinpointing your "when" and leveraging your natural energy in the best, most efficient way possible, is a secret that can give you an extra boost with no required extra effort on your part.

So, how do you determine your "when?"

Discovering your personal energy pattern

You probably have a pretty good idea of your daily energy patterns, but it doesn't hurt to get very specific so you can plan and utilize your time most effectively. Luckily, this is pretty easy to do, and all it requires is a little tracking on your part.

For the next few days (at least three), take note of your energy levels at different times during the day. I find this is easiest to do with the help of alarms or reminders on my phone. Set an alarm to go off every hour, on the hour during the hours you are awake.* Each time the alarm goes off, take a few seconds and think how energetic you feel at that moment and mark it down on a piece of paper, an index card, or on a document on your phone or computer. †

ENERGY TRACKER

Set an alarm to go off every half hour during the hours your are awake.
Each time the alarm goes off, note your energy level between 1 and 10.
1 means you're ready to sleep, 10 means your'e ready to take on the world.
Track for a minimum of three days (Use three different tracking sheets.)

PM			PM	
12:00 _____	6:00 _____	12:00 _____	6:00 _____
12:30 _____	6:30 _____	12:30 _____	6:30 _____
1:00 _____	7:00 _____	1:00 _____	7:00 _____
1:30 _____	7:30 _____	1:30 _____	7:30 _____
2:00 _____	8:00 _____	2:00 _____	8:00 _____
2:30 _____	8:30 _____	2:30 _____	8:30 _____
3:00 _____	9:00 _____	3:00 _____	9:00 _____
3:30 _____	9:30 _____	3:30 _____	9:30 _____
4:00 _____	10:00 _____	4:00 _____	10:00 _____
4:30 _____	10:30 _____	4:30 _____	10:30 _____
5:00 _____	11:00 _____	5:00 _____	11:00 _____
5:30 _____	11:30 _____	5:30 _____	11:30 _____

---

* Obviously, you wouldn't do this during the hours you are trying to sleep. Talk about a way to ruin your energy levels.

† Or use this tracker. Download it at EllenGoodwin.com/forms

How you define your energy level is up to you. I've found using a scale of 1-10 works pretty well. On this scale, a 1 means "I'm nearly comatose, a nap is definitely imminent," and a 10 means "Boom! I'm ready to take on the world (and I'm fairly sure I could win!)." Your definitions should be somewhat similar. When each hourly alarm goes off, pause, determine your energy level, mark your number down, and go about your day, until the next alarm goes off.

That's it. Just give yourself an energy level number every hour on the hour for at least three days. At the end of the third day, take some time to look at your numbers. It should be reasonably easy to see your peaks (the clusters of 8, 9, 10s) and valleys (the clusters of 1, 2, 3s) throughout the day. You now have your own personal energy map.

ENERGY TRACKER

Set an alarm to go off every half hour during the hours your are awake.
Each time the alarm goes off, note your energy level between 1 and 10.
1 means you're ready to sleep, 10 means your'e ready to take on the world.
Track for a minimum of three days (Use three different tracking sheets.)

PM   **PM**

Time	Level	Time	Level	Time	Level	Time	Level
12:00		6:00	7	12:00	7	6:00	6
12:30		6:30	8	12:30	6	6:30	7
1:00		7:00	8	1:00	5	7:00	7
1:30		7:30	9	1:30	5	7:30	8
2:00		8:00	9	2:00	3	8:00	8
2:30		8:30	10	2:30	3	8:30	5
3:00		9:00	10	3:00	2	9:00	3
3:30		9:30	10	3:30	1	9:30	1
4:00		10:00	10	4:00	3	10:00	
4:30		10:30	10	4:30	5	10:30	
5:00	7	11:00	8	5:00	5	11:00	
5:30	7	11:30	6	5:30	6	11:30	

To make the most of your energy map, start using your peak times to your advantage so they have the most impact on your day by either Ingesting an Amphibian or Do the Big Thing First.

Both of these tactics can be boiled down to: start your day by doing something you don't like, or by doing something that has an outsized influence on your day.

Do the thing that will impact your day the most

1. Ingest an Amphibian

You've probably heard of the idea of "Eating Your Frog," which is said to come from a quote by Mark Twain that says, "Eat a live frog every morning, and nothing worse will happen to you the rest of the day."* To Eat Your Frog, you are supposed to do your worst, most dreaded task first thing in the day before you do anything else. This way, the dreaded task doesn't get pushed off to the next day or the next, or the next. The task also doesn't get to take up residence in your brain or use up energy as you think about when you'll do it, how much you don't want to do it, and ways you can keep putting it off.

Doing your most dreaded task first thing in the morning can definitely give your day a boost, especially if you're the type of person who can easily jump into doing what they don't like first thing in the day. But, if you're not that kind of person, then it's easy to see how "Eating Your Frog" feels negative and can work against you, cause you to procrastinate and eat (no pun intended) into your precious store of energy.

How to eat

Let's say you hate cold calling—you're not alone. For most people, it's not the thing they want to jump into first thing in their day. But for your business to survive, you need to hit the phones and regularly do cold calling.

Those calls are your "frog" and you have to eat them before getting on with your day.

Because you hate them so much, you find a way to put them off. Unfortunately, since they are supposed to be the first thing you do during the day, you find yourself putting off starting any other substantive work, since starting anything other work would essentially be admitting you weren't "Eating Your Frog."

---

* Whether he actually said this is up for discussion. According to the Quote Investigator, there is no actual proof he ever said this, while there is proof that a French writer, Nicolas Chamfort, said something similar around 1795.

Instead, you do something that consumes time but isn't really useful. You are procrastinating and getting nothing done, all while using up valuable mental energy thinking about those calls and how you're not doing them. For you, dealing with your worst task the first thing in the morning isn't the best idea. It takes a lot of resolve and energy to do what you don't want to (especially first thing in your day), which makes it easy NOT to do.

If you're a person who feels like "Eating Your Frog" is a lovely motivational poster idea, which only works for the most inspired (and possibly most desperate) people, this isn't a good energy idea for you.

And, of course, that's ok. Personally, I like to give the whole frog thing a twist and go with a more positive spin. Instead of thinking of what is the worst or most dreaded task I've got to do today, I like to pick the one big thing that will do the most to help me achieve my outcomes for the day.

2. The Big Thing

When I plan out my day (ideally the night before), I look at what one Big Thing would give me the biggest boost towards achieving the outcomes in my day, and plan to do it first. I block out the time in my calendar and highlight it as my first task so I will do it automatically. This way, I won't take time to think about whether or not I'll do it. I'll just do it. I don't use up any energy thinking about it, which also eliminates any Moments of Choice that might arise.

When I accomplish the one Big Thing, I know I am starting the day correctly. I get a big burst of dopamine that adds a turbo boost to my day, and I've done something big that will help me achieve my outcomes for the day.

Usually, my Big Thing is some sort of exercise to get my brain and body going. For one of my clients, it means sitting and reviewing his client list and what they need for the day. For another, it means meditating, for a friend, it's writing 1,000 words of his novel. For you, it might mean time with your spouse or significant other, or reading, or checking in with three of your most important clients. If you're one of the people who enjoy cold calling, or simply the effects of it, then by all means make cold calling your Big Thing. Whatever you decide your Big Thing is, make sure it's something which affects the outcomes of your day in an energy-positive way.

If you're a person who likes to ramp up their day a little slower, but still want to make your energy work double time for you, don't despair. There's a plan for you as well called the Energy Snowball.

3. How a snowman can change your day

I grew up in Minnesota, where winters were really cold and really snowy. As kids, we spent a lot of time outside playing in the snow.* One of our favorite snowy pastimes was making snowmen.

Lots of snowmen.

For those of you who have never had the pleasure of making a snowman, let me give you a quick "how to." The best time to make a snowman is when you have sticky snow (trust me, it's a thing). You take a big handful of snow and pack it together to make a snowball about the size of a baseball. Then you put the snowball on the snow-covered ground and roll it around and around so it picks up more and more snow, making the ball bigger and bigger until you have a suitably sized snowball for the base of the snowman. Then you repeat the process to make the middle and small-sized snowballs required to build a respectable, regulation-sized snowman. Stack them all on top of each other, add some recognizable facial characteristics,† and you, my friend, have built a snowman.

Oddly enough, the process of building a snowman has a lot in common with building a successful, energy-leveraging day. Big things start out small. A six-foot tall snowman still starts with a four-inch, baseball-sized snowball. It's the same with your productive day.

The simple Energy Snowball plan:

Decide on something small you want to accomplish the first thing in your day. Honestly, it can be as simple as unloading the dishwasher, paying a bill,

---

* Looking back now, I'm thinking mom kicked us out to play so she could stay sane and have some alone time. Smart woman, my mom.

† Rocks and carrots come in handy for this. I personally have never seen a snowman with coal for eyes and a mouth. I believe that comes from another time and place.

making your bed, or jotting down some ideas for a project you're working on. This task is your four-inch initial snowball. You want this task to be something very small so you can easily succeed at it, while using up minimal amounts of energy. This doesn't have to be a brag-worthy success, it just needs to be a small success for you and you alone.

Do the easy task and enjoy the sense of accomplishment. The bed is made, the dishes are put away, you've taken care of a bill, and you've got a few ideas for your project. Well done.

Now, use this success to move on to accomplishing another small task on your list. Then another and another, using the compounding effect of your success to power you to the next thing.

Think of your success snowball getting bigger and bigger as you go through the day.

I have clients who take the snowball idea even further and visualize building the large snowball base of their snowman during a successful morning. They come back after lunch and build a medium-sized snowball during their afternoon, and then use time after work to build the smaller "head" sized snowball while spending time with family or friends.

The Energy Snowball is also a great way to tackle large projects you find yourself putting off precisely because they are so big. Instead of procrastinating on the project, snowball it.

Snowball a project

You won't have to rely on motivation to get started, or have to tackle a huge section of the project all at once. Instead, you just pick one small task you need to take care of, succeed at it, then use the success to move on to the next small task and the next. Each success should encourage you to keep going and succeed and accomplish more. With each accomplishment, your snowball starts to grow.

Whether you just need a way to ease into your day or you need to take on a big project, the Energy Snowball is a great way to leverage the compounding effect of building on your successes. If it helps to imagine building a snowman with your snowball successes, do it. Just please don't blame me if you find yourself humming "Frosty the Snowman" in July.

Any of these three techniques can be used as a way to make your peak energy times even more effective. There's one more tool you should keep in mind when it comes to your energy, and it's one that sounds counterintuitive, but it's a lifesaver. It's taking breaks.

Take a break already

Have you ever had one of those days where you have something you have to get done, so you've blocked out a large chunk of time to focus and work on it, and once you get going you are totally committed. Unfortunately, the longer you work, the more your enthusiasm wanes and the less you seem to be accomplishing. Yet, you keep pushing and trying to get more done.

Is it your imagination or are you slowing down? Here's a hint: you are in fact slowing down and the harder you work, the less you are getting done. Your effectiveness is diminishing as you're burning through your energy. You have hit the Diminishing Returns part of your task. When you feel this happening, for the sake of your energy levels, it's always time to take a break.

A friend of mine who does home repairs says he knows he's hit his wall of Diminishing Returns when frustration sets in and he can't get things to work correctly no matter what he tries. Hammers get dropped, screws don't fit and something easy that should take a few seconds to do ends up taking 10 minutes and still isn't completely correct.

When your car runs out of gas, you've got no choice but to get to a gas station and fill up the tank. When your phone or computer run out of battery, you have to charge them. Your brain and your body are no different. When you run out of energy, you have to pause to refill, in whatever way works for you. Otherwise, you're just pushing against an immovable, invisible, brick wall. Nothing is going to shift or change, and you're just going to end up getting more and more frustrated.

Diminishing Returns don't mean you're weak, unqualified, or aren't able to do things right. They mean you are human, and you need to rest and recharge.

Rest and Recharge

The easiest way to deal with Diminishing Returns is to stop and take a break, which is the opposite of your usual thinking. When you're in the middle of doing something, you buy into the idea of pushing through until the end, no matter what it looks like.

Mike, a friend of mine in college, was notorious for doing this. We used to excitedly pile into his car for road trips and compare notes about where we should stop along the way for lunch, or what random things we should stop and see along the way. Mike was always on board with our ideas.*

But usually, about two hours into the road trip, something in Mike shifted from "Taking our time and seeing and doing things along the way," into "There's no time to stop! We have to get there." Then, Mike would focus solely on getting to our destination, oblivious to having any fun or enjoying the trip. People could be starving or really needing a rest stop, but Mike was all intent on joylessly getting to the final stop. We certainly got there, but the returns on the trip diminished for everyone (probably even Mike.)

When Diminishing Returns start showing up, the only real answer is to stop what you are doing and take a break to let your brain and body reenergize again. For Mike, this could have meant pulling over, taking a brief walk, eating a snack, and reconnecting with his fellow passengers to reignite his excitement about the journey, not the destination.

For you, it can mean walking away from your task and briefly engaging in something else so your energy levels rebound.

What kind of breaks work best

The key to making your breaks effective is to make them the opposite of what you are doing so you get the maximum refreshment value.

Let's say you're working on something that requires mental energy, like writing, researching, problem-solving, or brainstorming. After working for an hour, it begins to feel like your brain is drained of ideas and nothing new is showing up. When you hit this point, instead of trying to force ideas, the best thing you can do is to just walk away from what you were doing and recharge. In this case, it means taking a break for 10-15 minutes, and doing something requiring physical energy as a way to allow mental energy to return.

During this break, you can crank out a few jumping jacks or put on a couple of your favorite songs and have a private dance party. You can move

---

* Because who doesn't want to see the World's Largest Ball of String?

some things around in the garage or pull some weeds. You can take a short walk and look at nature. Do something physical that requires minimal mental input. Trying to push through without a break will result in a less than stellar effort by you, and it will show. Physical activity will enable your brain to reenergize.

On the other hand, if you've been working on tasks involving physical labor and it's starting to take you twice as long to do anything, and everything feels heavier than it should and is taking longer and longer to do simple tasks, it's time to take a break. Recharge your physical energy by doing something requiring mental focus. There's no strenuous movement allowed, instead, use your brain and read a book, do a crossword puzzle, write an email, play a video game, or just watch some YouTube videos that make you laugh. Do this for at least 10 or 15 minutes as you reenergize your physical energy.

Recharging mental or physical energy requires being strong enough to recognize Diminishing Returns are affecting you and doing something about it. Take a break and do the opposite of what you were doing. It's like filling up your gas tank. Cars don't run on gas fumes, and you can't fully function on energy fumes.

It's human nature to want to push through to finish things, even when Diminishing Returns tell you otherwise. My friend Mike did. I know I find myself occasionally telling myself, "just ten more minutes and I'll be done," but every time I do that, the 10 minutes turns into 20 minutes of less than effective time. If I'd just taken a break and refreshed, then I could have actually finished the job in 10 minutes and had the energy to move onto something else.

So far in this chapter, you've learned the different patterns of energy that exist, how to determine your energy patterns, and how to leverage your energy throughout the day, so all of your energy issues are solved and you're going to be the most efficient person ever. Right?

Unfortunately, no. As you learned earlier, the enemy of Action is Procrastination. Energy has an enemy as well in the form of a villain who attempts to drain your energy whenever it can. This villain is known as Decision Fatigue.

Eliminate Decision Fatigue

Every time you have to make a decision, especially one where you are choosing from lots of options, you subject yourself to Decision Fatigue. Since energy is required to make each decision and the more choices you make, the more draining it can become.

Think of a time where you've had to make a lot of decisions. For example, let's say you were remodeling your kitchen and you had to make choices about what tile you wanted on the floor, decide on the paint color for the main wall, what handles and knobs worked best on the cabinets, what lighting you liked, what backsplash functioned best and whether you wanted a concrete or granite countertop. That's a lot of decisions to be making and a lot of energy is needed to make them. By the time you get to the end of your choices, you could easily be forgiven for not caring about anything. You've used up all your energy and Decision Fatigue has set in.

Decision Fatigue doesn't just apply to kitchen remodels. Too many choices means too many decisions, easily leading to Decision Fatigue. If you've had to make choices when buying a new car, planning a wedding, deciding how you wanted a website to look or even just deciding what you wanted to eat in a restaurant, you've experienced Decision Fatigue.

Once Decision Fatigue sets in, the energy needed to consciously analyze choices and make good decisions is gone.* So, the key to conserving your energy is to eliminate as many low-level decisions as possible throughout your day. With the low-level choices handled, you have conserved energy that is now available to use on higher-level decisions or tasks.

In Chapter Three, we looked at one way you can eliminate decision-making by rolling the dice or choosing things randomly. Rolling the dice can help you make decisions on what to wear, what kind of workout to do, what to eat, and what chores to do—all small choices that use up energy as you work through your day.

Another great way to eliminate daily decisions is by making a decision once and sticking with it.

1. Adopt a Daily Uniform

Think of Mark Zuckerberg, Barack Obama, Steve Jobs, and thousands of kids in private schools everywhere: they all wear (or wore) pretty much the same

---

* Which, in some cases, is exactly the point. If you're exhausted by making decisions, then it's easier for salespeople to get you to buy more.

thing each day. Not having to decide what to wear every day cuts down on Decision Fatigue as you try to get out of the door in the morning. Adopt a system of clothes that easily go together.*

You could use black as your base color and then pick two accent colors. Decide on an outfit you wear for each day of the week. Every Monday could be black pants and a gray shirt. Every Tuesday could be gray pants and a dark green shirt day. Put together a rotating series of clothing choices to get you through the week. It's not hard to do, and it's probably something you already do when you travel. To keep your luggage light, you figure out how to mix and match clothing to keep things minimal. Now, do the same thing when you aren't traveling.

You could also chose to wear only black socks, or white shirts, or blue jeans, or only two kinds of shoes. Whatever it takes to make getting dressed easy.

2. Eat the Same Thing

Eliminate choice making when it comes to what you eat. Decide to eat the same thing every day for one (or all) of your meals or have a weekly rotation of meals (if it's Tuesday, it's stir-fry!). Not only does this cut down on meal planning, it makes grocery shopping easier.

Make a list of your favorite restaurants, either for dine-in or delivery. Assign each of them a day. If you decide on a Tuesday that you don't feel like cooking, then your only choice is the restaurant you have designated as your Tuesday place.

Speaking of restaurants, think of how many decisions you have to make when you eat at a restaurant. Why not eliminate those choices by choosing to act like a neuroscientist?

Moran Cerf, a neuroscientist at Northwestern University, has a unique way of eliminating Decision Fatigue. No matter where he goes, he always orders the second restaurant special on the menu.[19] It doesn't matter what the special is, he orders it. Eighty percent of the time, he ends up with a food choice he enjoys, which is about the same odds he'd have if he had gone through the menu and made a decision. Not having to decide saves his energy.

---

* Think Garanimals for adults.

Not into the Specials of the Day? Then decide you'll always order the second salad, sandwich, or entrée on the menu.* Just make one decision and stick to it. You'll conserve energy, and who knows, you might end up trying (and enjoying) something you wouldn't have normally chosen.

Eliminating the small choices throughout your day goes a long way towards making sure you have the necessary energy to make larger and better decisions as needed.

Since you've already figured out your energy pattern, you already know there is going to be a part of your day where you have low energy and it's going to be hard to make decisions and continue to get things done. This is where having a Low-Energy Plan to call on is a good idea.

The Low-Energy Plan

You aren't a high-energy person all day. There are always going to be times when your energy levels decrease, and you feel draggy or not as energetic as you'd like. This happens right about the same time every day and is entirely natural.

During this low-energy time, you're probably not going to want to invest time (or non-existent energy) into making decisions or figuring out what you want to (or can) accomplish. With the lack of energy influencing your thoughts and actions, this can become a dangerous place. Depleted defenses make it much easier for the limbic system to take over and direct you to your comfort zone of doing the easiest, low-value, low-return task possible. Without really thinking about it, you find yourself on social media, playing video games, or mindlessly watching cat videos. You are distracted and procrastinating because you didn't have the energy to fight your limbic system. Instead of being frustrated by this daily, low-energy escapade, why not have a plan to make the most of it?

A preemptive Low-Energy Plan for situations just like this will prevent distractions from commandeering your attention, eliminate the procrastination that comes with it, and help to still use your time effectively.

Put your Low-Energy Plan together during the high-energy part of your day, when you can do this most easily. This plan should include tasks that aren't difficult to accomplish. They should be low-level tasks that can be achieved

---

* Or the third or the fourth.

quickly (so you'll feel successful). You could also add tasks that you don't want to do when you're high-energy because you'll be wasting good, productive energy on them. For each of the tasks on the list, you're going to set a timer for a short time to work on it.

Because there is a time frame, feel free to put a couple comfort zone items on the list as well, things like watching kitten videos for 10 minutes. This way, you'll still get things done, while appeasing the limbic system.

When your low-energy time hits, you now have a Low-Energy Plan to turn to that matches your energy intensity, so pick up the Plan, and start going through it, task by task. Some days this will be easy, other days it might be difficult. You'll know it's difficult when you find yourself trying to pick and choose the items which require the least amount of work. When this happens, it's a perfect situation for your limbic system to try to take over. Luckily, there's a way to stop this from happening.

Remember the dice we talked about in Dice, Dice, Baby in Chapter One? It's time to pull them out again and put them to work.

Number the items on your Low-Energy Plan, then roll the dice to determine what your first task is, set your timer and get started on it. As a bit of a bonus, making your Low-Energy Plan into a game of chance means you're just as likely to roll the number of one of your comfort zone tasks as you are another task.

Your low-energy time isn't going to last forever, but rather than let it be time you waste, put it to use on jobs that don't require a lot of thought. You'll eliminate Moments of Choice, continue to get things done, and keep your limbic system from taking over.

Your job is to manage your energy throughout the day by working with (and around) your energy highs and lows, taking effective breaks, guarding against Diminishing Returns and being stronger than the energy stealers that creep up during your day. But there's one more, very strong tool that you should be using to manage and even amplify your energy — Habits.

CHAPTER SEVEN ACTION TOOLBOX: ENERGY

DEFINITIONS IN THIS CHAPTER:

Chronotype:
A person's natural inclination with regard to the times of day when they prefer to sleep or when they are most alert or energetic.

Diminishing Returns
The point at which the level of profits or benefits gained is less than the amount of money or energy invested.

Decision Fatigue
The deteriorating quality of decisions made after a long session of decision-making.

TOOLS IN THIS CHAPTER:

Ingest an Amphibian:
Make the first task of the day, the task that you are least looking forward to doing. Do it and get it off your list and out of your brain. Then move on with your day, knowing you have succeeded.

The Big Thing:
Make the first task of your day, the one that will have the most impact on your day, and it will get your day off to a great start. Accomplishing this task will start the domino effect of one big task affecting the next big task, and so on.

Energy Snowball:
Build your energy like building a snowman. Start by accomplishing small things, which leads to an increase in dopamine. Like rolling snowballs, the energy accumulates.

Take a break:
When you are working harder than you are getting results from your efforts, take breaks to prevent Diminishing Returns. If you're doing physical labor, take a mental break and do mental activities like reading or doing crossword puzzles, if you're doing mental work, take a physical break and do physical activities like jumping jacks.

ENEMY OF ENERGY—DECISION FATIGUE:

Every time you make a decision, you use up a little energy. The more decisions you make, the more energy you consume. When you use up energy making lots of small decisions, it's harder to make big decisions. Eliminate low-level decision making by:

Adopting a daily uniform:

Eliminate options by making one decision and sticking with it. Choose the same outfit, same lunch, the same decision, and stick with it. This helps shorten time shopping for clothes, too.

Eating the same thing:

Eliminate daily choices when it comes to your food by deciding to eat the same thing every day, or the same foods on certain days. Eliminate decision-making at restaurants by deciding to eat the second special or the third sandwich.

Having Low-Energy Plan:

A plan you put together when you have high-energy to ensure you can still get things done during the low-energy portion of your day.

ACTION ITEMS:

Track your daily energy

Track your daily energy to determine when you have high energy ad low energy. Choose three consecutive days to track (it is best to pick days which are as close to "normal" for you as possible.)

Using the chart on page 154, (or download from EllenGoodwin.com/forms), track your energy for three days, then assess your data and determine your high and low energy times and your low energy times.

When are your high-energy times: _____

When are your low-energy times: _____

What are some things you should schedule during high-energy times:

_____

What are some things you could schedule during low-energy times:

_____

Frog or Big Thing?

Which way to do you want to start your day?

Think which is more appealing to you. Do you want to start your day doing the most difficult thing first or doing the thing which will have the most impact on your day?

Write your decision here: _____

Begin to plan out your days with this thought in mind.

_____

Build an Energy Snowball

Plan your day to build your energy. Think of five small tasks that you can easily succeed at and get the snowball going.

1. _____

2: _____

3: _____

4: _____

5: _____

Next, think of three to four tasks requiring more energy, which you will complete next (relying on your increasing levels of dopamine.)

1. _____

2: _____

3: _____

4: _____

Then think of one to two tasks which will require high energy, which you will have after building your energy by repeatedly succeeding.

1. _____

2: _____

Complete these tasks and enjoy the high energy level you've built.

Preplan your breaks

Eliminate Moments of Choice when break time rolls around by doing some "If/Then" break planning now. When complete, you'll have a list to refer to in the future.

If I'm doing something that requires mental energy, then here are some ways I can take physical breaks (for example: planking, folding laundry, doing jumping jacks.)

1. _____

2: _____

3: _____

4: _____

If I'm doing something that requires physical energy, then here are some ways I can take mental breaks (for example: do a crossword puzzle, read for 10 minutes, play a game.)

1. _____

2: _____

3: _____

4: _____

Plan a "Daily Uniform"

What are some ways you could "adopt a uniform" in your life?

Could it be wearing the same type of clothes every day? Eating the same foods? List what you could do and what it would look like. You can also think about why and how this uniform plan is going to help you conserve energy.

_____

_____

_____

CHAPTER EIGHT

Habits

A small daily task, if it be really daily,
will beat the labours of a spasmodic Hercules."
- Anthony Trollope, *author*

One of the most common habits people use daily is driving a car. Once you've gotten past drivers ed and have a year or so of driving under your belt, the physical act of driving starts to become a habit. Yes, you still have to pay attention to the traffic and pedestrians around you, but the physical act of driving is a habit. You don't have to think about putting on your seat belt, starting the vehicle, or the position of your feet on the pedals. Everything is automatic.

I drive a car with a manual, five-speed transmission. I have done this since I was 16. When I drive, I don't think about when my foot needs to press the clutch so I can shift. There is no conscious mental process involved. The act of moving my left foot and my right hand is so ingrained in my brain, if I stop to think about the process of shifting, it's actually harder for me. If I drive a car with an automatic transmission, I use up mental energy reminding myself I don't have to shift at stop signs or while stuck in traffic. Driving a stick-shift is second nature to me.

When I drive my car, I'm in stealth energy mode. Which is exactly what a habit is. It's automatic functioning that doesn't drain your energy, so you consistently have energy available for doing other things.

It would be easy for this chapter to be all about building good habits and eliminating bad habits exclusively. But I'm not looking at judging habits but rather how they affect your energy.

Daily habits deployed

How do you start your day? Are you one of those people who wrestle with the snooze alarm decision first thing when you wake up? "Should I hit the snooze? Should I not?" (or "Should I hit it five times and really screw up my day?") Do you likewise ask yourself "Should I get coffee first or brush my teeth?" "Put on my pants first or my socks?" "Eat food or watch the news?"

Chances are, each of these actions and the order you do them in, are already programmed into your head and you don't really think about them at all. There's no need to wrestle with each decision. You just do them. They are the habits you use to start your day.*

If you DID have to think through each one of them, you'd be mentally exhausted by the time you left the house. Don't believe me? Think about a time when you've had an unexpected wrench thrown into your day. You get up late. You're out of coffee. You have an argument with your five-year-old child (or your spouse acting like a five-year-old child). You have to meet a client at an unfamiliar location. Your car is out of gas. Your Uber is late.

As you handle each of these unexpected things without the safety net of a habit, mental energy is expended and the result is unanticipated and unappreciated brain fatigue. You've had to use up more energy than you would on a normal day, and you can feel the result. Now, you've got less mental energy to operate with so you might find yourself being snappy with people, less able to concentrate on a conversation with your coworkers, or unable to think of creative ideas in a brainstorming meeting.

Without habits to lean on and get you through your day, your stores of brain energy are depleted and it shows.

This is most definitely not a slam on you. This happens to everyone. Habits are there to enable us to get the maximum amount done with the minimum expenditure of energy.

---

* Good thing they are habits, since each of these is a Moment of Choice that could affect how your day goes.

As you learned in the last chapter, you want to keep your energy level as high as possible during the day, which is why you want to build, or keep, strong habits (and eliminate the bad, weak ones). This is exactly what we're going to look at.

The first important thing you need to know is: when it comes to habits, you've been lied to your entire life.

Lies, lies, lies

Somewhere along the line, you've heard the "fact" that it takes 21 days to build a new habit or get rid of a bad one. I put fact in quotation marks because it, like many other things you've been told over the years, is something you probably believe to be true, when it really isn't.

Long story short*: In 1960, a plastic surgeon by the name of Maxwell Maltz noted it took his patients a minimum of 21 days of looking at themselves with their new noses, chins, or eyelids, for the "old mental image to dissolve and a new one to jell." He noted this in a book he wrote, *Psycho-Cybernetics*, which sold 30 million copies. Even though he used the words "a minimum of 21 days," people ignored the "minimum" and kept the 21 days.

This meant now people had a number that they took to heart: 21 days, which is the same number of days it takes a chicken to hatch. Pretty remarkable. With this way of thinking, in three short weeks, you could establish a new habit or eliminate an old one, and you'd be on a path to a new (in some way) you.

Thus was born the idea of "21 Days to..." which has been the basis for magazine articles and books ever since. Think: "21 Days to Thinner Thighs,"or "21 Days to High-Performance Leadership." The number of books alone is staggering.[†] A recent check on Amazon revealed over 70,000 titles with "21 Days to..." in them. I haven't looked into each of the books, but I'm guessing at some point in the introduction of many of these books, the 21 days to a new habit "fact" is mentioned.

The unfortunate truth here is that it does not take 21 days to build a new habit. It actually can take much, much longer. A 2009 study[20] by Phillippa Lally at the University College in London found it takes between 18 and 254 days for a new habit to be formed, with the average being 66 days.

---

* Thanks to James Clear for this original research.
† I can't imagine how many magazine article titles there are.

Just over two months.

If you were counting on nailing down a new habit in 21 days, you are probably going to feel like a failure because it takes longer than you thought. But you're not a failure, you just have to expand your time line a little. Different habits take different amounts of time to build or replace. The harder the habit, the more time required.

Why this is a good thing

While you are probably now going to have to work a little longer to build or eliminate a habit, you are also going to be able to relax a little more than you thought. Lally's study also showed missing a day once in a while doesn't affect your ability to build new habits or eliminate old ones. And while this doesn't give you license to slack off, it does mean if you do slip up and miss a day, you have more time to get back on track or to repair any damage you might have done.

If you only have 21 days to cement in a new habit, each day shoulders a considerable burden. Each day represents about five percent of your 21-day total. Miss one day and you're five percent behind, miss two or three and you're in trouble. But if you miss one day out of 66 (or 254), the impact on your habit development is much less.

While it's okay to make a mistake, to miss a day, or to fall off the proverbial wagon, you just have to remember to get back on track. (Or as a friend of mine says, "you can miss one day, but if you miss two, you know something is wrong.")

Since it's going to take a little more time than you originally thought, the least we can do is make building or eliminating habits easy. And you probably already know which tool you need first: an Action Plan.

Habit achievement made easy

When it comes to habits, you're going to need an Action Plan (use the Repetitive Step Action Plan on page 18*). Since you can see your bright, shiny, new future self with this brand-new habit, you need a plan to get to this new future place.

Like all Action Plans, your plan needs to have an outcome in mind. Your outcome is what your new habit is going to look like, do for you, make you be, etc.

---

* Or download a plan at EllenGoodwin.com/forms.

For example, dropping your habit of looking at time-sucking online distractions in favor of timed, deep focus intervals throughout the day is not only going to allow you to take on new projects, but it's also going to help you significantly increase your monthly billable hours, and has the potential to radically improve your outlook on life.

Along with the outcomes, you're going to need to think about the process that is going to get you to your outcome. While you can visualize your ideal new self working diligently away, with all of your distractions properly blocked and notifications muted, if you don't have an Action Plan for how this is all going to happen, chances are, it won't. You need a road map, a fully fleshed-out plan to get there.

Like all Action Plans, this one not only needs to show you how you're going to achieve this new habit, it needs to also show you what you're going to do when (not if) you run into obstacles, how you're going to persevere when your enthusiasm flags, and where you're going to turn when you crave the comfort of the status quo you were so accustomed to.

The two kinds of habits

When it comes to building habits, whether they take 66 days or 254, there's really only two kinds of habits you can build: Towards Habits and Away Habits.

As you move toward doing something new, you are building a Towards Habit. If you are moving away from something you currently do, you are building an Away Habit. Look closely and you'll see in many situations the two types of habits are actually intertwined. For example, as you move Away from eating junk food, you move Towards eating healthier food. As you move Away from sitting on the couch watching television, you move Towards getting up and out and exercising more.

If you are moving Towards a new behavior, you want to make it easier to practice this new habit. If you're moving Away from an old routine or habit, you want to make it harder to continue doing what you used to do.

Make the easy hard and the hard easy

Think about how you've tried to build habits in the past. It doesn't matter if they were a moving Towards or a moving Away habit. Chances are you experienced the standard pattern of really being good with the change for a while, then slowly finding yourself reverting to your previous (now) undesired behavior. Your intentions were good, but the follow-up tripped you up. You could have increased your odds of success by making things either easier or harder.*

Let's say you wanted to end your habit of eating ice cream while watching television every night after dinner. You now wanted to establish a new habit of eating something healthy, like fruit. In this example, you're moving Away from ice cream and moving Towards healthy fruit choices. Just wanting to make the change isn't going to be enough. You're going to have to make it harder to do the things you were doing and easier to do the thing you want to do. What are some things you can try?

- Make your ice cream habit harder by not keeping ice cream in the house. If you want ice cream, you have to go buy it, which probably means you have to get in your car and drive somewhere to buy it. At the same time, make it easier to eat more fruit by stocking up on your favorites and making sure they are washed, chopped and ready to eat at all times.

- Make it harder to eat ice cream (and much less enjoyable) by forcing yourself to stand up and face a wall while you eat it. Make it easier to enjoy your new fruit habit by eating it while enjoying a favorite show or movie.

- Treat yourself like a kid and "ground" yourself in some way if you eat ice cream. Take away privileges you take for granted such as no Netflix for a week. "Unground" yourself by eating fruit and you get all the Netflix you want.

Easier and Harder

Now, obviously, making things easier and harder doesn't just work with ice cream and fruit. It can work with anything. (The key is a little preplanning and some precommitments.)

- Make it easier to work out in the morning by sleeping in your gym clothes (or having them already laid out for the morning) and having

---

* Don't feel bad. Now that you know, it's going to be much easier next time.

your workout gear already in the car. Also make sure the gym is close to your house. Make it harder to miss your workouts by setting up a "work out buddy system" where you have to pay your fitness buddy for every missed gym session.

- Make it harder to smoke a cigarette by keeping them in the freezer, or by not keeping any in the house at all. Again, you'd have to head to the store to buy more, or bum them off your friends or neighbors. Make it even harder by making sure everyone knows you are trying to quit, so if you tried to bum a cigarette off of them...well, you know. Make it easier to quit by having alternatives to cigarettes available, or by only hanging out with people who don't smoke.

- Make it easier to read by putting your book on or near your favorite chair. Make it harder to watch television by having someone hide the remote They can only return it after you've read for a predetermined amount of time.

- Make it easier to eat healthier by hiring someone (and paying them in advance) to make healthy food for you. Make it harder to eat junk food by having someone else in the household do the grocery shopping with strict instructions not to buy any junk food.

I could go on and on. It's all a matter of looking at what you want to be doing and coming up with options to make things easier or harder.

One of my friends wanted to move away from his habit of automatically drinking several beers when he got home from work. He wanted to move toward the habit of going for a run instead. His solution was not to keep his beer in the refrigerator.* All the beer at his house was kept on a shelf in the pantry. When he got home from work, he would put one, single, solitary beer in the fridge and go out for a run. Because it took a while for the beer to get cold, he had the time to get a good run in. He knew when the run was complete, the single can of beer would be cold and waiting for him. He would drink that one, but he wasn't interested in having more than one since the rest were warm.

---

* As a huge beer fan, I don't recommend this as a way to store beer, but as an Productivity trainer, I think it's an ideal way to build a habit.

Not the best way to store your beer, but an excellent way to make his Towards behavior easier and his Away behavior harder.

WORK ON ONE HABIT AT A TIME

WARNING: Please, for the sake of your beautiful brain, don't try to add or change too many habits in your life at once.

When you build a new habit, or eliminate a current one, you are building new neural pathways in your brain, which is great. You just can't try to add or subtract too many at once because you will do the one thing that you are trying to prevent: using up your energy. All the remembering of new actions and stopping of old actions is a huge energy drain.

So, take it easy when adding in new habits or eliminating current habits. Try to add in too many too fast and you'll fail at all of them. When you decide you are going to "drop-10-pounds-and-eat-only-healthy-food-while-thinking-only-kind-thoughts-all-while-looking-like-a-million-bucks-whenever-I-leave-the-house," you end up succeeding at nothing. You gain five pounds eating burgers drenched in ranch dressing while jealously checking out what the woman over the corner is wearing while you're wearing poorly fitting jeans and a ratty t-shirt and you haven't brushed your hair. Hey, I don't make this up. Science[21] backs me up on this as well. So, only one habit at a time, please.

It's like weight training for your brain. When you start lifting weights, 15 pounds can feel heavy, but after a while, 15 pounds feels like picking up five pounds. The same thing happens with your brain. As the habit becomes easier and easier for the brain to remember, it means the neural pathway is getting stronger, and requires less mental energy.

Start with one habit you want to build or eliminate. Build the mental muscle, then move on to the next habit.

Build an Anti-Friction Plan

By definition, friction is anything that slows you down or gets in the way of forward progress. Removing it can mean the difference between success or failure when it comes to habit-building (or habit removal), so getting rid of the friction is essential to your success.

Friction shows up in many different ways, and when it does, all progress stops. It happens with big habits and small, and it never fails to frustrate. Finding and calling out the friction is the first step, and answering questions is the next.

Recently, I encountered friction when I wanted to establish a consistent watering habit. Odd, I know, but stay with me.

I had new trees planted on the street side of my sidewalk, in the area affectionately known in my neighborhood as the "hell strip." There was no irrigation there, so there was no automatic sprinkler I could just turn on. If the trees were going to get watered, I needed to be the one watering them.

And that is where I encountered friction in the form of my garden hose.

Specifically, the friction was the rolling and unrolling of the hose so it could reach the trees. At one point in time, I had a hose reel with a crank on it that I used to roll up the hose. It wasn't a perfect solution because the hose would get twisted and kinked. The kinks would lead to cracks and splits, and eventually, I'd have to go and buy a new hose that didn't leak everywhere.

It was precisely at one of those "buying a new hose" phases where the hose reel also broke, and I replaced it with a hose hanger that I mounted on an outside wall of the house. Now, instead of cranking up the hose, I just had to loop it on the hanger.

While the hanger looked nice on the wall, it turned out to be even more work. Each time I used the hose, I had to wrestle it back onto the hanger, which meant I only watered the trees when I felt like they absolutely had to be watered (which I'm sure was much less than what they really needed).

Sometimes I would just fill up a bucket and hand water the trees, which again resulted in the trees getting less water than they should, and me splashing cold water on my legs as I walked from the faucet to the trees. While this was easier than wrestling with the hose, because of the time required to go back and forth, I wasn't consistent about doing it. It soon became apparent that if my trees were going to live, I had friction to remove.

Time to ask questions

To remove the friction and start building a consistent watering habit, I needed our old friend, the Action Plan. And not just any old Action Plan. I needed to develop an Anti-Friction Action Plan. I needed to look at what was impeding progress, i.e., my friction, and started asking questions:

What exactly was the friction I was encountering and how was it showing up?

What were some options I had to get rid of it?

Could I make the task easier?

Could I make it impossible to forget?

Could I automate it?

Could I schedule it?

Could I make it more fun?

For me, the hose was the source of friction.* I wanted to be a responsible homeowner with beautiful, healthy trees lining my sidewalk, but wrestling with the hose consistently just wasn't working for me.

The solution to eliminating the friction was in the answers.

Could I get rid of the friction? Yes. In theory, I could add sprinkler lines, but they would have to go under city sidewalks, and the process would be time-consuming and expensive. Could I make it easier? Absolutely. I could get a hand crank hose reel again, which was definitely easier than what I was now doing but easier only by a small amount. Could I make it impossible to forget? Sure, I could hire a gardener or a neighborhood kid and give them the responsibility to do it. Could I automate it? Yes. Again, I could hire someone and let them do it. Could I make it more fun? I could. I could get a hose that was lightweight and actually fun to deal with. And just like that, I had my answer.

---

* I know this is a first-world problem, but definitely a friction-filled problem nonetheless. Save the trees!

I purchased one of the hoses that expand when you turn the water on, then shrinks up to nothing when you turn the water off.* It's lightweight. I could store it in a garden pot if I wanted. Because it's so easy to use, it makes me laugh every time I use it, which is certainly not something I would have ever said about the old hose and reel system.

Without the friction of a bulky, vinyl hose, I actually don't mind watering anymore, so I now have a watering habit and my trees look great.

Obviously, friction doesn't only apply to watering trees. This was just one of my issues. Yours is going to be completely different.

You might find yourself encountering friction as you try to build a habit of eating more healthy foods or eating less of the foods that aren't so great for you. You might encounter friction as you attempt to add more exercise into your schedule. You might encounter friction as you try to build relationships with coworkers or clients. Maybe your friction is getting people to pay on time or a problem with cash flow in general.

When you encounter friction that slows you down or gets in the way of forward progress, it's time to start asking yourself some questions:

What exactly is the friction I am encountering, and how is it showing up?

What are some options I have to get rid of it?

Can I make the task easier?

Can I make it impossible to forget?

Can I automate it?

Can I schedule it?

Can I make it more fun?

Answer the questions, and you'll find your solution.

Friction happens, but it doesn't have to mean the end of forward progress. Instead, take a look at why it's happening, answer some questions, and put your Anti-Friction Action Plan in place and make changes.

Removing friction of any kind is essential when building new habits; so is removing excuses. Everyone wants to make changes but sometimes the easiest thing to make is an excuse. I'm just as guilty as the next person. Or, rather, I was

---

* I have no affiliation with the company that makes these hoses. I am just happy I live in a world where they exist.

(and yes, occasionally I still am). But there's an easy tactic you can use to work around excuses. It's called a Micro-Habit.

Micro-Habits

A Micro-Habit is the smallest possible, pain-free action you can take towards building a new, fully-fledged habit (or eliminating one you no longer like). The smallest action possible, which, in turn, means no excuses.

For example, let's say you wanted to impose some order on your eating habits so you decided to cut back on the amount of sugar you eat. Your Micro-Habit could be something as easy as throwing away one bite of your morning donut instead of eating the whole thing or putting a half teaspoon less sugar in your coffee.

Seriously, that's it. If you wanted to increase your exercise practice, your Micro-Habit could be doing one plank every day. You could work to improve your business by writing blog post ideas every day for one minute—an idea, not a fully-fledged post. Or you could decide to make one cold call every day at 10 a.m.

Almost sounds too easy, doesn't it?

Because Micro-Habits are small and easy, they virtually eliminate excuses. It's really not hard to do one plank or leave one bite of your donut on your plate. This makes it easier to get started on building your new habit, because honestly, there's no reason not to do it. "Write for one minute? I'm on it!"

When you succeed at your Micro-Habit task, your brain gets a hit of dopamine and starts to anticipate your future successes, which is exactly why one plank becomes two and three, and then you've formed a habit (same with eliminating sugar, writing, cold calling and more.)

Build your own Micro-Habit

Think about a habit you want to build (or eliminate). Decide on a very small action you can start doing daily. Then start doing it, with no anticipation of adding to it. Be happy and consistent with your chosen daily action. Your brain will tell you when it's time to start doing more.

One day, you'll feel like doing two planks or leaving two bites of your donut, or making two cold calls. Since the action is already in place, it will be easy to do just that. In a couple of days, you might decide two is easy and you'll move on to three. Move forward as you feel ready, and add in additional actions slowly as you build toward establishing your new habit (or eliminating an old one).

Yes, this might take you more than the 66 days we talked about, or it might take less time. It's important to remember that time is not the objective here, rather it's getting yourself in the practice of doing the actions that will eventually make up your habit (without having to deal with excuses showing up).

Micro-Habits in Action

Your one small action is much more powerful than you might think. Let's say you had a non-Micro-Habit goal to do 10 planks every day, but what happened during a jam-packed day when you didn't have the time or the physical or mental energy to complete those 10 planks? You didn't do them.

By standard definition, you have failed at your goal. If instead you had a Micro-Habit goal of one plank per day, chances are you would have found 30 seconds to do one plank. The mental energy needed for one plank is much less than needed for 10. One definition of a Micro-Habit is, it's so small that if you forgot to do it during the day and suddenly remembered it when you were already in bed, you could jump out of bed and do it quickly.

Another definition, is your Micro-Habit action should be so small, you would feel embarrassed telling a friend[22] what you are doing: "I'm doing one plank a day," "I'm eating one less bite of a donut," "I'm making one cold call a day." I know my friends would be less than impressed by these small efforts. But that's the point.

These are small, but ultimately, mighty actions.

The big, non-secret is here is that there is absolutely nothing stopping you from doing more than you have decided upon. You could do six cold calls today and seven tomorrow and then just one the following day and you still would have succeeded all three days.

You could do eight planks today, 12 tomorrow, and then just one the following day and you'd still be a success.

Think of your Micro-Habit as the on-ramp to fully-fledged habits. There are no drastic changes and no need for stress or excuses. There are just small, meaningful actions that increase over time to get you to where you want to be.

Now, while I'm a huge fan of Micro-Habits and have used them to establish and eliminate all sorts of habits, you might occasionally find there are times when you need to go even smaller.

When Micro-Habits are too much

For a long time, I assumed you started a Micro-Habit when you were ready to start building a new habit or eliminating an old one but weren't quite prepared to jump in with both feet, thus the idea of one plank a day. But one day, a client told me he wasn't even ready to start building a Micro-Habit because it felt like too much.

He needed something smaller than a Micro-Habit. He needed to get ready to get ready for a Micro-Habit. He needed a Micro-Mini-Habit.

How Micro-Mini-Habits work

When you start something new, one of the problems you can encounter is getting ahead of yourself and thinking of all the things that could go wrong. Those imagined issues can become an easy way to stop before you even get started. This isn't all that uncommon. It's just the three-year-old in your brain doing their best to keep you safe. They start to whisper in your ear, "If you start going to the gym, you might look stupid. You don't know what to do. People will laugh at you. It's best you stay home on the couch."

So before you've even taken the first step, you've stopped yourself. A Micro-Mini-Habit prevents this from happening since you start so slowly, so microscopically, your brain really has nothing to get alarmed about and slam the brakes on your progress.

Let's say you want to start going to the gym to workout. While you might like the idea of building a new habit, you're not ready to commit to it. Something is still holding you back. In this case, you need to get ready to get ready to get yourself in the gym working out.

Your Micro-Mini-Habit might be as simple as putting on your workout gear each morning for a week, just to get used to how it feels. Put it on, walk around the house for a couple of minutes, then take it off.

Then the next week you put on your workout gear and drive to the gym. You don't have to get out of the car, you only have to drive to the gym. Then the next week the Micro-Mini Action might be getting out of the car and walking into the gym. This doesn't mean you have to work out, you just have to step into the gym. At some point, you'll step into the gym and do your first exercise (not necessarily your first workout, remember, we're starting small here).

At this point, thanks to the Micro-Mini-Habit, you'll be ready to graduate to a Micro-Habit.

Micro-Mini Progress

You can use a Micro-Mini-Habit to start a habit of writing. In the beginning, all you would do each day, for a week, is sit down and open your writing notebook or your laptop. No writing, just opening up your notebook or laptop and then closing them. The next week you could do the same thing, but this time, you would also sit in front of the notebook or laptop for a couple of minutes, again, not writing anything. While this might seem odd, you are getting ready to get ready to write.

Eventually, the time comes when you are prepared to move from this Micro-Mini-Habit to a Micro-Habit. When this happens, and you feel ready to move forward, you can start writing for one minute a day and move up from there.

You can use Micro-Mini-Habits to declutter your house, learn a new language, build a new skill or revive an old one. The list is pretty much endless.

Using a Micro-Mini-Habit, or even a Micro-Habit, works so well because your actions are so small, your inner three-year-old can't really protest against them or cause you to procrastinate on them. They are so small, you can't really be afraid of them, so fear can't stop you. (How scary is opening up your laptop?) When you want to start working on a new habit, decide if you're ready to start, or if you need to get ready to get ready, then pick a Micro-Habit action, or your Micro-Mini-Action and get started.

While Micro-Habit actions are small enough to jump out of bed to do, not all actions are this way. What if you are struggling to remember to do the action that will build or remove a habit? That's where Habit Stacking is helpful.

Habit Stacking

With Habit Stacking, you use an existing habit as your cue to start building your new habit. Think of your existing habits as the anchor you use to establish your new habit.

Let's say you want to start meditating. As you start out, a meditation habit is going to require you to sit quietly for at least a couple of minutes. You're going to need to decide when during your day those minutes are going to be. You could decide you'll meditate when you have some extra time between clients. Unfortunately, with this plan, there will be times when meetings will run long or an unexpected crisis will appear. Although these would perfect times for a little calmness in your life, that's probably not going to happen.

You could decide on a time during your work day that is sometimes quiet, and hope nothing comes up in your schedule which interferes (but something inevitably does). Or you could look at what absolutely happens every day for you and anchor your new meditation practice to that.

What do you do every day (or at least one would hope you do)? Brush your teeth. You could use brushing your teeth as an anchor and Habit Stack your meditation habit on top of it. Each morning after you brush your teeth, you could sit for two minutes and meditate before getting on with your day. Or you could anchor meditation to getting out of bed, or getting coffee or any other set-in-stone habit that you have. It becomes a "When I do this, then I also do this" kind of thing, which makes it easy to remember to do.

Gratefully Stacking

A friend of mine wanted to add more positivity into her days by being more grateful. She could have done this by starting to write in a gratitude journal, or by taking five minutes before bed to think back through her day, but neither of those appealed to her. Instead, she decided to Habit Stack gratitude.

She thought about times during the day that would make sense to Habit Stack her gratefulness habit on, like every time her computer booted up, or when she filled her water bottle at the fridge, both daily things in her life. But ultimately, because she does a lot of driving, she decided each time she starts her car, she would take 15 seconds to be grateful for something in her life.

It's a random combination, but she swears it's been really helpful and made it easier for her to remember to be grateful. Each time she starts her car, she pauses to be grateful and further strengthens her gratitude habit. The stacking of a new habit on a preexisting habit is all that matters.

I've had entrepreneur clients who have wanted to build in business habits like writing, client development, continuing their education through dedicated reading, etc. So, they've taken Habit Stacking even further by setting a timer. When they perform their anchor habit, let's say sitting down at their desk after lunch, they immediately set a timer on their phone or use a kitchen timer and work on their new habit for a short, dedicated amount of time. The timer makes the work unemotional. It's just a thing to do for that amount of time, then they move on with their day.

When you stack a new habit onto an existing one, you have a built-in anchor that will increase the odds of successfully establishing a new, strong habit.

Making Habit Stacking easier

You can make it easier to remember your Habit Stacking plans by thinking "When/Then." With this phrase, you can easily remember your cue and your action, such as:

WHEN I brush my teeth in the morning, THEN I take my vitamins.

WHEN I walk the dog in the morning, THEN I meditate for 10 minutes after I hang up the leash.

WHEN I come in the front door, THEN I put my keys on the hall table.

Obviously, you won't always need to do this, but in the beginning, reminding yourself When/Then can really help you to cement your Habit Stacking.

Eliminating Friction, then building or eliminating habits using Micro (or Micro-Mini) Habits or Habit Stacking are all going to seriously upgrade your ability to conserve energy without a lot of effort on your part. That's the good news.

The bad news? Building and eliminating habits isn't a slam-dunk. There are villains out there that want to stop you from succeeding. The number one enemy of your habit-building (or eliminating) success is the What the Hell Effect.

The What the Hell Effect

The What the Hell Effect can be neatly summarized by the equation of "Indulge + Regret = Throw all your great efforts to the wind." While originally coined by diet researchers[23] to explain the phenomenon of the behavior after experiencing a diet set back, the What the Hell Effect doesn't just apply to food and can affect you any time you are trying to establish or eliminate a habit.*

The What the Hell Effect occurs when you give in to what you are trying to avoid. Whether it's food, booze, smoking, lying, Girl Scout cookies or a million other things. It's when you slip up once on your goal and use that slip-up as a reason (some say excuse) to tell yourself, "I've messed up, I might as well go all in and eat all the food/drink all the drinks/smoke all the cigarettes. I failed once. What the Hell? I'm going all in!"

I know you've experienced this before in your life. You just didn't have a catchy name for it, now you do. Remember the time you were on an unbeaten track record of consistently going to the gym, and you caught a cold and missed a week, and you never really got back on track? What the Hell in full effect. Or the time you were working on not drinking during the week, and there was a going away Happy Hour for Jenna in Accounting and you had a couple of glasses of wine and since it was ok then, well, "What the Hell was I thinking trying not to drink during the week?"

If building a new habit or eliminating an old one is a series of behaviors done over time, then you should be systematic and intentional about doing those behaviors. Unfortunately, when it comes to your habits at least, your life

---

* There's also another kind of "What the Hell Effect" often used when an unrelated form of exercise seemingly randomly influences a person's ability to perform another type of exercise. This is not that kind of What the Hell Effect.

is dynamic and changing and "things happen."* It's precisely because "things happen" that you encounter the challenge that is the What the Hell Effect.

The What the Hell Effect can easily derail your best efforts when it comes to habits, but there are ways to work around it and actually plan for it.

1. Change your habit

More often than not, the What the Hell Effect strikes when you are trying not to do something. This means you are working on an Away habit. You aren't eating certain foods, you aren't drinking, you aren't smoking, you aren't sitting on the couch playing video games. Because you are moving away from an established habit, it's very easy to be drawn back into it.

Remember, the three-year-old likes the comfort of the status quo. When you are moving away from the status quo, your inner three-year-old views this as being deprived of what it likes, so of course, it will do what it can to get you back. That's exactly why the What the Hell Effect is so pervasive. So, change your Away habit into a Towards habit as we discussed at the beginning of this chapter. When you are moving Towards something new, you are working to achieve something new, so there is no way for you to backslide, at least as your goal is defined. If your Toward goal is to go to the gym five times a week, you will be looking for ways to make it happen.

Yes, this is a little bit of a semantics ploy, but if you are thinking of ways to succeed at your Towards habit, you are less likely to be thinking about how you are deprived. Of course, it always helps to take away the power of the What the Hell Effect if you can...

2. Stop beating yourself up

The quickest way to take away the power of the What the Hell Effect is to stop and see how you are responding to what you see as a slip-up. True, you did eat a slice of cake or miss a gym session. But does this make you a bad person? Is there really a reason you need to feel guilty or to criticize yourself for what you did? Not really.

It's better to pause and look at what you did with a shred of self-compassion and realize you just did what any "normal" person would have done. If your best

---

* Actually, I prefer "things to happen" in my life. I don't want every single day to be exactly the same. You probably don't either.

friend came to you and said, "I blew my diet by having a piece of cake," would you start to yell at her? Would you tell her she was a loser and there was no way she was ever going to lose weight and she might as well give up now? Not if you're any kind of friend. You wouldn't think of doing that. So don't do it to yourself. Acknowledge you slipped up, but it doesn't mean you're a failure. Go back on the diet, drive (or better, run) to the gym. One slip-up does not make you a failure. Don't let the What the Hell Effect be that powerful!

To be stronger than the What the Hell Effect, it definitely helps to be prepared, and this is where If/Then Plans come in.

3. If/Then Plans

As you know from Chapter One (page 12), If/Then Plans are plans you put together before you need them. They are an integral part of Action Plans and the best way to be prepared for the What the Hell Effect.

Use your If/Then Plan to think of what situations you might encounter where you could easily stray from your best-laid plans. Now think of ways to get back on track. Boom! You have an If/Then Plan specifically designed to counter the What the Hell Effect. This will eliminate any Moments of Choice you might encounter as you try to figure out what to do, and they give you the means to easily and quickly take control of a situation so you can prevent or easily recover from a What the Hell moment. We all slip up. Having If/Then plans mean the slip-up is just a short detour and not a full-blown stop sign to your habit-building goals.

Habits, whether they are good or bad, are behaviors that we do without thinking about them, so cultivating and using them is one of the easiest ways to conserve energy. With strong habits in place, you can get more done during the day, without draining your energy. Even though building a habit is going to take you longer than 21 days, the building process doesn't have to be complicated. Start by using a Micro-Habit, or even a Micro-Mini Habit, then Habit Stack to make sure you remember to do your habit action.

Remember the What the Hell Effect is always waiting to trip up your habit-building efforts, but If/Then plans are there to keep you on track. Use the power of habits to leverage your energy as you move into the third powerful skill: Focus.

CHAPTER EIGHT ACTION TOOLBOX: HABITS

DEFINITIONS IN THIS CHAPTER:
What-The-Hell Effect:
The equation of "Indulge + Regret = Throw all your great efforts to the wind."

TOOLS IN THIS CHAPTER:
Two kinds of Habits: Moving Towards or Away:
When you build a new habit, you are either moving Towards something new or moving Away from something old. Usually, it's a combination of both. This is important to remember when trying to make changes.

Build an Anti-Friction Plan:
Discover where the friction is stopping you as you are building a habit, then start asking yourself a series of questions to figure out what will work to remove the friction.

Micro-habit:
Start building a habit by doing the smallest possible action every day. Pick an action that is so small, it will be impossible NOT to do. Repeat daily until you want to make the action larger.

Micro-Mini Habit:
Get ready to build a habit by going even smaller and doing tiny steps that will eventually help you to be ready to implement a Micro-Habit. Start very, very small, then gradually add in small actions. Eventually, you'll be ready to start building a Micro-Habit.

Habit Stacking:
Build new habits by anchoring new actions to already existing habits.

ENEMY OF HABIT BUILDING:
The What-the-Hell Effect, the reaction you have when you "slip-up" in your habit building and feel like you've failed, so you go all-in on your failure.

ACTION ITEMS

Are you Moving Towards or Away:

Think of the habit you are trying to build, is it a Towards habit or an Away habit? Now do some advance planning.

If it's a Towards habit, think of five things you could do to make building your habit easier.

For example: *Always have needed supplies easily accessible.*

1. _____

2: _____

3: _____

4: _____

5: _____

If it's an Away habit, think of five things you could do to make the performance of your habit harder to do.

For example: *Put things in hard to reach places.*

1. _____

2: _____

3: _____

4: _____

5: _____

Build an Anti-Friction plan

Think about where you are encountering friction as you attempt to build a new habit.

I am encountering friction when I: _____

_____

Now, answer these questions:

What exactly is the friction I am encountering, and how is it showing up?

_____

What are some options I have to get rid of it? _____

_____

Can I make the task easier? _____

Can I make it impossible to forget? _____

Can I automate it? _____

Can I schedule it? _____

Can I make it more fun? _____

Possible solutions: _____

_____

Experiment with the solutions to find what works for you. If necessary, ask the questions again and come up with additional options.

Build a Micro-Habit

Decide what habit you would like to start to build: _____

_____

Determine the smallest action you can take each day: _____

_____

Bonus: Decide when you are going to do this action: _____

Habit Stacking

Decide what habit you'd like to start to build _____

_____

Think about habits you already have that you could stack this new habit on.

Possible options: _____

_____

_____

_____

Pick one option and experiment for a week to see if it works. If not, pick one of the other options and experiment with it. Keep experimenting until you find what works best for you.

Plan for the What the Hell Effect
Since the What the Hell Effect can easily derail you, planning ahead is essential. Think of a habit you are working on, and how the What the Hell Effect can derail you. Come up with three different actions you could take to be stronger than the What the Hell Effect. Think in terms of When/Then: When this happens, then I will do this.

Habit:_____

1. When this happens:_____

   then I will do this: _____

2. When this happens: _____

   then I will do this: _____

3. When this happens: _____

   then I will do this: _____

FOCUS

In this third section, we look at the incredible skill of Focus which can give you an undisputed edge when it comes to getting things DONE.

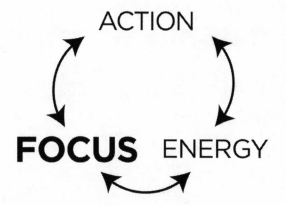

CHAPTER NINE

Focus

"Feed your focus; starve your distractions."
- Robin Arzon, *ultramarathoner, fitness coach & author*

Throughout history, people have gone out of their way to improve their attention and ability to focus. Oftentimes, they resorted to extreme measures to do so.

Victor Hugo, author of *Les Misérables* and *The Hunchback of Notre-Dame*, had his servant lock him in a room to work and take his clothes away. Naked and without a means to escape, all he could do was get his writing done. In his case, this was important because he was usually behind on a deadline for a book he had been paid to write, and quite often, he had already spent the money.

In every town she lived in, author and poet, Maya Angelou, would keep a hotel room strictly for writing, often renting it for months at a time, even if it was in her hometown. Arrangements were made for the room to be stripped down for her. No television, no refrigerator, no wi-fi, no art on the walls. She would bring in her writing notebooks, a bottle of sherry, and a deck of cards. That was it. It was there she lay on the bed, focused, and wrote without distractions.

Both knew the magic of Focus: it expands the perception of time and allows you to be in dedicated Action.

When I tell clients they are going to learn to Focus, I usually get some push back. "I don't have time to Focus all day. I've got distractions everywhere and my job and my...!"* I get it. No one has time for eight hours of pure attention and focus a day. I know I don't. It just can't be done.

Even if you've got a staff of 10 looking out for your every whim (and may I say right now, how awesome that would that be?) you are still physically unable to do pure Focus for that much time. Your poor brain would not be happy. But you know what? You don't have to Focus for hours and hours at a time in order to leverage its power. Because when it comes to Focus, size doesn't matter.

Four important Focus facts to remember:
1. Size doesn't matter

You don't have to seek out huge blocks of time to Focus. Instead of shooting for two full hours of Focus time (something you're rarely going to find), settle for two blocks of 15 minutes with a three-minute break in between. You'll be pleasantly surprised to see how much you can get done in 15 minutes when you dedicate your attention and Focus completely on one thing. Without distractions, it's kind of amazing how long 15 minutes really is. Just know 15 isn't a magic number. If you find yourself with seven minutes to Focus, use that time. Utilize whatever time you have in full, focused action. But don't discount (and waste) small pockets of time. One of the easiest ways to do this is to always be prepared.

2. Be prepared

Having a Focus Action Plan and knowing what you want to accomplish during your focus time, eliminates any chance of your limbic system hijacking your efforts. With no Moments of Choice to deal with, there is no chance for you to get off track and have your focus time to turn into distraction time.

For example, let's say you need to get a report written for work. Your Focus Action Plan (see next page) would break down the steps to follow to get the report completed, including what you want to cover, when to do research, who to speak to, and what kind of data needs to be covered. Looking at your Focus Action Plan, you could pick out one or two of the tasks to work on during your scheduled focus time.† Dedicate your attention to them, then move on to the next item on your plan the next time you have focus time.

---

* You might be thinking the same thing right now.
† Download your Focus Action Plan at EllenGoodwin.com/forms

FOCUS ACTION PLAN

PROJECT: _Write report on planned policy change_ **1**

GOAL: _Complete report for Board Meeting_ **2**

Focus Session Action Steps Session Time **3**		Possible Obstacles **4**	Possible Solutions **5**
Research 3 main areas: history of policy, policy details, and consequences, 3 sessions: 30 min/each		_Difficult to find needed information_	_Contact other departments_
Contact four experts 30 minutes		_Unavailable to talk_	_Have a list of alternative experts_
Draft Outline/Edit outline 30 minutes 30 minutes		_No quiet place to work_	_Schedule a conference room_
Write First draft 2 sessions: 45 min/each		_Missing needed information_	_Make list/plan session to get information_
Edit First draft Input changes 2 sessions: 45 min/each 45 mnutes		_Finding time_	_Block time on calendar_
Edit second draft Input changes 45 minutes 45 minutes		_Hunting down last-minute information_	_Ask for possible info ahead of time_

BREAK: _Walk around the block, 5 jumping jacks_

Filling in Your Focus Action Plan

Use this Action Plan as a way to make quick decisions about what to work on during Focus Sessions. Having a plan eliminates Moments of Choice.

1. What is the overall project you are focusing on?
2. What if the final full goal you are working towards?
3. What are the Actions you need to do, and how much time do you need to do them? These actions do not have to be in sequence. With larger Actions, break the sessions into several smaller blocks of time.
4. What possible obstacles might you encounter?
5. What possible solutions can you try?
6. What sort of breaks will you take after each session?

Or use a Mini Focus Action Plan

Depending on how long, and how many sessions of Focus I have planned, I sometimes turn to a Mini Focus Action Plan (example on the following page).

This Mini Focus Plan has a variety of items on it that I can work on, which is very helpful when something stops me from moving forward. So, if the expert I need to speak with isn't immediately available to answer a question, I move on to my next item on the Mini Focus Plan. Just because one person isn't available, doesn't mean all forward progress has to stop until they are available.

At the bottom of a Focus Action Plan and the Mini Focus Action Plan, I always put the word "Break" followed by what I will do at the end of my focus time. I do this both to make sure I take the right kind of break (physical/mental see page 160) and to remind myself of what I will do during the break. Sometimes it will be things like check email, or social media. Other times it will be a reward break where I do some exercises or read a few pages of a good book.

Also, know your focus plans don't have to be formal. A lot of the time I will just grab a Post-it Note and jot down my goals for my focus session as well as what my break will be, and I work from that.

MINI- FOCUS ACTION PLAN

GOAL: Complete research for presentation - 45 minutes

TASKS: Call with professor/expert

Look up 4 studies

Note authors info

Outline closing section

Make a list of questions for follow-up

BREAK: Read 10 pages of current fiction book

In addition to going into a focus session with a plan in mind, always have a blank piece of paper with you.* Without fail, while you are devoting all your attention to one thing, something new and (possibly) exciting will pop into

---

* This is much like the Back Burner List that was discussed in Chapter Five.

your brain. Maybe it's a new idea or you think of someone you're supposed to call, or you remember something you were supposed to do. Rather than give your attention to this new thought, write it down on your piece of paper. Don't let it become a source of distraction for you. Capture it so you can deal with it later, then get back to focusing.

3. Eliminate all your distractions

There are immutable laws that we live with, which we can and can't change. The Law of Gravity is one.* The Laws of Physics. And the Law of Focus that states: you can't focus with distractions, especially digital ones. They have to be eliminated—not just blocked—eliminated. If there's any chance you'll be distracted, you won't really be focusing. Your brain, not just the limbic system, never really goes to sleep.†

Remember the superior colliculus from page 68? Thanks to it, your brain is always looking for distractions. The goal of the superior colliculus is to move you toward or away from unexpected visual stimuli, so it activates the fight-or-flight response, which is the opposite physical state of being in focus.

When a notification pops up or something flashes on your screen, the superior colliculus springs into action, destroying any attention or focus. This tiny, overactive structure is why you need to eliminate all your distractions.

We talked about distractions earlier, so this really isn't anything new. For projects that don't require your computer or other electronics, turn off your phone and computer or physically remove yourself from their presence. Lock your phone in a drawer. Go and work in an empty office or coffee shop. Make it impossible to be disrupted. Just muting your computer and phone is not going to cut it. You can still see the screens, so you'll still be tempted. Temptation doesn't pair well with focus. Make focus time real, actual focus time. The phone and all your screens will be there when you get done. If you are working on your computer, only have open the program you are actively working in—no internet windows or email programs. This eliminates the distractions of alerts that may pop up.

---

* Gravity: It's not just a good idea, it's the law.
† Yes, you can quiet it down with meditation, as you'll soon see, but without medical intervention, it never really sleeps.

4. Be deliberate with your Focus

Since you know focus time is hard to come by, treat it as a delicate thing. Make sure you effectively and efficiently use the focus time you do have. The best way to do this is to Focus on the things that will give you the biggest bang for your buck. Unfortunately, this also means you will probably need to Focus on the things that are the hardest for you.

Let's face it, we all love the stuff we're good at, and we try to ignore or put off the things we aren't so good at. To use focus time most effectively, minimize the time you spend on the stuff you find easy and maximize the stuff that is harder for you to do.

When I work on new presentations and talks for conferences or corporate trainings, I usually find after I've put a few practice sessions in, I have the beginning of the talk down really well. This is because, during the first few practice sessions, I start practicing at the beginning of the talk and work my way to the end, sort of like reading a book. During my practice time, I invariably run into unexpected time constraints and I don't make it all the way to the end of the talk or presentation. Then the next time I practice, I start at the beginning again and work my way through. It took a speaking coach to point out what I was missing by practicing this way. I wasn't targeting the practice sessions in the way that it would help me the most.

Rather than going from start to finish, I needed to be working on the parts of the presentation I didn't know well—the parts that were, at this point, a little less familiar and a lot more difficult for me. Since this discovery, I always make it a point to pick the sections of my talks and presentations that I don't know as well and Focus on them during my focus sessions. This makes my focus time more productive and helpful.

Think it through

This isn't groundbreaking stuff. It's just something we need to be reminded of. Great athletes don't practice just what they are already good at. They also look at where they need to improve. They look at all the little things that can affect their performance.[24] Whether it's getting better coming out of the blocks in track, making better flip-turns in swimming or getting an extra inch or two in the vertical jump in basketball. (The list could go on and on, in every sport, there is something that can be worked on.) The point is, they find what needs to be improved and they use deliberate focus to improve it.

Great musicians don't often practice songs that they know already. They work on new songs, digging into the intricacies of a piece that's challenging to them. Classically trained musicians don't systematically work their way through long pieces of music from start to finish. They find a section they know needs work and they focus on it. They focus on the hard stuff because that's where they can make the most significant progress.

So, you may be thinking, "How exactly does this apply to my life? I'm not an athlete, and I'm certainly not performing in an orchestra any time soon."

Being deliberate with your very precious focus time means you do everything you can to make sure your time works for you. I'm not going to deny that it's more comfortable working on easy things. When things are easy, you're less likely to procrastinate on focusing on them. But if you're only doing things you're already good at, you aren't helping yourself improve.

When you start your focus time, be sure to look at whether you are leveraging your time by doing the things that may be the hardest for you. Start a focus session by having an outcome in mind that may be a bit of a stretch for you. Make sure that it's going to make a difference. It doesn't matter if you are working on something for your business, your home, your relationships, your health or your family. To make your time more effective, focus on the things that are currently difficult for you.

Focus is the lack of distractions. When distractions show up, Focus goes away. As we get distracted, we run into the prime enemy of Focus: Multitasking/Context Shifting.

The Enemy of Focus

The best type of Focus appears when you allow your brain to "stay in one room," which means you allow your energy and attention to stay on one type of activity, whether it's reading, writing, listening, researching, talking, tasting, or touching. As long as your brain is able to give full attention to one type of thing, you are fully engaged.

Multitasking* occurs when you flip back and forth between two activities, which are handled by two different regions of your brain. As a means of illustration, think of a time when you were reading something on your computer, and someone called you on the phone. You started listening, then talking, but you also kept reading. After a while you realized you had no idea of what was being said or what you were reading.

You were multitasking.

For a moment, imagine your brain is a house, and you can read only when you are in the living room and can speak and listen when you are in the bedroom. You can't read in the bedroom and you can't speak or listen in the living room. You must move each time you want to do one or the other task. You definitely can't do both in the kitchen. Each time you change rooms, you use up a little energy, and it takes a little time. The more times you shift back and forth between the rooms, the more energy you use and the more time it starts to take to shuffle back and forth between the rooms and to readjust and remember what you were doing in each room.

That is how multitasking takes place in your brain. It drains your mental energy and it makes Focus impossible since you can't focus if you're running between rooms in your brain. You have to keep your brain working in one room at a time.

When you Focus and keep yourself in one room, there's no pausing to remember what it was you were doing. There's no energy drain as you shift back and forth. It's the most efficient way to get things done. As you build focus sessions into your day, think of how you can keep your brain in one room at a time as often as possible.

Hocus Pocus, Let's All Focus

Focus is a lot like the clothes in your closet. When it comes to what you wear each day, you have options that work with different occasions, different temperatures, and different environments. You mix and match what works for you and what your day looks like. It's the same thing with focus. Different situations call for different strategies and tactics.

---

* Or Context Shifting. The two are interchangeable.

Some days you'll have the luxury of extended periods of time to Focus. Other days you'll be grabbing pockets of time whenever you can find them. And still other days you'll find yourself with varying amounts of time that you have to be proactive in seizing. With the right focus strategies, you can maximize any timing situation you run into.

Focus just doesn't have to be complicated for it to be effective. It can be as simple as setting a timer for 10 minutes, working with complete attention and Focus, then taking a break. Lather, rinse, repeat.

My favorite focus tool

As I've said in previous chapters, I'm a huge fan of old-school ticking kitchen timers.* I have them all over my house. And, besides my questionable taste in decor, they enable me to jump into Focus no matter where I am. Don't worry, you don't have to have a lot of timers like me.† You also have a perfectly good timer on your phone that you can use (as long as you don't use the proximity of your phone as a way to get distracted and give into a Moment of Choice). Timers of any kind allow you to track your focus time. More importantly, by focusing using a timer, the three-year-old in your brain knows your focus session is not going to last forever (or even take up most of your day).

When you set a timer, you are telling yourself this is the time for dedicated attention and Focus.

There's no deep magic to finding Focus. Set both a time frame and your timer, block distractions, do your task(s), and then move on.

There are lots of different methods for setting up timed focus sessions, but for any of them to be successful, it's important to remember and use one acronym: STING.‡

---

* I talked about timers on page 53. This time, I will wax poetic even more.
† I'm such a big fan of timers that my podcast partner gives me grief because he says I mention timers in every episode. He's not wrong.
‡ This does not refer to the lead singer of The Police or what a bee does.

STING stands for:

    Select one task

    Time yourself

    Ignore everything

    No breaks

    Give yourself a reward

Keep these five points in mind for all focus session

First, **Select** one task to work on so you avoid multitasking and keep your brain in one room. This will help you ignore distractions as well. While that one task is the most important task, it never hurts to have at least one additional task in mind in case you finish your selected task early or you run into a roadblock. Planning ahead and having a back-up task at the ready eliminates any Moments of Choice that might occur. You can keep going and don't waste any of your precious focus session time.

Second, set your **Timer** for an amount of time that feels good to you. In the next few pages, we'll look at some different timing methods and protocols you can use to guide your sessions. But remember, they are just guides. I never want you to feel like you have to have a set number of minutes to Focus. If you've got time to Focus, make it fit for you without worrying about it fitting in some other prearranged timing plan. If you can fit a 23-minute focus session in between afternoon meetings, do it! Don't put it off because it's not a perfect 25 minutes. Always use whatever time you have available to Focus. It's a precious commodity, use it as such.

Third, **Ignore** everything in order for your focus session to work. Everything. As you know, distractions mean multitasking, which takes you out of "the one room in your brain." While Focusing, ignore all distractions. Chances are pretty good they will be waiting for you when you get done.

Fourth, take *No* **Breaks**. Every time you take a break, you are leaving "the one room in your brain" so you will need to use time and energy to get back to that room. Work straight through from start to finish of your timed session.

And finally, when the timer dings or chirps or beeps or whatever it does to signal time is up, **Give** yourself a reward. What kind of reward is up to you. If chocolate motivates you, go for it. If a little physical activity is your thing, then jump up and give yourself a private two-minute dance party, do some jumping jacks, or walk around the block. Your call. If you want a quick social media check-in (with the emphasis on quick), do it. You just successfully completed a focus session, and completed or moved something forward in your world. Celebrate that!

Then, if necessary, set the timer again and begin another focus session.

In the beginning, when you're working to add focus sessions into your day, you might find it difficult. Just like any new habit you're adding to your life, it's going to feel uncomfortable. That's why, in the beginning, you start small. Maybe you only do one 30-minute focus session each day and see how it feels, or you can start small and do a 15-minute session. Or a couple of 10-minute sessions.

As you get more comfortable with Focusing, add in a couple more sessions each day. If it works to run focus sessions one after another, then do it. If it feels better and more effective to do a focus session in the morning and one in the afternoon, then do it. As you do them more often, you'll see how effective they are, how good the success dopamine feels, and you'll want to figure out ways to add more of them into your day (and your life). The key is to pick a task, set some sort of timer, and give it all your concentrated attention.

Six kinds of focus sessions

When scheduling focus sessions, it helps to break the time down into small chunks. The idea of Focusing for an hour or more can feel overwhelming, especially to the three-year-old in your limbic system, so start small. A 30-minute focus session requires you to ignore distractions for merely 1,800 seconds. That's it. Then you can go back to being distracted again.

For some people though, 30 minutes at a time is a lot to handle, so for the first two timing methods, Focus on 10 minute sessions. Just 600 seconds of Focus at a time.

1. The 10-Minute Time Chunk

There are some days when a 10-Minute Time Chunk is all you can slip into your schedule, or all you have the bandwidth for. But remember this: 10 minutes is always better than nothing.

A couple of years ago, we had some long-needed renovations done on our house. Unfortunately, I was working from home at the time so I could hear a worker at the back of the house building steps on the newly built deck, while another worker in the front of the house was putting new pickets on the front porch and another guy was sanding down the window sills in preparation for painting the entire house.

It was messy, noisy, disorganized, and not at all an environment conducive to Focusing in any way. Not surprisingly, my brain felt noisy, disorganized, and unfocused as well.

Since moving out of my office wasn't an option, during this disruptive period of time, I relied on the power of the 10-Minute Time Chunk every day.

A 10-Minute Time Chunk is exactly what it sounds like: a focus session of just 10 minutes. Knowing I only had to focus for 10 minutes at a time meant I needed to break my tasks into very small actions so I could accomplish them a little bit at a time. Ten minutes here. Ten minutes there.

The great thing about doing it this way was I felt successful for every 10 minutes of work. Some of my 10-minute tasks were physical things I needed to accomplish like sorting or filing. Other tasks were more mental: outlining blog posts, writing short articles, scheduling appointments.

Whatever it was, I just figured out what I could attempt to take care of in 10 minutes, and set my timer and got to work. The timer helped me to recognize this was focus time and block out the hammering and commotion going on outside. Because deep Focus wasn't really an option, I had to work with what I could.

Fitting in a few 10-minute sessions each hour ensured I got more done than I would have if I waited until my environment was perfect for Focusing. Ten minutes was really all I could really handle at the time, so leveraging it effectively made a huge difference.

Part of the power of the 10-Minute Time Chunk is acknowledging that your current situation precludes deep, extended focus time, but you aren't helpless. It's a proactive solution to an imperfect situation. Use a 10-Minute Time Chunk on days full of meetings, distractions, noise, or emotion. It's easier to get started and be successful when you know you just have to focus for 10 minutes at a time.

2. The (10+2)*5 plan*

The credit for this focus plan goes to Merlin Mann of 43Folders.com, who came up with this process 14 years ago.[25]

The (10+2)*5 plan is a pumped-up, much more robust version of the 10-Minute Time Chunk. With the (10+2)*5 plan, you do 10-minute sessions but instead of doing only one, you string together a series of five of them. You work for 10 minutes followed by a two-minute break then repeat four more times. In each 10-minute session, you move things forward in an energetic burst. If you do all five rounds, then at the end of an hour†, you've knocked out 50 solid minutes of work, 10 minutes at a time (and gotten in five short breaks as well).

The (10+2)*5 plan works really well on projects that are broken down into small chunks. For example, if you needed to write a report, you could use the first 10 minutes to outline the report. Then the second 10 minutes could be used to put three points on each outline point. The next 10 minutes you could really flesh out the first outline point. The next 10 minutes you could flesh out the second outline point, and well, you get the idea.

During each two-minute break, step away from your work and relax. Personally, I like to make the breaks physical and get up and do some jumping jacks, or squats or walk around.

While working in a series of 10-minute bursts, you never really get to relax. There's no middle stretch of time where you can coast on your work. Add in something physical for the break and the plan will keep you alert and active as you move from interval to break to interval.

The (10+2)*5 plan in action

The easiest ways I've found to do the (10+2)*5 plan is with an intervals timer. There are free ones available for both iOS and Android. The one I use is cleverly called "Intervals Timer." I create a custom "routine" (as the app calls different timing set-ups). My routine has five 10-minute intervals followed by

---

* While this sounds like a math problem, I promise there is absolutely no math involved.
† There is nothing magic about the hour of time. If you've only got 30 minutes, just set for three intervals. The point is to use focus and work in short bursts, and get as much done as you can in the time you have.

two-minute breaks. Each interval of time is signaled by the "ding-ding" of a boxing bell.

I find using a timer this way allows me to set up the timing for the whole hour at once, which works better than repeatedly setting and resetting the timer on my phone or a kitchen timer, for a couple of reasons.

First, if I have to reset the timer every 10 minutes or every two minutes, it's just inconvenient, so it's easy to give up on it. Second, every time I pick up my phone or kitchen timer to reset the time, I am giving myself a Moment of Choice. Do I set the timer and keep going? Or do I turn my attention elsewhere? Setting up the timer once eliminates any Moments of Choice I might encounter.

I've also found writing out a list of what I want to accomplish with my intervals really helps to keep me on track. The list enables me to move quickly and smoothly from one task to another as each gets finished, with no downtime trying to figure out what should come next.

I also make sure to have a blank piece of paper with me so I can write down the random thoughts that inevitably pop into my head while I'm focusing. Thoughts like "make an appointment to rotate the tires," are just a form of distraction, so the sooner they are out of my head and on a piece of paper, the sooner I can return to focus.

I think the (10+2)*5 plan is energizing. Accomplishing things bit-by-bit keeps the three-year-old in my brain happy as the dopamine hits keep coming and coming. I don't feel bogged down by having to be Focused for extended periods of time. And the dinging of the boxing bell keeps me amused.

3. Pomodoro Method

Another very popular timing plan you've probably heard of is the Pomodoro Method. It's named for the tomato-shaped timer it was founded on.

To "do a Pomodoro," you set the timer and work for 25 minutes. Then you take a five-minute break and repeat. At the end of an hour, you've focused for 50 minutes with 10 minutes off.*

There are whole websites and books written about the Pomodoro Method, but there is nothing magical about the tomato-shaped timer or the 25 minutes.

---

* Sounds a little familiar....

It's just a good amount of time to get into Focus and work. As you might imagine, there are other timing plans you can look at.

Pomodoro Alternatives

Longer timing sessions can help you get into the flow state where you are so involved in your task that you lose track of time. Flow is Focus at its best, but it's hard to get into flow if your timer keeps going off every 10-25 minutes. So, if you're working on something that requires more time to Focus, here are a couple of established timing plans you can explore.

The Rule of 52-17

Not so much a rule as the findings of a study[26] done by employee productivity tracking software company DeskTime. They found the most efficient workers worked on a 52/17 schedule. Using this rule, you work for a focused 52 minutes, then take a 17-minute break, then return for another 52 minutes. The longer focus time enables you to settle deeply into your task and work with purpose without worrying about interruptions. And the long 17-minute break gives you time to take care of almost anything you might have missed during your 52 minutes.

90/30 Plan

If you feel like 52 minutes isn't enough, consider the 90 minutes on, 30 minutes off plan. The idea behind this timing plan is our natural "ultradian" rhythms, a recurrent period or cycle throughout the 24-hour day. You sleep in 90-minute cycles, so why not work in them as well?

Following this plan, you structure your whole day in a series of 90 minutes of work, and 30 minutes of break sessions, which are essential in making this plan work. For most people, a schedule like this isn't really feasible, given the varying demands of their day, their coworkers, or their boss. But it is something to consider.

Experiment with these timing plans to find what works best for you. Some days the (10+2)*5 plan will be just the thing that allows you to get work done. Other days you might be super focused and work for 52 minutes at a time. Some days you might use one plan in the morning and another in the afternoon.

You can also put together your own timing solution. There is nothing set in stone with these numbers. If you want to do a 17/4 plan or a 27/8 plan, no one is going to stop you. As long as your focus time is deliberate and distraction-free, do what works for you.

4. Batching

The easiest way to think about Batching is how you already use it in your life (and probably don't recognize it). When you run out of something at home, most likely you put it on a list so you remember it the next time you go to the store. You don't run out and get that one item all by itself. Rather than running out to get a jar of mustard, you usually wait and go to the store when you have several items on your list. You are Batching getting groceries. It's the same with Batching your tasks and Focusing.

Batching is like a STING, since you set a timer and work for a predetermined amount of time with no distractions or breaks, and you can reward yourself if you'd like. But instead of doing one thing, you focus on doing one kind of like-minded thing. You can batch reading, researching, writing, inventing, building, speaking, or cleaning. Really, anything. The key is to use your time doing similar activities that utilize the "same room" in your brain.

Let's say you were going to Batch reading. During your timed session you might read a couple of blog posts, then a newspaper article, and then a few chapters in a book—different sources but all only reading. (And you don't even have to be reading about the same subject.)

You could Batch finances and pay bills, reconcile accounts, prepare invoices, and do expense reports. When I was a graphic designer, I would Batch photo research and photo retouching. I would set the timer and only research or make photos look nice. That was it. No answering emails, no checking social media, just solid photo work.

You might find it helps to write down three to five things you want to accomplish in your 30-minute Batching session.* When you finish one task, just move to the next task on your list, eliminating any Moments of Choice that could lead to becoming distracted.

You can find a way to Batch almost anything, just remember to make sure you are Focusing on like-minded tasks so you keep your brain in one room.

---

* Again, there is nothing magic about 30 minutes. It's just a suggested time frame for Batching, but if you want or need a longer or shorter time frame, do it.

5. Sprint

A Sprint could just as easily be called "Beat the Clock." Pick five or six tasks (they don't have to be related in any way), set a timer, and try to finish them before your time is up. That's it. The simplicity of a Sprint enables you to get a lot done for several reasons.

First, it allows you to overcome Parkinson's Law.* Since you only have a short time to do your task, you can't afford to get distracted and waste time. Second, you do your tasks sequentially so there are no Moments of Choice. You have a list to follow, there is no back and forth context-shifting. And third, Sprints build momentum as you get a dopamine hit each time you succeed at a task.

I find Sprints fun to do because I can knock a lot of things off my to-do list in a very short amount of time. Usually, these are things I've been putting off because they aren't a high priority for me. For you, they could be low-value, low-level tasks you've been putting off, they could be tasks you know you could easily get distracted on, or they could just be tasks you are tired of constantly seeing on your to-do list. Whatever they are, you can take care of them with a Sprint.

To do a Sprint, decide on five or six tasks to take care of, select a time frame (anything between five and 30 minutes is fair game), set a timer, and get started. Do the first task on your list. When it's complete, move to the second task, then the third. Your goal is to complete your list before the timer goes off.

Sprints work well because you are focused on both the time and the task. You have a sense of urgency to fuel your work.

6. Proactive Focus Time

The ability to be proactive with your time, even if it's only 15 minutes at a stretch, enables you to feel more in control, which in turn, means you get more done, and you're probably happier.

Unfortunately, reacting and responding to the impulses, wishes, and needs of others is how most days go. When you're reactive, you aren't in charge of your time, you've lost your autonomy, and are usually bouncing from one urgent "fire" to another.

---

* Work expands to fill the time available for it.

When this happens, there is no time for your brain to get quiet and Focus. Luckily, establishing a Proactive Hour where you can be in proactive mode only, can help you change that.

A Proactive Hour* allows you to Focus on things that will move you (or your business) forward. Not reacting to anyone or anything for a short amount of time is the whole idea behind your Proactive Hour. You don't talk with anyone, or respond to emails, calls, texts or instant messages. Everything you work on or do is instigated and initiated by you and you alone.

For a Proactive Hour to work, you need to have boundaries for both yourself and for others. You have to be firm that this is your time. For some people, the initial reaction to a Proactive Hour is that it is selfish and impossible to fit in their schedule. But, putting a Proactive Hour into place is really no different than scheduling any other type of appointment. During a Proactive Hour, you are in a one-on-one meeting with yourself.

Look at it this way, if you were taking a yoga class, you wouldn't expect people to barge in and demand you take a phone call or answer an email. Yoga is definitely Proactive time. A Proactive Hour quiets the external noises and allows you to think and focus more clearly.

Building a Proactive Hour

Now it's time to focus on things that apply to you. Start your Proactive Hour by turning off all distractions and blocking anyone or anything that is going to cause you to react. Think about what's important to your life, whether it's personal, business, family or something else, then proactively work on what you decide.

Just like any other form of focus, as you go through your Proactive Hour, things are going to start popping up in your brain that have the potential to steal your attention. While you're diligently doing research on a project that you are championing, you'll suddenly remember you were supposed to call a client today, or schedule a doctor's appointment, or take snacks to the

---

* I know blocking out a whole hour can be hard, so feel free to start with a Proactive Quarter-Hour or a Proactive Half-Hour and increase the time as you feel comfortable. Do what works best for you. For the sake of this section, I'll still call it a Proactive Hour, and you can substitute in the time frame which works best for you.

soccer game after work. Just like any other type of focus session, jot down these thoughts down so you don't forget them, then go back to what you were doing.

As you get more comfortable, add more time to your Proactive time. Be in charge, be efficient and be Proactive.

Alternative Timing

While it would be great to have a Proactive Hour every day, for you, this may not be feasible. But that doesn't mean you should dismiss the idea completely. If you can only do one Proactive Hour a week, that's okay. Any Proactive time is great. Not only will you get more done by having uninterrupted Focus, but you'll also benefit from the feeling of being in charge of your time and from the reduced stress of dealing with the demands and time frames of others.

A client of mine blocks out non-negotiable Proactive Hours in her calendar every couple of weeks. She labels them in various ways such as "training," "consults," and "one-on-one meetings." Keeping those hours for herself has enabled her to focus on more complex, high-value tasks that are making a huge difference in her career.

These six different kinds of Focus Sessions give you a good starting point for adding Focus into your life. Since Focus is an essential skill if you want to get things done, it's important you experiment with these tools to find out what works best for you. Don't worry if it feels hard at first to Focus. Just like building a muscle, building the power to Focus can take a while. There is one thing, though, that can help you: Meditation.

Build your ability to focus

One of the most misunderstood (and most powerful) tools for Focus is meditation. I say misunderstood because people tend to think it's a lot harder than it looks, and they misunderstand its role in Focus.

Meditation, among other things, decreases both anxiety and activity in the region of the brain responsible for mind wandering.[27] Meditation can increase working memory capacity,[28] and because it can help your limbic system to settle down, it improves your ability to Focus.

True confession time: I am not a great meditator. I know I should do it. I know how much it helps me tune in and Focus in a much better way. But, just because I know these things, doesn't mean I am consistent in doing it.

Why is that? Because the two sides of my brain are constantly fighting when it comes to meditating. The antsy, "let's get going" fight-or-flight three-year-old in my limbic system doesn't want to settle down. It wants to go full tilt towards whatever I am working on.*

My limbic system says "no!" to meditation, while the prefrontal cortex, which is responsible for keeping me in line,† knows just sitting quietly will elevate our (me, my limbic system and I) ability to focus in both the short-term and long-term. So, the overarching goal is to get the prefrontal cortex into the driver's seat. Usually, I do this through bargaining with the three-year-old, and my main tool is, of course, a timer.‡

I make a deal with my limbic system that I only have to meditate for five to 10 minutes. That's it. Five to 10 minutes is short, and sweet, and effective. Both the use of the timer and the short amount of meditation work perfectly for me.

What I'm really telling you here is, if I can do it, you can do it because you only have to meditate for a short amount of time, really short. But, it will still be helpful and effective. If you want to settle in for 20 minutes, half an hour or longer, good for you and your Focus. But don't scare yourself into thinking you have to meditate for a huge block of time, which will negatively impact your already fully packed day. (That sort of defeats the whole purpose.)

If you want to try meditation in order to Focus better, it is only as difficult as you choose to make it (and really, isn't that the whole story in life?)

---

* This is a common complaint of those with ADD and ADHD, neither of which I have, but I have lots of colleagues who do live with it and leverage it for their greater good. Peter Shankman wrote a book called "Faster Than Normal," which explains how he uses his ADHD as a superpower. It's a great book. Definitely read it. He doesn't meditate, instead, he exercises to quiet his brain.

† The prefrontal cortex is responsible for your "executive functions."

‡ Since I don't want to be listening to ticking while meditating, I usually use a meditation timer like Enso, Aura, or Insight Timer or I set a timer on my phone with a gentle chime to tell me when my time is up.

Meditation 101: Make it easy

You don't have to have a special location to meditate. You don't need special clothes. You don't need a chant. You don't need a special Tibetan gong or chime. You don't need special music or incense. You just need a quiet space where you can be undisturbed for five minutes (or more).

Sit as comfortably as you can. You can sit in a chair with your feet on the floor. You can sit on the floor and curl your feet under you. Do whatever is most comfortable, but don't lay down, it's too easy to go from meditation to sleep, which can be an issue if you're doing this at work.

Now, close your eyes, or don't. If you chose not to close your eyes, find something you can focus on so your mind doesn't wander. You can softly focus on a spot on the wall or a chosen object that means something special to you. Some people focus on the flame of a candle. Others some other inanimate object. It's all up to you to decide what works for you.

With your eyes in whatever state you want them to be, start listening to your breathing. Breathe in slowly. Breathe out slowly. Feel the breath as it moves through you. Keep doing this until your timer goes off.

That, in a nutshell, is meditation. (And yes, you can make it much more involved. If you want to go deeper check out some of the books listed in the resource section of this book.)

Your brain is not a fan

When you meditate, thoughts will show up. Thoughts about things you need to do, things you did in the past, things that might happen which scare you, things you wish you could do over, things you've done that have embarrassed you, and of course, the nagging question of what you want for dinner tonight. All of these thoughts, and lucky you, a whole lot more will show up. Isn't your brain supposed to be quiet when you're meditating? In theory, yes. But it rarely is, which is one of the main reasons people think they are doing it wrong.

But guess what? You are doing it exactly right! Those thoughts show up because the brain doesn't want to be quiet. Remember the limbic system not wanting to meditate AT ALL? Well, now that you're actually doing it, it is rebelling in the only way it can, by bringing everything up it possibly can in an effort to get you to stop.

As you meditate, you just have to brush those thoughts away. Which is sort of the whole purpose of meditation. Brush them away then refocus on your breath. The best advice I ever got on disruptive thoughts is to just acknowledge they are there. Think of them as floating on clouds. You see the thought, you acknowledge it, then you mentally brush them away. Or let it drift away. Then go back to peacefully concentrating on your breathing. The peacefulness should last about another 0.05 seconds before the next disruptive thought tries to interrupt and you do the same, acknowledgment and brush it away.

This is what meditation is like, and it's perfectly normal.

You are not going to be able to sit and have a perfectly blank mind for five or 10 or 30 minutes. Your brain rocks and rolls and does crazy things 24 hours a day, 365 days a year, which is obviously a very good thing. It's also the reason why, when you are meditating, it can't simply shut down. Eventually, like a toddler taking a nap, it starts to quiet down just enough for things to begin to sort themselves out and become clearer. It's not like the heavens open up and clarity comes to you on the wings of angels. Well, not at least every time. But sometimes it's close, which is why meditation is important in the first place.

Why do you think they call it Practice?

No one is perfect at meditation. Ok, maybe some monks who do it for hours and hours a day. But that's not you.*

Expecting yourself to be perfect at meditation undermines what it is all about. You don't have to be perfect at it, or even really good at it. You just need to do it. In theory, you need to be good at driving to be out on the streets and highways. You need to be good at your job to keep getting a paycheck, and you need to be good at managing your money so you can keep eating on a regular basis, but you don't have to be good at meditating. You just need to take the time to sit quietly and let your brain relax. Five minutes at a time.

One of my favorite things about meditating is the way it allows random connections to appear between different parts of life. When my brain quiets down, it's like a 1,000-piece puzzle starting to take shape. Pieces start to come together that I never thought of as being related.

---

* Unless you are one of those monks, which in that case, thanks for picking up this book and I hope you enjoy reading it between your meditation sessions. You impress the hell out of me.

One time, I was trying to figure out who I could reach out to help me get in front of a business I wanted to work with. Research wasn't helping, so I put the idea aside. The next morning when I was meditating, the answer just showed up. A woman I knew from years ago was the direct contact I needed. While still friendly with this woman, I hadn't been thinking of her and hadn't been mulling how to contact her. Her name just surfaced as I meditated, as the person I needed to reach out to.

This is not an isolated incident. Talk with anyone who meditates and they will share stories of things "just coming together" when they quieted their mind. I like to think of meditation as a bit of a brain reset that allows me to focus better. When I meditate before work, I don't get as distracted, I have more clarity, and I'm able to do a deeper dive into my tasks than I might have been able to do before.

Meditation can be the best five minutes (or more if you feel like it) you spend today. There's no required way to do it. There's no one way to do it. Free form it as it feels best to you. But do it. Your brain will thank you. Your Focus will thank you.

When Focus is combined with Action and Energy, you can become unstoppable. Building strong Focus isn't difficult. You don't need to Focus for hours at a time, you just need to know what you need to Focus on, clear your distractions, and be deliberate with your focus time. Keep your three-year-old in check by using a timer, minimize Moments of Choice, and experiment with different timing plans, then build your ability to concentrate by adding meditation into your life.

Adding dedicated focus time into your day will allow you to expand your perception of time, and will enable you to accomplish more with the time you have available.

CHAPTER NINE ACTION TOOLBOX: FOCUS

TOOLS IN THIS CHAPTER:

Important Focus Facts to remember:

Size doesn't matter:

Never dismiss the power of small amounts of Focus time. While large chunks of time are useful, you can still get a lot done in ten minutes.

Be prepared:

Always go into a focus session knowing what you want to accomplish. Take a moment and write down on a Post-it Note what you want to get done, so if you get distracted, you can remind yourself of your task and stay on track. Also, write down what you'll do during your break.

Eliminate your distractions:

Eliminate anything that could distract you, whether digital, human or anything in between

Be deliberate:

Don't rely on hoping there will be a time in your day to Focus. Plan and schedule time when you will put distractions aside and Focus.

ENEMY OF FOCUS—MULTITASKING:

Multitasking is like trying to be in two rooms of your house at once. It can't be done. To Focus, you need to eliminate multitasking and keep your brain in one room.

Timers:

One of the best tools for Focus. Use an old-fashioned kitchen timer or a timer on your phone. Decide how long you are going to Focus and ignore distractions and get started. String together several focus sessions by using an Interval Timer on your phone or computer.

STING:

The acronym used to always guide you when going into a focus session. STING stands for:

Select one thing

Time yourself

Ignore everything else

No breaks

Give yourself a reward

Timing Methods/Protocols

10-Minute Time Chunk:

Plan for 10 minutes of Focus throughout the day. Very helpful in situations where large amounts of uninterrupted time aren't available, such as a day filled with meetings or distractions you can't control.

(10+2)*5:

A timing protocol where you work for five sessions of 10 minutes of focus with two-minute breaks in between. Great for doing short sprints of work that don't need intense Focus.

Pomodoro Method:

Popular timing method named after a tomato-shaped timer. Work for 25 minutes, take a timed, 5-minute break, then repeat as necessary.

Batching:

Focus by doing a time-block filled with a series of like-minded tasks, such as reading, financial work, writing, or research. During your timed session, you move from task to task without changing the type of task you are doing.

Sprint:

A short, timed session, where you do a series of tasks in an effort to "Beat the Clock." Tasks don't have to be like-minded, the goal is to eliminate distractions and procrastination by keeping within the time goal, and getting everything accomplished.

Proactive Focus Time:

Build a Proactive Hour where you can Focus on what you need to accomplish, and you don't react to anything or anyone.

Build your Focus with meditation:

Learn to meditate and improve your ability to Focus. Sit quietly for five minutes and breathe. Let thoughts come into your brain, then send them away. Practice every day, forever.

ACTION ITEMS

Focus Action Plan

For every focus session, answer these questions before setting the timer and beginning. (Using a Post-It Note can help you to corral your thoughts.)

During this time I am going to work on:

_____

If I finish before my time is up, I will work on:

_____

Break: When my focus session is over, I will enjoy a break by doing:

_____

```
┌─────────────────────────────────────────────┐
│ MINI- FOCUS ACTION PLAN                       │
│ GOAL:                                         │
│ _____   │
│ TASKS:                                        │
│                                               │
│                                               │
│                                               │
│                                               │
│                                               │
│                                               │
│                                               │
│                                               │
│ _____   │
│ BREAK:                                        │
└─────────────────────────────────────────────┘
```

Plan for Focus Sessions

Think about how the different Focus timing protocols would work for you and what you could do during the different time periods. Keep these in mind when planning out focus times.

10-Minute Time Chunk (example: *do dishes, write three bullet points*)

_____   _____

_____   _____

10+2*5 (example: *outline paper, brainstorming*)

_____   _____

_____   _____

Pomodoro Method (example: *work on a section of presentation, draft emails*)

_____   _____

_____   _____

45/15 (example: *edit videos, deep research*)

_____   _____

_____   _____

_____   _____

Batching Plan

When you Batch, you concentrate on like-minded tasks for a dedicated amount of time. Before you start a Batching Session, decide what type of task you are going to do, and make a list so you eliminate any Moments of Choice that might occur.

Batch Session Activity:_____

Length of Batch Session: _____

Actions: _____

Sprinting Plan

Sprints can be shorter than Batching Sessions if you want (think "Beat the Clock"), but they don't have to be. The tasks you do during a Sprint don't have to be like-minded. As with a Batching Session, you should have a concrete plan for what you want to accomplish.

Length of Sprint Session: _____

Tasks to accomplish during that time: _____

_____

_____

_____

_____

Proactive Hour

Proactive Hours are a great way to focus on yourself, your projects, and your goals. Like any focus period, knowing what you want to work on, and accomplish, is the key to making the session work for you. Practice being Proactive by planning your Proactive Hour here.

My Proactive Hour:

When: _____

Where:_____

Duration: _____

What I will work on: _____

_____

_____

GOALS

In the preceding three sections, you've learned the about the trifecta of Action, Energy, and Focus and how to leverage it to your advantage. You've studied how to be in Action to prevent procrastination, how to work with your Energy to your greater good, and how to use Focus to expand time. Now we take all of that information and use it to achieve goals and get things DONE.

CHAPTER TEN

Moving Goals Forward

Blame your effort, not your ability
when you don't succeed.

- Anonymous

Everyone has goals. Some goals are big: running a marathon, graduating from college, or opening a new business. Some are much smaller: going to the gym before work, crossing five items off your to-do list by the end of the day, finishing reading a book, or completing a level on a video game.

What can goals do for you? They can change your life. They can make you happier. They can give you inspiration and give your life direction. They allow you to dream of what your life could be like. They give you a connection to the future. They give you a filter by which to live your life so you can focus and cut through the distractions and to do things you want to do.

One things goals aren't? Easy. Especially big goals. A friend of mine told me once "You can't tip a refrigerator over on the first try." It applies here as well. It's hard to nail down a big goal in one try. There are minor victories, then defeats, then bigger victories, and then defeats, and so on and so on. The victories inspire us. The defeats deflate us. But the key is always to keep going. Which, I know, is sometimes a lot easier to say than do.

The whole study of goal setting and goal achieving gives us entire sections of books in the library or the bookstore. (Seriously, there are thousands of books written about goal setting and achieving, so if you want to dig deeper than this chapter, I invite you to do so. Some of my favorite books are listed in the resource section. While I am not the world's foremost authority on goals, I do know a lot.)

When you are truly specific with your goals, you are able to really focus on what you need to do each day to move towards achieving those goals.

Deciding what you want

Defining and deciding on your own goals should be easy, and for the most part, it is, but when it's not done right, you defeat the goal of goal setting. Wishy-washy just doesn't cut it. You can't just want to be a writer. What kind of writer? A technical writer is much different than a writer of children's books, which is different from someone who blogs, which is much different than someone who writes speeches. They are all writers, but they all write differently. These kinds of distinctions are everything when it comes to defining your goals, which is why it's so very important to be specific about what your goals are.

The Joy of Specificity

Right now, you might be thinking "I can't be that specific. There are too many options out there. How could I pin things down?"* Really? How could you not? These are your goals and your life. Specificity is the name of the game. Besides, you CAN be specific. You do it all the time, and I can prove it.

Look at what foods you like and don't like.

Think about it. We all know what we want and don't want when it comes to food. I don't like peppers: green, red, yellow, orange, it doesn't matter. If I'm reading a menu and I see that peppers are in a dish, I quickly move on to the next item on the menu. If I'm checking out a recipe to try and peppers are one of the ingredients, I turn the page. Pretty specific. I know I don't like peppers. I know I don't want them. It's that simple.

I know it sounds like I'm finicky, but you know what? It's my life and I get to eat want what I want. Because I'm specific, I never make anything with peppers in it, and I never order anything with peppers in it. I never have to spend part of the meal picking peppers out of a dish (and failing to get all of

---

* Or you're thinking about what you want for lunch. Which is good as well, since thinking about lunch can help you answer a very important question in this chapter.

them so there is that one surprise bite of pepper which ruins the whole meal for me). Finicky or specific, either way, I enjoy my food my way.

It's the same with you and the goals in your life. You have every right to be finicky. As a matter of fact, I'd be disappointed if you weren't. You have to be just as specific with your goals so that you are working towards something you really love and want and not sidetracked and distracted by something that's just so-so.

So, the big question is: how do you really decide and get crystal clear about your goals?

You decide what you want by deciding exactly what you don't want.

I don't want bell peppers. What do I want? Broccoli. It's that simple. Really.* For someone else, it might be "I don't want to be living paycheck to paycheck. What do I want? To be paid what I'm worth, so X amount of money per year/month/week." For someone else it could be "I don't want to be working for someone else. What do I want? To be running my own mobile dog grooming business, working four days a week, living in a house by the beach in Southern California." This is how you go about deciding and declaring what your goals are.

You decide what you don't want, then figure out exactly what you do want. Don't leave these decision up to chance. Take a few minutes right now to get started. As you know already, once you get started, thanks to the Zeigarnik Effect, chances are you'll keep going until you've gotten everything done. One of the easiest ways to decide on what you want and don't want is to do a simple exercise.

Figuring it all out

A word of caution about this exercise though: when you do it, you may find out that you don't actually want what you think you've been wanting and working towards. Surprise! You may find that secretly you have been wanting something completely and utterly different from what you always thought you wanted. This can actually be a huge relief. Once you know with clarity, where you want to go, the road to that goal is much, much easier to navigate.

---

* And yes, I have bigger goals in life. Peppers are just here to provide me with a very clear example.

Exercise: What do you want?*

To start the exercise, take a blank piece of paper and fold it in the middle, the long way. Draw a line down the fold. On the top of the left side of the paper, write "DON'T WANT." On the top of the right side, write "WANT."

DON'T WANT	WANT
I don't want to work in an office with 9-to-5 hours	I want to work in an friendly, open environment with flexible, outcome-based hours
I don't want to feel like I'm out of shape	I want to be able to run two miles in less than 20 minutes
I don't want to be limited by a set salary	I want to be making $X amount every month within 12 months from now

Now comes the fun part. Set aside some time to start writing down what you don't want. On the left side of paper list whatever you don't like now, what you don't want in the future, what you've had in the past you never want to see again.

Knock yourself out.

For example, maybe you don't want to work in an office with 9-to-5 hours. Write it down in the left-hand column. In the right-hand column write down what you do want "Work in an friendly, open environment with flexible, outcome-based hours."

Maybe you don't want to feel like you're out of shape. Write it down. In the right-hand column, write what you do want "To be able to run two miles in less than 20 minutes." Be as specific as you possibly can be. I can't emphasize this enough. Get down to very small, serious details.

---

* I learned this years ago from a wonderful coach and all-around fantastic human being, Erin Matlock.

Now do it again. What else don't you want? Write it down. Then write down what you do want. Keep doing this until you run out of things you don't want.

How long should this exercise take? Just as much time as it takes for you to specifically decide what you want. Sometimes this comes easily and you can do it in five minutes. Sometimes it works best to do it a little at a time with space for reflection time built in.

Some of my clients find this exercise works best as a right-before-bed activity. Each night they write down one Don't Want and one Want and then sleep on it. Others find if they wait a day between writing what they Don't Want and what they do Want, they are able to be more thoughtful and specific. Some write the Don't Wants in the morning then let their thoughts percolate and write their Wants in the afternoon. Honestly, it's up to you and how you want to work on your Don't Wants and Wants.

Your list can have lots of items on it or just a few. There are no quantity minimums or limits. This is your life. You get to want what you want and work towards what counts for you.

When you have completed your list, fold the paper so the only thing you can see is the WANT column. These are now the only specific goals you should be concentrating on.

If your list is long, and there are lots of things on your Want list, take some time to prioritize them* and determine what is the number one Want you are ready to be working on. Keep your Want list for future use, but for now, only concentrate on your number one Want.

Then move onto your Why.

Figure out your Why

When you set a goal, you need to have a good reason Why you want to achieve it. You need to know Why it's important. Knowing Why makes it much more likely that you will do the things you need to do to make this goal a reality. Knowing your Why gives more definition to your daily actions as you set about achieving your goal. A Why makes your goal much less abstract and it stops, in advance, any arguments that the inner three-year-old might bring up.

---

* Consider using a bracket as discussed on page 39.

It's not enough to say, "I am starting a new online business." Why do you want to start this business? What will you get out of it? Will it give you freedom? Will it provide for your family? Is it something you've dreamed about your whole life? Why do you even care about it? Once you have your Why, you're well on your way towards achieving your specific goal,* all you need now is a plan.

There are all sorts of Goal Achieving Plans you can follow when you're ready to start achieving your goals.† One of the most popular is the concept of SMART Goals. However, it isn't perfect.

The problem with SMART Goals

When you Google "Goals," one of the first things that always comes up is SMART Goals. Somewhere along the line, this became THE way to set up goals. Just for the record, it is not THE way to set up goals. It is A way.‡ It's a pretty good way, sort of, the set-up just needs a little tweaking.

SMART is a mnemonic device that's designed to help you remember that your goals should be:

Specific

Measurable

Attainable

Realistic

Time-bound

Setting up a goal using this framework surely has to be a recipe for success. Except, it's not.

When you set up a SMART Goal, it's really great that you now have a goal that is very Specific, is Measurable with a precise Timeline you can track. But, in my experience, things go completely sideways when you get to the part where you decide if your goal is both Attainable and Realistic. Let's look at those terms.

---

* When I put together an Action Plan, I always make sure there is a place for me to list my Why. This is an easy way to keep the Why in front of me and to remind me of why my goal is important.

† Of course, you can set your own up using the Action Plans from Chapter One.

‡ SMART is not the only mnemonic you can use when setting goals. Two others are CLEAR and FAST. All three provide a framework to follow to achieve your goals.

Is your goal Attainable?

My question here is: attainable in whose book? This term can lead to two different things. First, it can cause you to aim too low and set a goal that is guaranteed to be Attainable so you will achieve your SMART Goal. The only problem is, you'll be setting a goal you know you can achieve without much effort, so that you aren't going to be pushing yourself to achieve more. You're sacrificing growth in the name of guaranteed success. You're going for the easy Gold Star of Accomplishment rather than the life lesson of expanding your reach.

It's like setting your goal to be County Champion (of whatever your particular sport, skill or hobby happens to be) when you could set your goal to be the World Champion. You might not ultimately succeed at being the World Champion, but you'll definitely stretch and grow and learn more than if you just settled for County Champion.

Second, a purely Attainable goal limits you. Goals that seem crazy or completely impossible are the way we change our worlds. What's more important—achieving a too-small goal or trying to achieve something we're not sure we can do? Both of them move you forward, but in one case it's just a baby-step—in the other, it's a hop-skip-and-a-very-enthusiastic-jump-forward. So, which one do you want in your life? (Hint: the whole hop-skip-jump thing is way more fun, exciting, terrifying and satisfying.) Deciding if your goal is Attainable is a surefire way to remain small, when you need to be shooting for the stars.

Is your goal Realistic?

In the strict context of SMART goals, this is expected to be a yes or no answer. Don't be fooled. It's just another way to keep your goals small. You'd like to think "Yes, of course, my goal is infinitely Realistic," but who knows what is truly Realistic?

Every day people achieve goals that no one ever believed were Realistic: best-selling books get written, Olympic heroes are crowned, and people recover from horrifying accidents. Were these ever Realistic goals? Not at all. They were pie-in-the-sky goals that people went for without limiting themselves by worrying if they were Realistic.

Asking if your goal is both Attainable and Realistic limits your inspiration, your enthusiasm and quite possibly your future. So, I propose a change to the whole SMART Goals concept.

Replace Attainable and Realistic with Action and Response

Attainable needs to change to Action Plan, as in "I have an Action Plan to do this," and Realistic needs to be replaced with Response as in "I have a Response Plan for the inevitable obstacles which are going to show up as I move forward."

You know how I love my Action Plans and their power when it comes to working toward goals

Subbing Action and Response into the SMART mix proactively takes care of two problems that show up when working towards goals: knowing what steps are needed to move forward, and knowing how to overcome obstacles that get in your way.

The good thing is the two kinds of plans don't have to be dull and boring. You just need a little imagination and creativity to make your ideas and plans into something that inspires you and makes you want to follow through.

Developing an Action Plan* gives you a very specific track to follow so you aren't winging it as you go along. You want your Action Plan to have defined steps that guide you as you move from where you are to where you want to be. So, before you start working on your goal, think about what you need to do first, second, third. Where might you need help? Who could you look to for help? Put all of this information into your Action Plan.

Action Plans are really the roadmaps of how you plan to achieve your goals. They give you the step-by-step direction to get to where you want to go. Of course, Action Plans are nothing if you just look at them and don't follow them, you have to be proactive about achieving your goal.

Setting Up Response Plans

As you move forward towards your goals, obstacles will invariably show up in your path. Steve Jobs didn't build Apple in one, seamless, obstacle-free step. Sir Richard Branson, Martha Stewart, and the owner of your favorite restaurant down the street all encountered obstacles on the way to success, and

---

* See Chapter One, pages 16-20.

somehow they overcame them and so will you. Remember the whole "rocking the refrigerator?" This is exactly what is happening here. Because the path to goal achievement is never straight, you need to be ready with a Response Plan that details what twists and turns and roadblocks and obstacles you might encounter and your options and solutions to move past them.

You know what really helps with a Response Plan? Looking at others who have achieved what you're trying to achieve and how they dealt with the obstacles that showed up.

Who has done what you're trying to do? What problems did they encounter? How did they overcome them? How would that same obstacle impact you? What are some options you could use that would enable you to keep going?

Using this information, make an "IF this happens, THEN I will respond like this" list. (You're already familiar with doing this.) If you're ready before obstacles show up, then you're prepared for them and less likely to be stopped in your tracks.

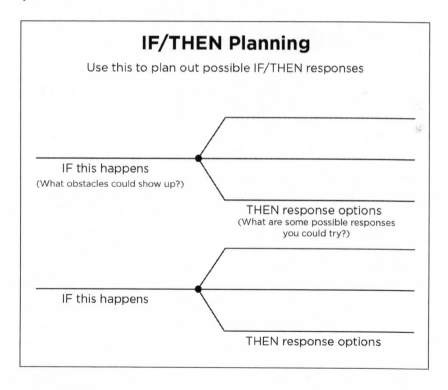

IF/THEN Planning
Use this to plan out possible IF/THEN responses

IF this happens
(What obstacles could show up?)

THEN response options
(What are some possible responses
you could try?)

IF this happens

THEN response options

Replacing Attainable and Realistic with Action and Response in the SMART Goals plan will make you much more likely to achieve your goal. You're no longer limiting what you can achieve by deciding if your goal is Attainable or Realistic. Instead, you're shooting for the stars with big goals, fully prepared for whatever you might encounter on your way to achievement. Plan your SMART Goals so they now look like this.

Once you've got your SMART plan written down, and please make sure it IS written down somewhere, you need to be looking at your goals whenever possible, then the next obvious step is to start working on them. For some people, this might be where the first big STOP sign pops up. (Remember that starting is often the hardest part). So, instead of thinking of achieving your goal as one big thing, imagine the whole process as a video game.*

Achieving your goal the video game way

A video game usually opens with a big flashy title, then a path or timeline shows you what level you're on, what levels you've already crushed, and what levels you are looking forward to. At this point, you might also have the opportunity to grab a daily log-in reward before you're off and running.

As you progress through the game you acquire more skills and hit new milestones for which you are rewarded. Then, of course, the game gets harder, the obstacles get tougher, and the learning curve gets steeper. Sometimes you have to repeat levels, but eventually, you succeed and move forward.

Depending on the game, you might only get a limited amount of time or a limited number of lives, and when you've run through them, you have to sit back and take a breather until everything is replenished. The next time you return to the game, the quest for success continues.

Does any of this sound familiar?

While your life might not be as flashy, dangerous, educational, or goofy as a video game, it does follow the same sort of format that gives you a guide to achieving real-world goals.

---

* Although sometimes achieving goals feels like a more frantic game of pinball, one where the "TILT" sign is only seconds from appearing.

The Flashy Open

As the game opens, the lights, the sounds, and the colors are all designed to excite and entice you to jump in and start playing. Never discount how much your brain loves visual excitement! Would the opening be as fun if it were silent and in black and white? Probably not. Take the cue and make sure your goal is big and flashy and exciting. Find a colorful picture that represents your goal and use it as your screensaver or your home screen, so that you see it repeatedly throughout the day. Print it out as a poster and hang it near your desk, or put it on your wall at home. Make sure it is enticing and causes you to be excited every time you start working toward your goal.

The Path and Milestones

Video games have a path or timeline that show you where you are in the game or what level you are on, and indicates your progress, so far, and points out predefined milestones up ahead for you to shoot for. Your goal should be like this as well. In a game, it's impossible to successfully jump from Level 4 to Level 24, so the path lays out a visual representation of where you are and where you are going. It also allows you to see where you've been and how far you've come. So, devise your own way to track where you are and how you're doing. Whether you do a daily chart with Red & green dots* or Don't Break the Chain† or a different way that you come up with, just track where you've been and where you're going.

The power of milestones can't be overstated. If your final goal is a long way from where your starting point is, there's going to come a time where you're probably going to get discouraged, bored or uninspired. It happens to everyone. You're well past the beginning where you were excited about what you were going to accomplish, and you've still got a ways to go before you get to the end.

This is the spot where it's easy to just give up. So setting milestones, or mini-goals to achieve, is going to be just the thing to keep you interested, motivated, and inspired. Break what's left of your goal down into concrete mini-goals and work towards them. If you wanted to write a book, your

---

* See page 133.
† See page 134.

milestones could be a simple as writing 1,000 words a day for four days, or finishing a chapter, or making a sketch of what you think the cover should look like. Next, you not only shoot for those milestones, but celebrate as you achieve each and every one of them.

Limits

All video games have some sort of limits. Whether it's a one-minute sprint, a certain number of lives, or a timed battle, there is always some type of limit. Your goal should have the same thing. You've probably heard the sayings "A goal without a deadline is just a dream." So, set a deadline for yourself. Make it one that challenges you a little. Make sure though, that it's not impossible. While it would be great to say "I will gain 10 pounds of muscle by next Tuesday," or "I will make one million dollars by Friday," for most mortals, those aren't really achievable time frames. If you're going to have a goal, you have to have a timeframe for achieving it. Make it one that you'll be happy to work towards. In the game of (real) life, you only get one life, so use it wisely.

Rewards

Whether you get an instant reward for just showing up or rewards as you move past levels and milestones, rewards are essential to video games. If we're being honest, a lot of times they are precisely the reason you play. You strive to achieve the rewards, whether it's more lives, more time, more power, or a silly cat video that makes you smile. All of your efforts are concentrated on achieving some reward.

It should be the same in real life. There should always be rewards along the way as you work towards your goal. I honestly think that workdays would be a lot more fun with random rewards sprinkled in along the way. Rewards are a great way to celebrate the achievement of milestones since they encourage your ongoing success.

Repeating a level

Sometimes it's hard to succeed at a level, both in a game and in real life. As long as you keep repeating the level, you're learning something, and it's likely that it is something that will help you eventually succeed. Chances are you're going to need this new skill as you move forward, so what looked like failure was really just a chance for you to really learn the information that you're going to need as the obstacles get tougher and the learning curve gets steeper.

Keep playing

A few years ago, when I was complaining to one of my coaches about the difficulty I was having achieving a specific goal, she told me to just "play and have fun" with it.

She wanted me to relax and quit pushing so hard. Not only was I making things harder than I needed them to be, but I was also sucking all the fun out of my path to success. Once I took her advice, everything changed. Roadblocks that I had unknowingly thrown in my own way, started to vanish. Things became easier. I found the joy and excitement about my goal that I had forgotten and it felt like everything started to fall into place.

"Play and have fun" is the perfect finish to imagining your goal achievement as a video game. Video games are designed to be challenging and fun. They can delight you and frustrate you, just the same as working towards goals, but if you relax and play and have fun, you get out of your own way. You stop pushing so hard and your path can become much, much easier.

Moving into Goal Achieving Action

Once you have your goals nailed down, next comes the fun part: actually moving into Action to achieve them. The following six steps are guaranteed to help you. They've always helped me and my clients swear by them. Now it's your turn. Achieving your goals doesn't require rocket science.* It's just doing things step by step.

1. Have an Action Plan (this one goes without saying)

You know your goal, now set up your plan. You saw the basics in Chapter One. Start putting one together now. Once you have your Action Plan in place, you're going to make it stronger and have it work even harder by:

2. Sticking to a schedule

According to author, James Clear, "Professionals stick to a schedule, amateurs let life get in the way." To succeed at your goals, you need to have an ironclad

---

* Unless, of course, your goal really is building rockets.

(but not impossible) schedule. Why? Because a schedule gives you a timeline to stick to and eliminates the wishful thinking of "I'll do this when I have time." (Because if we're all being honest here, "When I have time" is just another way of saying "this ain't ever happening.")

Obviously, the schedule you choose is up to you. Whether it's practicing music every morning for an hour, writing every day at 8 a.m., meditating for five minutes at noon, going for a run after work, or studying a new skill for 10 minutes before bedtime, having a specific time to do your thing means you can do it without needing momentum or enthusiasm to get started. You just do what you're supposed to do when you're supposed to do it. Using an If/Then plan to schedule your time works really well: "If it's 8 a.m., Then I am at my desk writing." Decide on your best time, and commit to doing your work at that time.

Of course, this doesn't mean that every scheduled session will be fantastic. They aren't all going to be. Sometimes you'll screw up, sometimes it won't be what you really want to be doing, but you do it anyway. Author, Steven Pressfield, talks about this in *The War of Art*. Every day, he goes to his office at 9 a.m. and writes for four hours. Sometimes what he writes is great, sometimes it's terrible. But he puts in his four hours.* You don't let life get in the way of working toward your goal: schedule it, and follow the schedule.

More than anything, having a schedule enables you to:

3. Be consistent

Consistency is doing your small actions repeatedly in a way that eventually leads to a big, successful outcome. Think about it this way—what's going to be more effective: doing 100 push-ups one Saturday a month or 10 push-ups every day?

Unless you're in great shape, 100 push-ups are going to be really hard to do and since it's not something that sounds like a lot of fun, you'll probably procrastinate on doing them. But dropping and doing 10 push-ups every day? That's infinitely more achievable and the compound effect of doing them each day will quickly be seen and felt.

I like to think of consistency as the skill that leads to the Brick Wall of Goal Success.

---

* Writing is his job, so don't let the four-hour figure scare you.

Each time you perform a small consistent action, it's like adding a brick to a wall you are building. In the beginning, a brick a day doesn't seem like much, but over time you build an enormous, solid wall of achievement.

In the 2018 Winter Olympics in South Korea, one of the U.S Ski Team's most powerful members was Olympic Gold Medal alpine ski racer, Mikaela Shiffrin. She was a 22-year-old phenom in the skiing world and went into the Olympics with the potential to ski away with five gold medals.*

In middle school, Mikaela began attending The Burke Mountain Academy (a boarding school in Vermont for ski racers). While there, Mikaela built up a consistent habit of "sneaking in" five extra ski runs every day. While everyone was starting to wrap up their day, she would do those five extra runs. And those five extra runs she took every day turned eventually turned into hundreds of extra runs every season and thousands of extra runs over the course of her childhood.[29]

What's important to notice here is that she took those extra runs every day. Not just five extra runs when she wanted to. Or 10 extra runs on the weekend.

She took them every day. She stuck to a schedule and she was consistent with her small action of five extra ski runs.

She didn't immediately see the results of her actions and efforts, but they definitely added up to the point where she was an Olympic caliber skier.

Big results come from small actions

When Mikaela started doing the extra five runs a day, she was years away from skiing in the Olympics. The effect each extra run had on her was incremental at best, but her consistent actions added up.

Is she the gold medal-winning skier she is today ONLY because of those five extra runs a day? Definitely not. But without those consistent extra runs, she might not have the edge she now has. Each time she consistently practiced, she put another brick on her Wall of Goal Success.

4. Track the Right Thing

As you move towards your goals, it's important to not only track your progress, but to also make sure you're tracking the Right Thing.

---

* Due to weather-related issues, she left the Olympics with two medals, a gold and a silver, and went on later that year to win her second World Cup Overall title.

The Right Thing is the one action that moves you towards your desired outcome most efficiently and effectively.

A friend of mine is working to become a better drummer, so he's tracking the progress of his daily practice. He doesn't track the number of times he sits down to practice, instead, he tracks the number of practices where he works on specific issues with his drumming. While it is essential for him to do daily practice, it's even more important to him to spend time working to overcome specific issues he has identified with his drumming. This means he is tracking the dedicated practices where he works on difficult parts of songs, or a technique he's trying to master, rather than the times he just sits down to practice a song he already knows.

Tracking explained

Let's say your goal is to get stronger. Specifically, you want to be able to bench press X amount of pounds for 10 repetitions. You could track the number of times you go to the gym each week, but a more powerful action to track would be the workouts where you focus on bench pressing with more weight or for more reps, or both. Why? Just tracking the number of times you go to the gym doesn't accurately reflect working towards your goal. There are probably days where you do cardio instead of weights, or you show up but don't push yourself. True, you have made it to the gym, but you haven't really moved towards your stated goal. Track the Right Thing that directly applies to your goal.

Deciding on what specific action you're going to track is one of the essential steps needed to achieve your goal. Tracking the Right Action gives you more direction and focus. How do you decide what is the Right Thing to track? Look at the actions you are taking towards your goal. Is there one action that stands out as affecting your progress more than others (as per the example, heavier weights versus just showing up at the gym)? Start tracking it.

As always, you don't have to make the perfect tracking choice right away. You can pick an action and track it for awhile and then reassess whether it's working for you or not. Don't let deciding on the perfect action to track stop you from picking an action and getting started.

5. Make Mistakes

In March of last year, I gave a presentation about setting and achieving goals to one of my most demanding audiences ever: a troop of Girl Scouts winding down their annual cookie sale season. Each of these young entrepreneurs had just spent a few weeks working on hitting both their personal sales goals and the sales goals of the troop.

These young ladies knew about achieving goals like nobody's business.

They had been knocking on doors, stopping people on the sidewalk, and stalking shoppers as they entered and exited grocery stores, all in the name of more cookie sales. Some had already achieved their sales goals, some were in the final push to succeed in the next five days, but all were ready to learn more secrets about achieving goals, not only so they could do better next year, but so they could do better on all their goals going forward. We discussed the importance of being in Action and having an Action Plan, and how Action can be a scary thing.

Just like asking strangers to buy cookies from you, being in Action can mean attempting something that you've never tried before or aren't sure how to do, all while not knowing what the outcome is going to be. As an added bonus, there is a very real possibility that what you are doing could be a mistake. It's the fear of the mistakes that can hold you back because "everyone" knows mistakes aren't allowed when you're achieving goals.

Ding! Ding!

You have just hit on one of the biggest lies when it comes to achieving goals. Making mistakes doesn't mean that you won't be able to achieve your goal or that you don't know what you're doing. Mistakes aren't bad things. They ARE going to happen and, as that whole troop of Girl Scouts now knows, it's absolutely ok to make mistakes on your path to goal achievement.

Learning from your mistakes

Here's the thing: when you try something and it doesn't work, you always learn something. True, it's disappointing when you think you have the right answer and it turns out you don't. The key is to remember that the information you learned from each mistake is just a data point. It's nothing judgmental, it's nothing that says you are a failure or a terrible person. It's just a guidepost that tells you that this bit of Action doesn't work, so try something different.

Making mistakes means that you are trying new things and learning as you go. Whether it's selling Girl Scout cookies, getting new clients, or starting a new business, or building a new habit, there is going to be trial and error involved on the way to successful achievement of your goals. It would be great if the path to achievement was one direct line from beginning to end. The truth is that it's an up-and-down-curve-to-the-left-curve-to-the-right roller coaster of a ride. Mistakes don't stop the ride, they are just part of it.

At the end of my presentation to the Girl Scouts, I asked them what was the one that they would remember the most about achieving goals (mind you, these included things such as breaking goals into bite-sized pieces, asking for help when needed, and having a plan for when things got frustrating). Their number one, overall favorite discovery was that it was okay to make mistakes (one even wrote "okay to make misteaks" on her worksheet.) Knowing that it was okay to make mistakes was something they had never considered.

Maybe it's something you've never considered either.

There is no reason to fear mistakes. They are going to happen and they are just data points to guide you. Be bold as you work towards achieving new goals. Be in uncharted action territory as you try new things. Know that you are human and mistakes will be made. Remember that the mistakes are there to help guide you to success.

Achieving goals is an important skill that combines everything you now know about the trifecta of Action, Energy and Focus. When you're working towards goals of any kind, you're going to have opportunities to procrastinate, you'll hit Diminishing Returns, and fall victim to Decision Fatigue. You'll have days where the What the Hell Effect will try to take you off your path, and multitasking will seem like the best idea you've ever heard of. Stay strong. You now know how to approach and conquer all of these villains, and more. You know how Action will move you forward, how Energy will keep you going, and how Focus will give your efforts much-needed intensity. You are on the way to getting things DONE and no one can stop you.

CHAPTER TEN ACTION TOOLBOX: GOALS

TOOLS IN THIS CHAPTER:

Decide what you want by deciding what you don't want:
Take time to decide what you want your goal(s) to be by determining what you don't want. It's like knowing what foods you will and won't eat, but better for your goals.

Problem with SMART Goals:
SMART Goals break down into goals that are Specific, Measurable, Achievable, Realistic, and Time-based. Rather than deciding if your goal is Achievable or Realistic, change it to Action Plan and Response Plan, so you have a road map to follow when things go wrong.

Achieving Goals Like a Video Game:
Following the structure of a video game—build your goal with the flashy open, the path of what you've accomplished and what's up ahead, limits and rewards—is a great way to approach and work on goals.

Moving into Goal-Achieving Action:
Have an Action Plan:
Build an Action Plan that focuses on the small wins rather than achieving one big success. Small victories, done repeatedly, will ultimately mean a big win.

Stick to a Schedule:
Have a schedule for working towards your goal. Plan when you will work toward your goal.

Be consistent:
Do the small actions consistently as a way to achieve big goals.

Track the Right Things:
While it's essential to track your progress, it's even more critical to track the things that affect your goal the most. Don't just track your efforts, track the right efforts.

Learning from your mistakes:
As you make progress on your goals, mistakes are going to happen. Rather than becoming upset, take the time to learn from the mistakes. Recognize each error as a data point, and add it to the information you already have.

_____

ACTION ITEMS
Decide what you don't want
If you haven't done the exercise on page 234, now is a great time to go back and do it. Take a blank piece of paper and fold it in the middle, the long way. Draw a line down the fold. On the top of the left side of the paper, write "DON'T WANT" on the top of the right side write "WANT."

On the left side of the paper, start writing down what you don't want. Write whatever you don't like now, what you don't want in the future, what you've had in the past you never want to see again. In the right-hand column, write what you do want. Be as specific as you possibly can be.

Now do it again. What else do you not want? Write it down. Then write down what you do want. Keep doing this until you run out of things you don't want.

When you have completed your list, fold the paper so the only thing you can see is the WANT column. These are now the only specific goals you should be concentrating on.

_____

What's Your Why

When you set up a goal, it's a good idea to know what you're going to do, but knowing your "Why" gives your goal more strength, and gives you a deeper understanding of your motivations.

Think of your goal, then come up with the Whys of your goal. The deeper you deep, the stronger and more truthful your Why.

Goal: _____

Whys: _____

_____

Choose the Why that resonates the deepest with you and add it to any Action Plans you currently have.

Set up an Action Plan

When working towards any goal, it's important to have an Action Plan for achieving it. Pick one of the three types of Action Plans found on pages 16-20, and begin filling it out (blank copies of all the Action Plans can be downloaded at EllenGoodwin.com/forms).

Decide what you want to achieve, the steps you need to take to get there, what obstacles you might encounter, and how you will respond to them. Be sure to include your Why and then get started.

―――――――――

Set up a Response Plan

A Goal Response Plan is really an If/Then Plan. It's you, planning ahead, so you know what to do when your goal-achieving is threatened by outside forces. As always, knowing what you will do before you need to do it, eliminates procrastination-causing Moments of Choice.

Example: *IF early morning meetings get in my way of going to the gym, THEN I will take my work out gear with me to work and go to the gym before heading home.*

If I encounter _____

Then I will _____

If I encounter _____

Then I will _____

If I encounter _____

Then I will _____

Stick to a Schedule

Decide how and when you are going to work towards your goal. You may have to experiment to find the timing that works best for you. Consider "stacking" your schedule on top of something you already do during the day.

Example:

Goal: *Learn French*
Action: *Learn 10 new words every day*
Schedule: *Seven days a week*
Time: *11:30 a.m. for 15 minutes*

Goal: _____

Action: _____

Schedule: _____

Time: _____

Goal: _____

Action: _____

Schedule: _____

Time: _____

Goal: _____

Action: _____

Schedule: _____

Time: _____

Track the Right Thing

Merely tracking your actions doesn't guarantee success. Tracking the Right Things gives your actions more power. With respect to your goal, what one action has the most power? For example, it's not just going to the gym, it's working on lifting more weight. Take some time and think about what one action or task has a disproportionate effect on what you are working towards. Then decide how you are going to track it.

Example:

My Right Thing is: reading recent studies in my area of expertise
I will start tracking it by: putting an X on the calendar every day when I finish 30 minutes of reading

My Right Thing is: _____

_____

I will start tracking it by: _____

_____

Throughout this book, you have learned the importance of being in Action, and why Moments of Choice should always be avoided. You've learned to Jump In when you aren't ready and to ignore perfectionism like the plague. You've learned how to be stronger than the three-year-old in your brain who loves to say no, how to be organized with your time, and ruthless with your distractions. You've learned how to make your outcomes happen, and how to make your goals concrete. You've learned the strength of accountability (in all forms) and why consistency is the key to building habits and accomplishing goals.

You've learned how to manage your Energy and leverage the power of habits to make things happen. You've learned that Focus has the power to expand your perception of time and to exponentially improve your ability to get things done.

You've learned when you bring all these skills together, you can accomplish goals and make big changes.

More than anything you have learned that you can successfully work when no one is watching. You, my friend, are now fully equipped to take everything you have learned and go out and get things DONE.

CHAPTER ELEVEN

Action Toolbox Recaps and Fast Action Guide

CHAPTER ONE: ACTION BASICS

DEFINITIONS IN THIS CHAPTER

Limbic System

The region of your brain responsible for your emotions, your memories, and your fight or flight response. This is the part of your brain that wants you to stay in the safety of your comfort zone, where everything is safe, secure, and non-challenging. Your limbic system is like a naughty three-year-old, saying "no, no, no" when you need to get things done, or you want to try something new.

Dopamine

The neurotransmitter, a chemical released by neurons in your brain, responsible for the pleasure response, acting as a motivational factor in tasks such as when you complete a task.

Moments of Choice

Moments of Choice are a point in time where you have to choose what you are going to do. Many times, this comes down to a choice between two or more things. Do you click on an email, or do you continue to focus on what you were working on? Do you choose to do X, or Y, or possibly even Z? Moments of Choice are a gateway to distraction and procrastination.

TOOLS IN THIS CHAPTER

Draw Your Line-In-the-Sand:

Eliminate procrastination by setting up a deadline where all motion stops, and you move into Action on your project or goal.

Jump In When You're Not Ready:

Instead of waiting for everything to be perfect, take a deep breath and jump into action by starting, knowing that Action is how things get accomplished.

Action Plan:

A series of pre-planned, small steps paired with pre-emptive Implementation Intentions, otherwise known as If/Then plans, designed to get you from where you are to where you want to be.

If/Then Plans:

Also known as Implementation Intentions, these precommitments determine what you will do if a triggering event occurs. They can be used to plan ahead for life obstacles or to commit to doing something in the future.

ENEMY OF ACTION:

The three-year-old in your limbic system which loves Distractions and Moments of Choice. The three-year-old wants to keep you safe and in the status quo. All Action Plans and strategies and tools in this book are designed to help you overcome the three-year-old.

CHAPTER 2: HOW TO GET STARTED

DEFINITIONS IN THIS CHAPTER

Zeigarnik Effect

A cognitive bias. Humans are motivated to complete tasks rather than having them partially done.

TOOLS IN THIS CHAPTER

Games you can choose from to overcome procrastination by getting started:

Color My World:

Pick a color (or a shape) and count how many times you see it while doing a low-value task such as running errands, attending meetings, doing household chores, or even taking a walk.

Dice, Dice, Baby:

Remove emotions and choices from decision-making. Number your options, roll the dice, then perform the option which corresponds to the dice roll.

Go Fish:

Remove choices from decision-making. Write each of your options on separate slips of paper, put the slips in a bowl or hat, then pull one out. Do whatever is listed on the paper. Then pull out another and repeat. Keep going until all the slips are removed and completed.

Pin-the-Tail on the To-Do:

Write each of your tasks on a separate Post-it Note, put all the notes on a vertical surface, such as a wall, a door or a whiteboard, close or cover your eyes and point. Do the task that is listed on the note you pointed to. Continue until all the notes have been chosen and completed. (Bonus points if you spin around first.)

Bracket Your Options:

Set up a bracket, like ones used in sports tournaments, of your options, then go through to determine the priority of the alternatives. Like March Madness, but not as frantic.

Eliminate Perfectionism by:

Do a Shitty First Draft:

Do the first draft of a project, a new skill, an exercise, knowing that your first efforts will not be perfect but, they will be done, and you can improve on them from where you are.

Adopt a Beginner's Mind:
Accept that you are a beginner when you try new things and know that it is ok not to know everything...yet.

Pick a Place and Start:
Rather than spending time and energy trying to find the perfect place to start, pick a place, not necessarily THE perfect place, and start, confident that it will eventually get you to your desired outcome.

Get Small to Start:
Break your tasks, large or small, into the smallest task possible. Perform the small task, then move on to the next small task, and the next, knowing that the small tasks all contribute to the success of the big task.

One Timer to Rule Them All:
Set a timer for five minutes and start working. Work for just those five minutes, and then you are done. Most of the time, you will keep going because of the Zeigarnik Effect.

Leverage the Stops:
Stop working on your project in the middle of a step, making it easier to jump in and get moving when you return to the project. Again, leverage the Zeigarnik effect and close your loops. (Just think about leaving breadcrumbs for your future self to follow.)

Build a Starting Ritual:
Put together a small ritual that you use to tell yourself it's time to start, whether it's putting on a particular piece of clothing or jewelry, sitting in a certain place, or listening to a specific playlist. Do something that tells you, "Now is the time to start."

Hows:
Not knowing your Hows is no reason not to get started. You didn't know how to walk when you were a baby, but you learned. As an adult, there are teachers, coaches, and trainers who will help you with the Hows. Approach your Hows as small steps to move forward.

Restarting Ritual:
Develop a ritual you can follow when you find yourself off track and need to get restarted. Identify that you are off track, remind yourself of this, then consciously move back onto the track to action.

CHAPTER THREE: DISTRACTIONS

DEFINITIONS IN THIS CHAPTER

Distractions of Choice

The distractions in your life that you choose. Your devices all fall neatly into this category.

Unexpected Distractions

The distractions that show up in your life, such as coworkers popping into your office, phone calls, and unexpected problems that take time to resolve.

Superior Colliculus

A paired structure located on your optical nerve designed for reacting to visual stimuli.

TOOLS IN THIS CHAPTER

Become ten percent less distracted by making it harder to be distracted. Put together ways to make it 20 seconds harder to use your cellphone, computer, television.

Make it Awkward:

Make it awkward to give in to your distractions of choice by only doing them when you ARE not comfortable. Walk around, stand in the corner, wear a motorcycle helmet, wear mittens—do whatever you need to do to make the performance of your distraction less than optimal.

Schedule Your Distractions:

Set a timer for the last five minutes of each hour and only allow yourself to give in to Distractions of Choice during this time.

Leverage Hard Deadlines:

Use the power of hard deadlines to get things done. If you don't have a hard deadline, then set one up. Shorten the time available to get things done.

Work Like You're on an Airplane:

Schedule work time as if you were taking an airplane flight. Plan on being where no one can bother you with an email, or by coming into your office. Settle into deep focus and get things done.

Go to the Extreme:

Give someone the power to be in charge of the things that distract you. Have them hide remotes or anything else that's a distraction, or have them decide log-in passwords, and agree not to give them to you until you've done your work.

CHAPTER FOUR: ACCOUNTABILITY

DEFINITIONS IN THIS CHAPTER

The Observer Effect or Hawthorne Effect:

People modify their behavior when they know they are being observed.

Fear of Loss/Loss Aversion:

Being more motivated to hang on to what you already have, rather than getting something you don't currently have.

Precommitments:

A commitment made in the future that makes it harder for your future self to sabotage your efforts.

TOOLS IN THIS CHAPTER

Power of the Group/Social Accountability:

Leverage groups to become accountable. Tell people what you're going to do, and by when, then follow through and let them know.

Accountability Partner:

Have one-on-one accountability with a person/coach/teacher, which may include daily check-in calls, or weekly get-togethers to stay on track. Tell them what you are going to do, then report back in when you've accomplished it.

Put Your Money Where Your Mouth Is:

With the help of an Accountability Partner, set up a plan where you must pay money to a person, group, charity, or organization that you don't believe in if you don't finish your predetermined task on time.

Put Some Skin In The Game:

Plan out milestones to achieve on your way to your goals and attach an amount of money to each one. For each one you hit, you keep your money. For each one you miss, your money goes to a person, group, charity, or organization that you don't believe in.

CHAPTER FIVE: ORGANIZATION

DEFINITIONS IN THIS CHAPTER

Planning Fallacy:
A cognitive bias that causes humans to consistently underestimate the amount of time necessary to complete tasks.

Parkinson's Law:
A task expands to fill the time available for it.

TOOLS IN THIS CHAPTER

Plan Your Day the Night Before:
Take time at the end of your workday, or the end of the day, to plan out exactly what needs to happen the next day. Set up whatever plan works for you, then jump into your next day at full tilt, completely eliminating any option of procrastination.

Think about Friday on Monday:
Think about what you need to have done by the end of the week, then back-time your schedule to ensure everything gets done.

Plan for Your Outcomes:
Decide what your desired outcomes for the day are. List them on a Post-it Note, schedule your day in a way that the Outcomes are achieved.

Back Burner List:
A list of ideas and thoughts that pop up during the day that need to be acknowledged and remembered, but that you don't need to drop everything and take care of immediately.

The To-Don't List:
An ongoing list of tasks and obligations that are a hard "No" for you. These tasks and responsibilities are no longer attractive, are time-wasters, or no longer serve your desired goals. When they pop up in your life, refer to your To-Don't list and say No.

Honor Your Free Time:
Plan out your free time, not only when it's going to happen, but also exactly what you are going to do. Then hold to that schedule like it's a doctor's appointment.

Mind the Gap:

Eliminate the gaps in your day that are Moments of Choice, where you can get easily distracted and start procrastinating. Choose from:

Have a Ritual or Routine to Mind the Gap:

Establish a ritual or routine that helps you to identify gaps and then smoothly move past them without getting distracted. Don't leave this up to choice; when you see a gap, call it out so it can't waste your time.

Build a Habit:

Put together a habit that takes you through the gap without getting lost in it.

Establish Personal Rules:

Set up personal rules for how you deal with gaps. Follow them whenever you encounter a gap.

Recite a Mantra:

Have a Mantra or an affirmation that you repeat to yourself to keep from falling into a gap. Something as simple as "This is a gap, and I don't have to fall into it" will work.

CHAPTER SIX: PUTTING THINGS OFF

DEFINITIONS IN THIS CHAPTER

Hyperbolic Discounting

A term from Behavioral Economics that says we can easily see ourselves today, but not in the future.

Present Bias

The tendency of people to give stronger weight to payoffs that are closer to the present time when considering trade-offs between two future moments.

TOOLS IN THIS CHAPTER

Make friends with your Future self:

Because your future self is a stranger to you, and as humans, we don't like strangers, use an Aging app to get an idea of what you might look like in the future. When you know what your future self looks like, it's easier to do things that will benefit you in a future time.

Use Precommitments:

Decide ahead of time when you are going to do things that will benefit your future self. Make it even easier by automating activities, which eliminates the need for making choices.

Keep Things in Front of You:

Keep actions and goals in front of you and top of mind, so you are more likely to accomplish them.

What gets measured, gets done:

Track, measure, and follow your daily progress, so you don't forget and go off track. Choose from:

Red dots vs. green dots:

Decide what things you want to change or track in your life. Decide what daily success looks like for each item you follow. At the end of the day, put a green dot on a calendar if you succeeded, and put a red dot if you didn't. At the end of a week, or month, tally the dots to see how you are doing.

Don't Break the Chain:

Each day you succeed at a predetermined task, make a red "X" on a calendar. Try to keep the X's going by continuing to succeed. The goal is an unbroken chain of red Xs.

Make your goals concrete:
Find a way to keep your goal or a representation of it in front of you every day. Use a picture, a saying, or chart, anything to make far off goals a part of your everyday experience.

CHAPTER SEVEN: ENERGY

DEFINITIONS IN THIS CHAPTER

Chronotype:

A person's natural inclination with regard to the times of day when they prefer to sleep or when they are most alert or energetic.

Diminishing Returns

The point at which the level of profits or benefits gained is less than the amount of money or energy invested.

Decision Fatigue

The deteriorating quality of decisions made after a long session of decision-making.

TOOLS IN THIS CHAPTER:

Ingest an Amphibian:

Make the first task of the day, the task that you are least looking forward to doing. Do it and get it off your list and out of your brain. Then move on with your day, knowing you have succeeded.

The Big Thing:

Make the first task of your day, the one that will have the most impact on your day, and it will get your day off to a great start. Accomplishing this task will start the domino effect of one big task affecting the next big task, and so on.

Energy Snowball:

Build your energy like building a snowman. Start by accomplishing small things, which leads to an increase in dopamine. Like rolling snowballs, the energy accumulates.

Take a break:

When you are working harder than you are getting results from your efforts, take breaks to prevent Diminishing Returns. If you're doing physical labor, take a mental break and do mental activities like reading or doing crossword puzzles, if you're doing mental work, take a physical break and do physical activities like jumping jacks.

ENEMY OF ENERGY—DECISION FATIGUE:

Every time you make a decision, you use up a little energy. The more decisions you make, the more energy you consume. When you use up energy making lots of small decisions, it's harder to make big decisions. Eliminate low-level decision making by:

Adopting a daily uniform:

Eliminate options by making one decision and sticking with it. Choose the same outfit, same lunch, the same decision, and stick with it. This helps shorten time shopping for clothes, too.

Eating the same thing:

Eliminate daily choices when it comes to your food by deciding to eat the same thing every day, or the same meals on certain days. Eliminate decision-making at restaurants by deciding to eat the second special or the third sandwich.

Having Low-Energy Plan:

A plan you put together when you have high-energy to ensure you can still get things done during the low-energy portion of your day.

CHAPTER EIGHT: HABITS

DEFINITIONS IN THIS CHAPTER
What-The-Hell Effect:
The equation of "Indulge + Regret = Throw all your great efforts to the wind."

TOOLS IN THIS CHAPTER:
Two kinds of Habits: Moving Towards or Away:
When you build a new habit, you are either moving Towards something new or moving Away from something old. Usually, it's a combination of both. This is important to remember when trying to make changes.

Build an Anti-Friction Plan:
Discover where the friction is stopping you as you are building a habit, then start asking yourself a series of questions to figure out what will work to remove the friction.

Micro-habit:
Start building a habit by doing the smallest possible action every day. Pick an action that is so small, it will be impossible NOT to do. Repeat daily until you want to make the action larger.

Micro-Mini Habit:
Get ready to build a habit by going even smaller and doing tiny steps that will eventually help you to be ready to implement a Micro-Habit. Start very, very small, then gradually add in small actions. Eventually, you'll be ready to start building a Micro-Habit.

Habit Stacking:
Build new habits by anchoring new actions to already existing habits.

ENEMY OF HABIT BUILDING:
The What-the-Hell Effect, the reaction you have when you "slip-up" in your habit building and feel like you've failed, so you go all-in on your failure.

CHAPTER NINE: FOCUS

TOOLS IN THIS CHAPTER:

Important Focus Facts to remember:

Size doesn't matter:

Never dismiss the power of small amounts of focus time. While large chunks of time are useful, you can still get a lot done in ten minutes.

Be prepared:

Always go into a focus session, knowing what you want to accomplish. Take a moment and write down on a Post-it Note what you want to get done, so if you get distracted, you can remind yourself of your task and stay on track. Also, write down what you'll do during your break.

Eliminate your distractions:

Eliminate anything that could distract you, whether digital, human or anything in between

Be deliberate:

Don't rely on hoping there will be a time in your day to Focus. Plan and schedule time when you will put distractions aside and Focus.

ENEMY OF FOCUS—MULTITASKING:

Multitasking is like trying to be in two rooms of your house at once. It can't be done. To Focus, you need to eliminate multitasking and keep your brain in one room.

Timers:

One of the best tools for Focus. Use an old-fashioned kitchen timer or a timer on your phone. Decide how long you are going to Focus and ignore distractions and get started. String together several focus sessions by using an Interval Timer on your phone or computer.

STING:

The acronym used to always guide you when going into a focus session. STING stands for:

Select one thing
Time yourself
Ignore everything else
No breaks
Give yourself a reward

Timing Methods/Protocols
10-Minute Time Chunk:
Plan for 10 minutes of Focus throughout the day. Very helpful in situations where large amounts of uninterrupted time aren't available, such as a day filled with meetings or distractions you can't control.

(10+2)*5:
A timing protocol where you work for five sessions of 10 minutes of focus with two-minute breaks in between. Great for doing short sprints of work that don't need intense Focus.

Pomodoro Method:
Popular timing method named after a tomato-shaped timer. Work for 25 minutes, take a timed, 5-minute break, then repeat as necessary.

Batching:
Focus by doing a time-block filled with a series of like-minded tasks, such as reading, financial work, writing, or research. During your timed session, you move from task to task without changing the type of task you are doing.

Sprint:
A short, timed session, where you do a series of tasks in an effort to "Beat the Clock." Tasks don't have to be like-minded, the goal is to eliminate distractions and procrastination by keeping within the time goal, and getting everything accomplished.

Proactive Focus Time:
Build a Proactive Hour where you can Focus on what you need to accomplish, and you don't react to anything or anyone.

Build your focus with meditation:
Learn to meditate and improve your ability to Focus. Sit quietly for five minutes and breathe. Let thoughts come into your brain, then send them away. Practice every day, forever.

CHAPTER TEN: GOALS

TOOLS IN THIS CHAPTER:

Decide what you want by deciding what you don't want:

Take time to decide what you want your goal(s) to be by determining what you don't want. It's like knowing what foods you will and won't eat, but better for your goals.

Problem with SMART Goals:

SMART Goals break down into goals that are Specific, Measurable, Achievable, Realistic, and Time-based. Rather than deciding if your goal is Achievable or Realistic, change it to Action Plan and Response Plan, so you have a road map to follow when things go wrong.

Achieving Goals Like a Video Game:

Following the structure of a video game, build your goal with the flashy open, the path of what you've accomplished, and what's up ahead, limits and rewards, is a great way to approach and work on goals.

Moving into Goal-Achieving Action:

Have an Action Plan:

Build an Action Plan that focuses on the small wins rather than achieving one big success. Small victories, done repeatedly, will ultimately mean a big win.

Stick to a Schedule:

Have a schedule for working towards your goal. Plan when you will work toward your goal.

Be consistent:

Do the small actions consistently as a way to achieve big goals.

Track the Right Things:

While it's essential to track your progress, it's even more critical to track the things that affect your goal the most. Don't just track your efforts, track the right efforts.

Learning from your mistakes:

As you make progress on your goals, mistakes are going to happen. Rather than becoming upset, take the time to learn from the mistakes. Recognize each error as a data point, and add it to the information you already have.

FAST ACTION GUIDE

1. **Help! I always seem to have great plans and goals, but I never follow through on them. What can I do?**

   The important thing to remember is your brain sees planning (motion) as the same thing as doing (action), so when you plan, your brain sees you as having already accomplished everything. When you plan, you are in motion, and nothing is getting accomplished. When you are in Action, things get done.

   - For a quick review of Action versus motion, see page 2.

   - When you plan, for anything, you also need to think of what obstacles might show up, and how you will deal with them. When you know your response ahead of time, you're less likely to give up when the going gets tough. (If/Then plans page 12).

   - Be better prepared to stay on track with your plans and goals by setting up Action Plans (page 16) to follow.

   - Increase the probability of doing the daily work and follow through by keeping your plans and goals in front of you and tracking them (page 245).

2. **How can I quiet my brain so I can get things done?**

   Four things you can immediately do: limit distractions, know what you want to accomplish, set timers, and start meditating.

   - Whenever possible, make your distractions harder to do (page. 70) or schedule them (page 76).

   - Minimize Moments of Choice (page 22).

   - Start with a clear direction each day, either by using an Outcome List (page 110) or a list you've put together the night before (page 108).

   - Plan timed Focus sessions where you work for short periods of uninterrupted time (page 201), which allows you to keep your brain in one room (page 205).

   - Start adding some simple meditation into your day (page 217).

3. **I procrastinate by doing semi-productive things, which is sort of helpful, but I'm not getting the things done that I need to.**

    You are having issues with getting started, common cause of procrastination. (Procrastination shows up in all sorts of ways—check out Chapters Two through Six for more information.)

    - Make getting started easier by making a game out of your task (page 32) or setting a timer (page 52).

    - Take the pressure off yourself by ignoring perfectionism (page 41).

    - Set up a Starting Ritual (page 55) so you eliminate the option of giving in to the semi-productive tasks.

    - If you are procrastinating because you are overwhelmed by the size or complexity of your project or task, start breaking it down into small chunks and work on it little by little (page 49).

4. **What are some techniques I can use to increase my productivity when I'm working from home?**

    Congratulations! You want to work better when no one is watching! There are lots of things you can start doing.

    - Know what you want to accomplish each day by putting together a daily Outcome List (page 110).

    - Set boundaries by putting together a To-Don't List so you know what to say No to (page 115).

    - Block distractions (page 69) or have a plan to make them either more difficult to do (page 71) or awkward to do (page 74).

    - Make timers your friend. Time both work and Focus sessions to keep your day on track (page 207).

    - Make sure someone knows that you are trying to accomplish by adding outside accountability into your day (page 89).

5. How do I organize my time so I can get a lot done in a short amount of time?

Chapter Five covers organizing to overcome procrastination and will have a more in-depth look at your answers, but in a nutshell:

- Put together a Mini Action Plan (page 14), so you know exactly what you want to accomplish with your block of time.

- If you just have a few things to get done, try a Sprint (page 215) or a Batching session (page 214).

- Determine an order of importance by taking all the tasks on your to-do list and Bracketing them (page 39).

- Eliminate Moments of Choice by numbering your tasks and rolling the dice (page 34) to decide the order you will work on them.

- Know precisely what you need to get done, prioritize the most important, or the most time-sensitive, then systematically work your way through. If you have a lot of tasks, make a Master List of all of them, then take the top five or six tasks and put them on a separate list. Do the tasks, then pick the next five or six tasks. You can learn the details on page 138.

6. I feel like I run out of steam every afternoon around 3 p.m.

Chapter Seven was made just for you! It's all about managing your energy so you can get things done. Because we all have different energy rhythms, knowing, and working with yours, instead of against it, is vital.

- Discover your energy patterns by tracking your energy levels (page 154). Use this information to leverage your high and low energy times of the day.

- Eliminate Decision Fatigue by limiting your choices throughout the day (page 162) or by randomizing your options (page 34).

- Use high energy times to set up plans for when you have low energy (page 165).

- Take breaks throughout the day (page 160).

7. How can I improve or increase my ability to Focus?

Chapter Nine covers, in depth, everything Focus related.

- Learn the essential facts about Focus (page 200).

- Timers (either analog or digital) are your friend when it comes to blocking out time for Focus, and there are lots of different timing protocols you can use (page 209). Pick one or two that resonate with you and start incorporating them into your day.

- Eliminate multitasking by keeping your brain in one room (page 205).

- Set up a Focus Action Plan (page 201) and follow it.

- Make sure you are focusing on the right things (page 204).

- Increase your ability to Focus by adding meditation to your day (page 217).

8. My life needs some structure! How can I start building better habits?

Habits, both good and bad, are all covered in Chapter Eight, so if you have time, check out that chapter first.

- Determine if the habit you want to build is a Towards habit or an Away habit (page 175).

- Build your habit utilizing a Micro-habit (page 182) or Habit Stacking (page 186).

- You can build an Action Plan for your habit (page 18) or put together a tracking plan (page 132), so it stays at the top of your mind.

- Be aware of and plan for the What the Hell Effect, which can stop your habit-building progress (page 188).

9. **How can I avoid distractions**

If you have time, check out Chapter Three. It covers procrastination-causing distractions and how you can be stronger than them.

- Become aware of the distractions which show up in your day by tracking them (page 66).

- Make distractions of all kinds, 20% harder to do (page 70).

- Make Distractions of Choice (the Distractions you choose to engage in), awkward as a way to limit your performance of them (page 74).

- Plan ahead by putting together preemptive If/Then plans designed to quickly get you back on track when a distraction shows up (page 12).

- It's harder to give in to distractions if you know you have to report your progress to someone, so put some accountability into your day by getting an Accountability partner (page 92) or by Putting Your Money Where Your Mouth Is (page 94).

- Quit giving distractions time to appear by eliminating Moments of Choice where ever you can (page 22).

10. **How do I stay on track to achieve long-term goals and outcomes (especially when I get distracted and bored)?**

Chapter Six is all about overcoming procrastination when your goal is to far away.

- One of the most reliable tools you can use to stay on track is an Action Plan, which helps you prepare for the things that might stop your progress. There are several kinds you can put together (page 16).

- Make your goal concrete, and keep it in front of you every day (page 136).

- Set up a tracking plan to follow your progress (page 132) and keep you inspired.

- Become friends with your future self (page 129), so your actions today will benefit your future self (rather than your current self).

11. **Either because of myself or because of others, I have trouble sticking to my schedule, what can I do?**

Interruptions, distractions, and life can throw the best-laid plans right out of the window. Being prepared is your best defense.

- Plan for what you can by having If/Then plans in place (page 16).

- Build a Restarting Plan (page 57).

- Mind the Gaps in your day (page 118).

- Schedule your day the night before, so you know what you'd like to accomplish (page 108).

- Know your desired outcomes (page 110).

- Enlist outside help in the form of accountability of all kinds (page 89).

12. **What are the five tools I absolutely have to have to successfully accomplish things every day?**

1. A plan to be stronger than your easily distracted limbic system (i.e. the three-year-old that lives in your brain.) This plan should include: knowing what you want to accomplish each day (page 110), a plan to ignore distractions (page 69), and a way to keep your goals concrete (page 136).

2. A way to minimize Moments of Choice (page 22) where ever they show up, including Minding the Gap (page 118) and randomizing choices (page 34-38).

3. An idea of what obstacles you will encounter during the day and possible solutions to overcome them (page 12).

4. Timers. Whether they are on your phone, computer, stove, or an old-fashioned kitchen timer. Having a way to time yourself is a great way to get started (page 50). It's also essential for timing focus sessions where you direct your attention towards what you need to accomplish for the day (page 207).

5. A thorough understanding of your energy levels so you can schedule your day to take advantage of your high-energy times of the day (page 152).

CHAPTER TWELVE

Resources

Important Note: I have no affiliation
with any of the resources listed in this chapter.

CHAPTER ONE
BASICS

If/Then Plans and Action Plans - Download full-size versions at EllenGoodwin.
com/forms

CHAPTER TWO
PROCRASTINATION: GETTING STARTED

Random Number Generator - Easy way to choose random numbers, set up passwords, or decide numbers for the lottery. iOS. Free. App store.

Random Number Generator - Same as above. You can also put names on a list and randomly pick them, or set up to run in dice mode. Android. $1.49

Random Number Generator Plus - Roll up to 20 dice, pick numbers, flip coins, all by shaking your phone. iOS, Android. Free.

BOOKS MENTIONED IN THIS CHAPTER
Bird by Bird by Anne Lamott

PODCAST MENTIONED IN THIS CHAPTER
The Faster, Easier, Better Show Podcast. On iTunes

CHAPTER THREE
PROCRASTINATION: DISTRACTIONS

COMPUTER TRACKERS AND BLOCKERS

Freedom - Set times to block you most distracting sites. iOS, Android, Mac, Windows, iPad, iPhone. 7 sessions free. Upgrade pricing starts at $6.99/month. www.freedom.to

SelfControl - Blocks sites for a predetermined amount of time with no way to override them. Mac. Free. www.selfcontrolapp.com

KeepMeOut - Online app that reminds you when you've been visiting certain sites too much. Tracks how often you click on your chosen sites and gives you usage charts so you can keep track of your clicking patterns over time. All platforms. Free. www.keepmeout.com

Focus - Block websites, hide applications, schedule focus time, track productivity, and configure breaks. Mac. Free 7-day trial. Prices start at $19 for one time purchase. www.heyfocus.com.

Kill News Feed - Eliminate Facebook newsfeed with this Chrome extension. You can still go to Groups, or to individual timelines but otherwise, there is nothing to scroll through. Mac or PC. Free. Chrome extension.

FocusWriter - Turn your computer into a typewriter, (with optional typewriter sounds) by blocking everything. Timers, word counts, optional spell check and live stats. All platforms. Free (but accepts tips). www.gottcode.org/focuswriter

CELLPHONE TRACKERS AND BLOCKERS

Forest - A simple, gamified focus timer designed to help you ignore your phone. Determine how long you'd like to go without phone interruption then plan a virtual seed. As long as you don't attempt to pick up your phone, the seed starts growing into a tree. If you pick up your phone, your tree dies. iOS, $1.99, Android, Free. Browser for Chrome & Firefox.

Flora: Focus Habit Tracker - Focus timer for groups. Functions much the same as Forest. Everyone in the group is tied to one plant, which grows as long as no one in the group uses their phone. iOS Free. App store.

Space - Usage tracker. Receive "nudge messages" throughout the day, designed to help you find balance. Does not block you from using your phone. An optional 60-day program is available to make you more mindful of your phone usage. iOS, Android, Chrome. Free. SpacePro, with added features: $8.99/3 months, $14.99/6 months. www.findyourphonelifebalance.com

Space: You Need a Breather - Uses a combination of neuroscience and artificial intelligence to bring mindfulness to your phone usage. Each time you attempt to use an app, a "moment of zen" message pops up, designed to make you pause before you give up your precious focus. iOS, Android, Chrome. Free. www.youjustneedspace.com

Siempo - Eliminates the visual appeal of your phone by replacing your home screen with a minimalist black and white screen populated with simple representative icons. Schedules how and when you receive notifications. Every time you unlock your phone a short intention phrase pops up designed to make you more mindful of your phone use. Android. Free. www.getsiempo.com

Moments - Measures and records screen time and app use with the goal of reducing both. If you can't reduce use on your own, for an additional fee, subscribe and receive Moment Coaching which includes short, daily exercises and tools to help you be more present. iOS, Android. Free. Upgrade to Moment Coach for $7.99. www.inthemoment.io

Flipd - Schedule blocks of time to lock apps or everything on your phone. Schedule recurring personal locked-out times or join different community groups and do lock-out time together. Listen to focus tracks or mindfulness coaching. iOS, Android. Free. Premium is $29.99/year and offers more customization and content. www.flipdapp.com

Your own phone - Schedule time to set daily limits or block apps without needing outside help. On an iPhone you have Downtime, and on an Android (9 and above) you have DigitalWellBeing.

MINIMALIST CELLPHONES
Light Phone II - Minimalist phone designed for only the basics of calls, messages, timing and alarms. https://www.thelightphone.com/

Palm Phone - Designed to be used as a secondary phone or to use when you don't want to carry a larger, full-featured phone. https://palm.com/pages/product

EMAIL HELP
Unroll.me - Identify unneeded email subscriptions then have them rolled all together in to one daily email. Available for computer or for iOS, Android. Free. www.unroll.me

TRACK COMPUTER TIME

ManicTime - Track computer usage and work time. Windows, Mac, Linux, Android. Free. Pro version is $67/year. www.manictime.com

RescueTime - Track time spent on applications, websites, and social media, and block distractions. Free 14 day trial. Premium starts at $6/month. www.rescuetime.com

TimeSink - Tracks how much time you use on various tasks and apps. Can also time non-computer activities. $5 on App Store or at www.manytricks.com/timesink

VIDEO CONFERENCING SERVICES

Zoom - Secure video conferencing for online meetings. Syncs across devices and calendars. Offers additional services including webinars and phone systems. Basic plan is free. www.zoom.us

Join.me - Video conferencing. Syncs across devices and calendars. Try for free. Plans start at $10 per month. www.join.me

CHAPTER FOUR
ACCOUNTABILITY

PUT YOUR MONEY WHERE YOUR MOUTH IS

StickK - Set a goal and stay on track with financial incentive. Pricing varies depending on how much money you put up against yourself. www.stickk.com

Beeminder - Set quantifiable goals and pay money if you don't reach them. Your data is charted on a "Yellow Brick Road" so you can see how your actions are trending. Pull in data from all types of sources such as Zapier, Garmin, and Fitbit. Different pricing plans depending on your goals. If you stay on track with any goals, you don't pay anything. www.beeminder.com

BOOKS MENTIONED IN THIS CHAPTER

Think and Grow Rich by Napoleon Hill

CHAPTER FIVE
PROCRASTINATION: ORGANIZATION

TO-DO LISTS

Carrot - Cross things off your list to be rewarded. If you fail Carrot reprimands you. Carrot also has additional apps to keep you on track for exercise, food, and an alarm clock. Mac. $2.99. App Store.

Any.do - Be rewarded for finishing items on your to-do list. Syncs across all devices, helps to organize your life with a calendar app and customized reminders. iOS, Android, Chrome and web. Basic app is free. Upgrade to Premium for $5.99/month. www.any.do.

Vitamin-R - Set up goals with clear objectives, eliminate distractions, stay focused, log tasks, take timed breaks, and track your time. Mac. Free 14-day trial. Paid service starts at one-time cost of $24.95. https://www.publicspace.net/Vitamin-R/

Remember The Milk - List all your tasks and due dates, receive automatic reminders via email, text, or Twitter of tasks and deadlines. Mac, Window, Linux, iPhone, iPad, Android phones and tablets, Blackberry10, and Fire. The basic site is free. Upgrade for $39.99/year. www.rememberthemilk.com

ToDoist - Manage tasks create lists, email, color code and manage tasks with friends. Helps to focus on goals, capture and organize tasks, remember deadlines and track progress. Synchronizes across all devices. Free to start, then $3/month.

SUGGESTED BOOKS

The Procrastination Habit by Piers Steel, Ph.D.

Decisive: How to Make Better Choices in Life and Work by Chip Heath and Dan Heath

CHAPTER SIX
TOO FAR DOWN THE ROAD

Aging Booth - See yourself 20 years in the future, then take care of your future self. iOS and Android. Free.

Oldify - Swap current age for one 20 to 100 years in the future. Make funny faces or body gestures, as well as animations which you can share. iOS, Android. Free with in-app purchases. www.oldify.net.

Life Advisor: Personal Test - Discover how you will look in the future. Can also do tailored assessment reports. iOS. Free with in app purchases. App Store.

Chains.cc - Based on "Don't Break the Chain." Form groups around a common goal such as meditation, early rising, not smoking, stretching. Online service is free. iPhone app is $1.99.

PEOPLE MENTIONED IN THIS CHAPTER

Lee Silber - Efficiency Expert, Author, Speaker, and podcast co-host. Contact Lee at LeeSilber@LeeSilber.com. www.LeeSilber.com

CHAPTER SEVEN
ENERGY

BOOKS MENTIONED IN THE IS CHAPTER

When: The Scientific Secrets of Perfect Timing by Daniel Pink

SUGGESTED BOOKS

The Willpower Instinct: How Self Control Works, Why It Matters and What You Can Do To Get More Of It by Kelly McGonigal, Ph.D.

Willpower: Rediscovering the Greatest Human Strength by Roy Baumeister and John Tierney

CHAPTER EIGHT
HABITS

TRACKING

Habitseed - Select a habit you want to change over the course of 21 days* and plant a virtual seed. Receive daily reminders to check in with your progress. Each day you succeed, your seed grows a little bit more into a tree. If you don't succeed, your tree withers and dies. iOS, Android. 99¢.

Habitica - Habit building and productivity Role Playing Game (RPG) website. In-game rewards and punishments. Work on areas such as Health, Work, School, Goals, Chores. Work towards new habits (ex. walking 15 minutes everyday) or away from existing habits (ex. cut down on swearing, quit smoking). iOS, Android. Free. www.Habitica.com

HabitMinder - More than 50 pre-defined positive and healthy habits to get started. Track sessions, see daily progress, view stats. Then customize. iPhone, iPad, iPod Touch, iOS. Prices vary starting at $9.99. www.habitminder.com

Productive - Build a routine of positive, life-changing habits. Set goals and track progress. Clear, easy to use interface. Subscribe for more features including unlimited number of habits to track and upgraded reminders. iOS. Free to start. Upgrades start at $6.99/month.

---

* Yep. They went with 21 days!

BOOKS MENTIONED IN THIS CHAPTER
Psycho-Cybernetics by Maxwell Maltz

SUGGESTED BOOKS
The Power of Habit by Charles Duhigg

Atomic Habits by James Clear

Habit Stacking by S. J. Scott

Mini Habits: Smaller Habits, Bigger Results by Stephen Guise

Better Than Before: Mastering the Habits of Our Everyday Lives by Gretchen Rubin

59 Seconds: Think a Little, Change a Lot by Richard Wiseman

CHAPTER NINE
FOCUS

TIMERS
Interval Timer - HIIT Workouts - Set intervals, with breaks and timer sounds. Track work and rest periods for all types of focus sessions (and sports). Customizable. Runs when the screen is locked. iOS, Android. Free, upgrade for $2.99.

Focus Booster - Based on the Pomodoro Method. Visually track time with a colored time bar or track via audio and a ticking clock. Subscription starts at $2.99/month. www.FocusBoosterapp.com.

Focus Time - Set focus periods of up to 59 minutes with break times up to 15 minutes. Automatically time, tracks and graphs your progress. iPhone, iPad and Mac. $4.99 - $9.99. www.FocusTimeapp.com.

Pomodone - Pomodoro timer which tracks your focus. Integrates with Basecamp, MS Teams, Asana, Wunderlist, ClickUp, Toggl. Starts at $2.29 per month. Mac, Windows, Linux, iOS, Android. https://pomodoneapp.com

Procraster - Tackle one project at a time. If you get stuck, Procraster will give you advice for working through the blockage. All data is stored in the cloud and available to sync between your devices. iOS. $1.99. www.procrasterapp.com

BREAKS
TimeOut - Break reminder which sets up customized breaks and micro-breaks. Mac. Free with in-app purchases. www.dejal.com/timeout

FadeTop - At regular intervals your desktop will fade to a bluish color so you can take a break. Breaks can be scheduled, or will just occur when the app sees which you are working too long. Free. Windows. www.fadetop.com.

MEDITATION

Insight Timer - Learn how to meditate, listen to guided meditations (over 27,000 available), set up timed meditations - complete with bell ringing. iOS and Android. Free. Insight Premium is $5/month.

Headspace - The "gym membership for your mind" which eases you into mindfulness meditation. Follow a free initial series of 10-minute meditations on your phone, tablet or computer, and learn the basics of mindfulness meditation and begin to see how meditation can impact your life. $7.99 - $12.99/month. www.headspace.com

Aura - Meditation timer. Includes mindfulness mediations, life coaching, stories, music to help with stress, anxiety, or sleeping issues. Offers a variety of voices and types of meditation. Gamifies creation of good habits. $47/year. iPhone, iPad, iOS. www.aurahealth.io

BOOK MENTIONED IN THIS CHAPTER

Faster Than Normal: Turbocharge Your Focus, Productivity and Success with The Secrets of the ADHD Brain by Peter Shankman

Accompanying podcast is Faster Than Normal on iTunes.

SUGGESTED BOOKS

Making Space: Creating a Home Meditation Practice by Thich Nhat Hanh.

Zen Mind, Beginners Mind by Shunryo Suzuki.

Wherever You Go, There You Are by Jon Kabat-Zin

CHAPTER TEN
GOAL TRACKING

42goals.com - Simple app for tracking and logging your daily goals and activities. Web. Free. $5/month for Premium version. www.42goals.com

Lifetick.com - Goal setting and tracking software. Set up goals, track progress, get reports, share goals with family, friends and colleagues. Web. $39/year. www.lifetick.com

Goalscape - Visual goal setting for success. Break down challenges and get a clear picture of goals, priorities and progress. manage goal lists, create a clear goal structure, visually assign importance and track progress, share and collaborate. Free 14-day trial. From $6/month. OSX, Windows, Cloud, mobile. www.goalscape.com

BOOKS MENTIONED IN THIS CHAPTER
The War of Art by Steven Pressfield

SUGGESTED BOOKS
Goals by Brian Tracy

The Slight Edge by Jeff Olson

The Success Principles by Jack Canfield

Notes

1   Peter M. Gollwitzer (1999), "Implementation Intentions: Strong Effects of Simple Plans," *American Psychologist* 54:493-503.

2   Jonathan Gottschall, Ph.D., "Crappy First Drafts of Great Books," Psychology Today, March 27, 2012, https://www.psychologytoday.com/us/blog/the-storytelling-animal/201203/crappy-first-drafts-great-books.

3   John Waters, "Why John Waters Swears by His Motivating 'Writing Sweater,'" *Wall Street Journal*, June 4, 2019, D3.

4   Ravi Mehta, Rui (Juliet) Zhu, Amar Cheema, "Ambient noise study: Is Noise Always Bad? Exploring the Effects of Ambient Noise on Creative Cognition," *Journal of Consumer Research*, Vol. 39, No. 4 (December 2012), pp. 784-799, Oxford University Press

5   Gloria Mark, Daniela Gudith, Ulrich Klocke, "The Cost of Interrupted Work: More Speed and Stress," Conference: Proceedings of the 2008 Conference on Human Factors in Computing Systems, CHI 2008, 2008, Florence, Italy, April 5-10, 2008. https://www.ics.uci.edu/~gmark/chi08-mark.pdf

6   Adrian F. Ward, Ayelet Gneezy, Maarten W. Bos, "Brain Drain: The Mere Presence of One's Own Smartphone Reduces Available Cognitive Capacity," *Journal of the Association for Consumer Research* 2017, 2:2, 140-154

7   Seungyeon Lee, Myeong W. Kim, Ian M. McDonough, Jessica S. Mendoza, Min Sung Kim, "The Effects of Cell Phone Use and Emotion Regulation Style on College Students' Learning," *Applied Cognitive Psychology*. Volume 31, Issue 3, May/June 2017. 360-366.

8   Michael R. Ent, Roy F. Baumeister, Dianne M. Tice, "Trait self-control and the avoidance of temptation," *Personality & Individual Differences*, Feb 2014, 12-15.

9   James Clear, "How to Automate a Habit and Never Think About It Again," James Clear, accessed July 25, 2019, https://jamesclear.com/how-to-automate-a-habit

10 J. McCambridge, J. Witton, DR Elbourne, "Systematic review of the Hawthorne effect: new concepts are needed to study research participation effects," *Journal of Clinical Epidemiol.* 2014 Mar; 67(3):267-77. doi: 10.1016/j.jclinepi.2013.08.015. Epub 2013 Nov 22.

11 WC Wang, CH Kao, TC Huan, et al. "Free Time Management Contributes to Better Quality of Life: A Study of Undergraduate Students in Taiwan," *Journal of Happiness Studies* (2011) 12: 561. doi:10.1007/s10902-010-9217-7

12 Hal E. Hershfield, Taya R. Cohen, Leigh Thompson, "Short Horizons and Tempting Situations: Lack of Continuity to Our Future Selves Leads to Unethical Decision Making and Behavior," *Organizational Behavior and Human Decision Processes* 112, no. 2 (2012): 298-310, doi:10.106/j.obhdp.2011.11.002

13 T. O'Donoghue, M. Rabin, "Doing it now or later," *American Economic Review,* 89(1), (1999): 103-124.

14 Gina Trapani, "Jerry Seinfeld's Productivity Secret," lifehacker, July 24, 2017, https://lifehacker.com/jerry-seinfelds-productivity-secret-281626

15 Mark Muraven, Dianne M. Tice, Roy F. Baumeister, "Self-control as limited resource: regulatory depletion patterns," *Journal of Personality and Social Psychology,* (1998 Mar); 74(3):774-89.

16 Daniel M. Wegner, David J. Schneider, , S.R. Carter, III, and T.L. White, "Paradoxical effects of thought suppression," *Journal of Personality and Social Psychology,* 53 (1987): 636-647/

17 Evan C. Carter, Lilly M. Kofler, Danierl E. Forster, Michael E. McCullough. "A Series of Meta-Analytic Tests of the Depletion Effect: Self-Control Does Not Seem to Rely on a Limited Resource," *Journal of Experimental Psychology,* 2015 http://local. psy.miami.edu/faculty/mmccullough/Papers/EgoDepletionMetaAnalysis_Text_Revision_for_circulation.pdf

18 Daniel H. Pink, *When. The Scientific Secrets to Perfect Timing.* (New York: Riverdale Books, 2017), 9-47.

19   Chris Weller, "A neuroscientist explains why he always picks the 2nd menu item on a list of specials," *Business Insider*, July 28, 2017, https://www.businessinsider.com/neuroscientist-decision-making-hack-restaurants-2017-7

20   Phillippa Lally, Cornelia H. M. Van Jaarsveld, Henry W. W. Pott, Jane Wardle, "How are habits formed: Modeling habit formation in the real world," *European Journal of Social Psychology*. 40. (2010):10.1002/ejsp.674. https://onlinelibrary.wiley.com/doi/abs/10.1002/ejsp.674

21   Amy N. Dalton, Stephen A. Spiller, "Too Much of a Good Thing: The Benefits of Implementation Intentions Depend on the Number of Goals," *Journal of Consumer Research*, Vol. 39, No. 3 (October 2012), pp. 600-614. https://www.jstor.org/stable/10.1086/664500?seq=1#page_scan_tab_contents

22   Stephen Guise, *Mini Habits: Smaller Habits, Bigger Results (Volume 1)*, (Createspace, 2013).

23   Janet Polivy, C. Peter Herman, Rajbir Deo, "Getting a bigger slice of the pie. Effects on eating and emotion in restrained and unrestrained eaters," Appetite, 55:3, (December 2010):426-430. https://doi.org/10.1016/j.appet.2010.07.015

24   K. Anders Ericsson, Jim Pool, *Peak: Secrets from the New Science of Expertise* (New York: Houghton Mifflin Harcourt, 2016), 98-99.

25   Merlin Mann, "Procrastination hack: "(10+2)*5," 43Folders, October 11, 2005, http://www.43folders.com/2005/10/11/procrastination-hack-1025.

26   Julia Gifford, "The secret of the 10% most productive people? Breaking!," DeskTime, May 14, 2018, https://desktime.com/blog/17-52-ratio-most-productive-people.

27   Judson A. Brewer, Patrick D. Worhunsky, Jeremy R. Gray, Yi-Yuan Tang, Jochen Weber, Hedy Kober, "Meditation experience is associated with differences in default mode network activity and connectivity," *PNAS* 108 (50) (December 13, 2011): 20254-20259; https://doi.org/10.1073/pnas.1112029108

28   Amishi P. Jha, Elizabeth A. Stanley, Anastasia Kiyonaga, Ling Wong, Lois Gelfand, "Examining the Protective Effects of Mindfulness Training On Working Memory Capacity and Affective Experience," *Emotion*, Vol. 10, No. 1, (2010):54-64. http://citeseerx.ist.psu.edu/viewdoc/download?doi=10.1.1.329.2557&rep=rep1&type=pdf

29 Ben Cohen, "Mikaela Shiffrin Learned to Ski in Vail. She Learned to Race in Vermont," *Wall Street Journal*, February 12, 2018, A13.

ACKNOWLEDGEMENTS

Thank you to all my family and friends. I'm not listing everyone here because I know I would unintentionally leave someone out and feel terrible for it. Just know I appreciate and love every one of you.

Thank you to my early readers: Adrimire Dominguez, Courtney Biehl, Gabriella Riberio, Heather Gaynor, Israel Savage, Monisha Kapur, Russell Jones, and Tara Zimnick-Calico. Your input and thoughts were instrumental in shaping this book into the one you hold in your hands.

Thank you to Peter Shankman and all the members of Shankminds for their ideas, and constant support.

Thank you to my coaches, past, and present who have encouraged and pushed me to become who I am (even when I resisted being pushed.)

Thank you to everyone who has shared their productivity struggles with me and who have allowed me to help and learn from them.

Last, but certainly not least, a huge thank you to my husband, Chris, for being my best fan, and a very patient cheerleader.

ABOUT THE AUTHOR

Through the course of a successful career as an advertising creative, Ellen Goodwin learned the elusive secrets to getting things done when no one was watching. She now shares this information through speaking engagements, corporate trainings, coaching, and writing.

Ellen is the co-host of the Faster, Easier, Better Show podcast, and a graduate of Gustavus Adolphus College. She lives in sunny San Diego with her husband.

Ellen is available for keynote presentations, seminars, and workshops. Please contact her at Ellen@EllenGoodwin.com for availability.

Made in the USA
San Bernardino, CA
09 January 2020